Wild Shore

Wild Shore

EXPLORING LAKE SUPERIOR BY KAYAK

Greg Breining

University of Minnesota Press
Minneapolis • London

For additional maps, color photographs, and more information about Kayaking in the Upper Midwest, see the University of Minnesota Press web site at http://www.upress. umn.edu/wildshore.

All photographs throughout the book were taken by the author unless otherwise credited.

Map by Parrot Graphics

Published by the University of Minnesota Press
111 Third Avenue South, Suite 290
Minneapolis, MN 55401-2520

Library of Congress Cataloging-in-Publication Data

Breining, Greg.
    Wild shore : exploring Lake Superior by kayak / Greg Breining.
        p.   cm.
    Includes bibliographical references (p.).
    ISBN 0-8166-3141-7 — ISBN 0-8166-3142-5 (pbk.)
    1. Kayak touring—Superior, Lake.   2. Superior, Lake—Description and travel.
    I. Title.
    GV776.05 .B74 2000
    917.74'904'43—dc21

                                                            00-009081

Printed in the United States of America on acid-free paper

11 10 09 08 07 06 05 04 03 02 01 00   10 9 8 7 6 5 4 3 2 1

To Susan

And I think over again
My small adventures
When with a shore wind I drifted out
In my kayak
And thought I was in danger.
My fears,
Those small ones
That I thought so big,
For all the vital things
I had to get and to reach.

And yet, there is only
One great thing,
The only thing:
To live to see in huts and on journeys
The great day that dawns,
And the light that fills the world.

— Eskimo song, in *Eskimo Realities*
by Edmund Carpenter

Contents

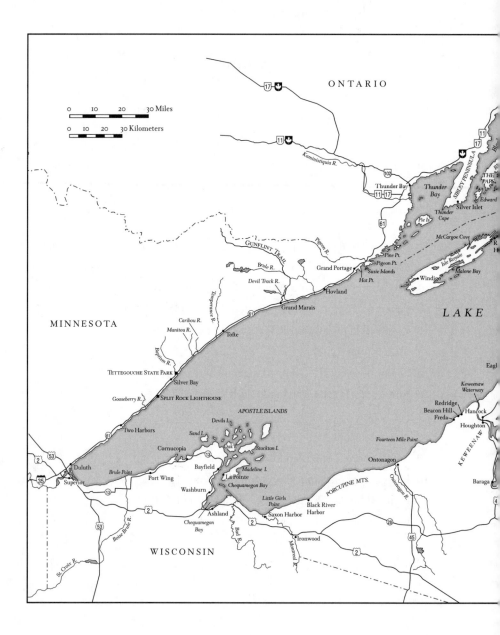

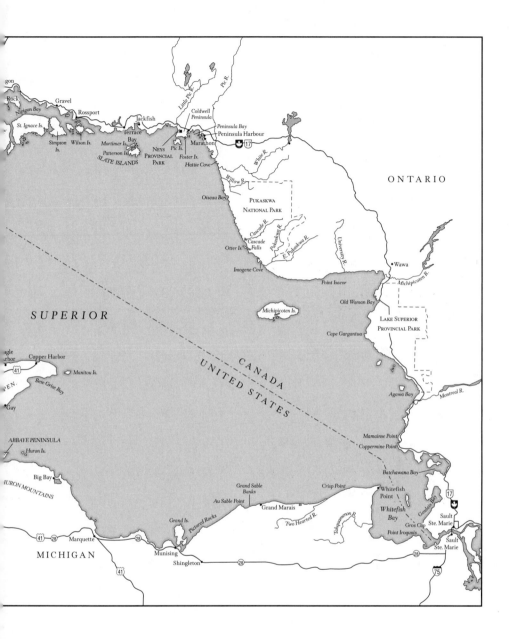

Acknowledgments

I WOULD LIKE TO THANK Midwest Mountaineering in Minneapolis and We-no-nah Canoe in Winona, Minnesota, for helping with equipment, and John Amren and Jennifer Stoltz of Cascade Kayaks in Grand Marais for providing a way station for trips to the northern shore of the lake.

Thanks also to public servants on both sides of the border, especially employees of various natural resource agencies who provided information about Superior and helped with my travels.

I'm indebted to the many kind people I met who gave me a lift or otherwise helped me get around the lake.

Finally, I would like to thank the several friends, especially Susan, who gave logistical support and traveled with me, despite the danger that I might quote them.

The Thin Blue Line

A STONE SAILED OUT in a puny arc and plunked silently into the water, the sound failing to rise above the whoosh and hiss of wind and surf. The horizon mocked the meager distance of the boy's throw. It was not like throwing a stone across a pond, or even into a lake, where the flight might suggest some fraction of the distance to the far shore. No, the thin blue line spelled infinity, and the arc of the rock represented no meaningful fraction at all—only a vague wish to reach infinitely far.

It was fall on the Minnesota shore of Lake Superior, the North Shore as we call it. I was the young boy—gangly, modestly athletic, infatuated with fishing and the outdoors, and too willing, perhaps, to let my dreams remain dreams. Each fall my family spent a weekend in a cabin perched on concrete blocks less than thirty feet from the lake. When waves broke on the cobble beach and splattered the windows, I imagined they might wash the cabin to sea.

We would clamber over a point at the edge of the bay and look into the clear water to the green rocks below. We would drive to Canada to see the Sleeping Giant at the entrance to Port Arthur. We would hike the rushing rapids of the Brule River. In the evenings, we would roast wieners on the beach. The rocks were smooth and somewhat flat. I would throw them into the lake by the hundreds, and Dad told me I soon might not have any left.

An old fisherman owned the resort. I remember only white hair and whiskers and squinting eyes. He told me how to catch trout in a nearby river. With a fly rod and grasshoppers, I watched the shadowed current and the occasional glint of a white belly. But I never caught a trout, not until much later.

As I grew older, I explored on my own. I paddled a whitewater kayak down the steep rapids of rivers with names of mystery and darkness, such as Manitou, Presque Isle, and Devil Track. In aimless ramblings motivated by vague yearning and melancholy, I drove to Michigan's Upper Peninsula— Nick Adams's country, land of the Big Two-Hearted River. I worked as a newspaper reporter in Duluth. In my time off I waded the North Shore streams. I actually began to catch trout.

Still, I saw the lake only in glimpses: the cliffs and points, the foaming cascades of the rivers that ran to the lake, the unblinking horizon. I did not know what lay beyond the highway, in the hidden bays and islands, and along the remote shores where there were no roads. I still did not understand what I was looking for and why the end of the day and the end of travel were so lonely.

One day, I paddled a sea kayak. All graceful lines and curves, the hull carved the water with barely a whisper and turned at the touch of a paddle. With waterproof cargo holds fore and aft, it would hold enough food and gear for a week or more. How does it feel to travel days on end with no fixed schedule? I wondered. What happens to your sense of distance when every mile is earned by a thousand strokes of the paddle? A plan began to form as I imagined paddling on and on, never having to turn back.

It wouldn't do, I thought, to circle the lake in a single thousand-mile marathon. That had been done, by explorers and voyageurs, Ojibwa and Cree, and by nameless tribes in the distant past who had traveled the lakes in birch-bark canoes. More recently, several kayakers have circumnavigated the lake, some in less than a month. There was nothing to prove by doing it again.

Nor did I have the time or temperament for it. I couldn't take off two months from work and family. And I knew that after a few days on the water, I would begin to race around the lake, logging fifty-mile days in a mad rush toward home, driven by impatience, loneliness, and anxiety. I'd miss much of what I had set out to see. As one friend told me, paddling around Lake Superior takes no time at all if you stay far enough from shore.

Instead, my travels would be poky and taken in stages—a week here, two weeks there. I would start at Sault Sainte Marie, at the eastern tip of the lake, because it had been a gateway for so many people, including the Ojibwa, the French, the British, and later the Americans. As historian

Grace Lee Nute wrote in *Lake Superior*, the Sault was "the focus of the entire life of the lake. Here the great body of water was first discovered; here passed all the great explorers, almost without exception; here were some of the earliest settlements, mission and fur-trading posts; and to it came all the commerce of the lake."

I would make my way around the lake in consecutive stages, to give the illusion of traveling continuously, but if I missed a few miles here or there, so what? Mainly, I wanted to nose around and ask questions. I'd travel when I was able and lay up when I found something interesting. I would paddle with others for safety when I could, and travel alone when I had to. I wanted to see the lake from the waterline, to talk to people who knew it, to find out what the lake meant to them through their own stories. I wanted to know the lake, to the extent possible in this modern age, as those who had come before had known it.

In doing that, I thought I might learn something of myself. I had not camped alone very often, especially in the wilderness. Would I be brave when I was caught out on the lake with a rising wind and no good place to land? How would I fare on nights alone, when loneliness calls out like a wolf?

Over the years, my mind had prepared me for this trip, even without my realizing it. I had often thought of the artist George Morrison. He grew up on the Grand Portage Indian Reservation on Lake Superior. He left the reservation for Minneapolis, then went to New York and abroad, becoming known throughout the United States and Europe. His painting evolved into the flat, colorful abstract expressionism so celebrated in midcentury. He thought of his paintings as "endless space." As he said in his autobiography, *Turning the Feather Around*, "the painting seems as if it could go on and on in all directions." What better image for the lake on whose shores he grew up? Later, his works organized around a thin flat line, the horizon that identified all these works as landscapes. The single line represented the objective, natural world.

For his Horizon series, a collection of small, abstract landscape paintings, Morrison wrote, "I seek the power of the rock, the magic of the water, the religion of the tree, the color of the wind, and the enigma of the horizon."

That, by a different means, is what I would do.

CHAPTER 1

East Shore: Sault Sainte Marie
to Old Woman Bay

GOULAIS BAY formed a beautiful funnel. To the south, Gros Cap loomed massive and purple above Superior. To the north, hills rose lush and fertile, as though we paddled in the humid tropics. Between these headlands, from the west-southwest, poured a howling wind. To stand in it would be hard enough. To paddle into it sucked the life right out of you.

Susan had never kayaked on big water before. I worried not so much for her safety as her spirit. We had just set out on the lake, only one hour into a ten-day trip, and here we were, nearly paralyzed by the wind. I felt as though I were trying to pull through quicksand. Forward progress was a matter of faith.

The three miles across the bay took well over an hour. Finally gaining shelter behind Goulais Point, we followed the shore to find a campsite. Cabins and homes ringed much of the bay, and this land seemed privately owned as well. Eventually we paddled up to a man standing on shore, as though he were waiting just for us.

"Do you know of somewhere on shore where we can camp?"

"No, not really." It was getting late. I wanted him to say: *Yes, of course, camp in my yard.*

A younger man emerged from the woods. I asked if there was camping nearby. "Down the shore it's just bush," he said. "There's crown and tribal land. You can probably find some place."

We paddled past a vacant lot with a rusted car on blocks. Beyond, the woods stood thick as fur, with only a rocky beach. Then we finally spotted a clearing. We landed and explored; it appeared to be an old road and a clearing that was once an old homesite, now covered with club mosses and trilliums. Mosquitoes closed in immediately. We set up the tent and Susan

lay down, exhausted. I built a small fire for dinner. Our first day we had paddled only five miles. If that were to be our pattern, we would never make
Michipicoten in ten days. For that matter, to paddle around Superior would
take three years.

Sault Sainte Marie, as it had been for so many before us, was our gateway to
Superior. Susan and I had driven in from Michigan's Upper Peninsula, crossing from Sault Sainte Marie, Michigan, to Sault Sainte Marie, Ontario, on
U.S. 75. The two-lane bridge twisted high in the air between the two cities,
spanning the fretwork of locks, piers, dams, canals, and industrial works
that allowed thousand-foot ore boats and oceangoing freighters to pass
from Superior (named so by the French because it has the highest elevation
among the Great Lakes) down the St. Mary's River and into Lake Huron.
Rapids once filled the river. The Ojibwa called the area *Bawating*, "place of
the rapids." They fished the fast water in their birch-bark canoes. As the
sternman nosed upstream through the eddies, the bowman would search
the turbulence for the dark, refracted forms of whitefish, scooping them
from their resting spots with a long-handled net. "I watched with a mixture
of admiration and terror several little canoes which were fishing in the
midst of the boiling surge, dancing and popping about like corks," wrote
Anna Jameson in the mid-1800s. "The manner in which they keep their position upon a footing of a few inches, is to me as incomprehensible as the
beauty of their forms and attitudes, swayed by every movement and turn
of their dancing, fragile barks."

   The population of Bawating would swell at the peak of the whitefish run,
when fishing was easiest. Other tribes, less expert fishers than the Ojibwa,
would trade for fish, dried and smoked. It was at Bawating in 1671 that the
French claimed all of North America west of Montreal for France. Simon-
Francis Daumont, Sieur de Saint Lusson, summoned the Indians, erected
a huge wooden cross and hoisted a cedar pole bearing the escutcheon of
Louis XIV. Jesuit black robes led a procession. Father Claude Allouez proclaimed the king "more terrible than thunder: the earth trembles, the air and
sea are set on fire by the discharges of his cannon." Hymns were sung and
muskets were fired. By one account, the "Indians were left literally speech-
less." The spectacle ended with Te Deum (*We praise thee, O God!*) "on behalf
of those poor peoples, that they were now the subjects of so great and

powerful a monarch." Later some Indians tore the king's escutcheon from the cedar pole.

When geologist Louis Agassiz passed through in the summer of 1848, he described the U.S. side of the Sault as a "long straggling village, extending in all some two or three miles. . . . The most striking feature of the place is the number of dram-shops and bowling-alleys." The Canadian shore of the St. Mary's River, with poorer access to the water, was even drearier.

These days, nearly a hundred thousand residents live at the Sault, most of them on the Canadian side. Sault Sainte Marie, Ontario, transports an American back in time. Like many cities of northwestern Ontario, it seems trapped in the commercial shadow of the United States, like something from the Ashcan School, with overhead wires strung everywhere, angled streets, a few old stone buildings and brick storefronts. We drove along the waterfront, past the tentlike pavilion set up for the lock tours, through the moribund downtown, by the Richardsonian Romanesque Sault Sainte Marie Museum on the corner of East and Queen. Old houses, a brownstone church, more Richardsonian mishmash. Finally somewhere near the Algoma Steel mill, we admitted we were lost and asked for directions at Beaver Gas. Soon we were on the road north, through the outskirts of prefab buildings, vacant lots, and bulldozed ground, into the green hills and long vistas toward Hayden and Goulais River.

I had wanted to bypass the shipping lanes of the Sault, where fishing boats, runabouts, sailboats, cabin cruisers, oceangoing freighters, and thousand-foot ore boats squeezed down the narrow throat of the St. Mary's River. And I decided to avoid cities, which were difficult by kayak. Except for an intimate view of the harbor, what could you see by kayak that you couldn't see better by car or on foot? Better, I thought, to launch at the next bay to the north, near the small town of Goulais River and paddle a couple of miles down its namesake stream to Superior. Goulais River offered the additional advantage of lying close to the highway. Once we finished our trip, I could ride the Greyhound or hitchhike back to our car.

We turned off the highway at Goulais River and drove to the government dock on the slow, sandy river. As we arrived, boys launched Jet Skis and roared downstream toward the lake. Across the road were houses, cabins, and small resorts. We walked to the nearest house, where we found a man working in his garage. His name was Tee Ed, he said. He sewed fabric tops for boats. He was short, slight, quick.

"Where could we park a car while we paddle up the coast for nine days?"

"You could park right in that grassy spot over there."

I offered him ten dollars.

"For nine days? That's just over a dollar a day to have someone watch over your car, here where it's safe."

I paid him twenty dollars. We unloaded the boats and piled our gear on the dock. The volume of gear clearly overwhelmed the two kayaks, so we began to ruthlessly winnow the equipment. As we worked, two teenage girls walked over.

"How far are you going to paddle?"

"To Wawa."

"Get outta here!"

"Look at all the food they're taking," her companion said. "They could paddle to Wawa."

Sleeping pads, cook kit, water bottles, rain jackets, waterproof bags stuffed with sleeping bags, waterproof bags stuffed with clothes—everything packed into a kayak must pass through a hatch. Even the larger rear hatch won't swallow anything bigger than a small watermelon. Much of a kayak's storage capacity lies in the long tapered ends, where we jammed tent poles and shoes. The process seemed without form, as though we merely presided over a pile of junk on the dock. Then, unexpectedly, the last piece of gear disappeared and we climbed into our boats and pushed off.

Susan dropped her rudder and, still a novice at paddling, plowed into the bank. A teenage boy at the landing guided her back into the channel. This was inauspicious and to her, I'm sure, embarrassing. I wondered if we had bitten off more than we could chew.

We paddled down the river as Jet Skis and a jet boat ripped by. Then, suddenly, we saw the lake, filled with whitecaps that broke over the long delta at the river's mouth. We landed on a sand flat to pull on our wetsuits. We would give it our best.

I had met Susan a year earlier. She was married then, soon to be divorced. She had been born in Japan. Her mother was Japanese and grew up spearing flatfish in the shallows of Tokyo Bay. Her father was a military policeman. I knew I was interested when I learned she liked to fly-fish. The following spring, during a lunch stop on a kayak trip, I watched her poke through the duff on the forest floor to look for spring ephemerals. I think I fell in love when she named the plants in Latin. I figured she would enjoy this trip, but my reasons for inviting her were partly selfish: I wanted the company. I thought we would be safe enough. For many miles the shoreline consisted of protected bays, where the lake was relatively warm. What better place to learn?

That was the theory. Then we emerged from the mouth of the river and the wind hit like a snowplow.

That night Susan said the paddle across Goulais Bay had worried her, not out of concern for our safety, but because she feared she would hold me back. Don't worry, I said. When time ran out, we'd pull out at the nearest road and I'd hitchhike back to the car.

We awoke early to sneak out onto the lake while it was calm. Susan emerged from the tent.

"Were you comfortable?" I asked.

"How would I know? I was unconscious."

The wind rose as we rounded Goulais Point. Soon whitecaps danced across the open lake as we angled into the wind. The breeze annoyed me. It made tough work of paddling and if the waves grew much larger, they would force us off the lake. Ile Parisienne lay about six miles off to our left, low and green. We looked up ahead for Maple Island, but could not see it. The gradual rounding of the shoreline on my map appeared from the perspective of our boats to be a series of jagged points. *Surely we must have rounded that point by now!* But we hadn't, and the fact that Maple Island hadn't yet emerged from behind the shore was our proof. Slowed by the wind and teased by this illusion, we seemed to crawl up the shore. Finally Maple Island appeared. An hour later we pulled even with it. An hour after that we found shelter behind Rudderhead Point. Exhausted, we landed on a hard sand beach in the lee of the point. We snacked while ravens flapped lazily overhead and a ring-billed gull begged for pieces of bagel. In the shelter of the cove the lake was beautiful, aglitter with diamond waves. North and South Sandy Islands were visible in the hazy distance. My foul mood evaporated; suddenly I felt fortunate to be here.

We paddled out of the sheltering bay, once again into the wind. For the rest of the day, we accomplished nothing more than rounding Rudderhead Point as the waves crashed among the rocky shoals that extended several hundred yards into the lake. In Batchawana Bay we found a clearing on a small island about two hundred yards from shore. We built a small fire and cooked among large boulders on an otherwise gentle gravel beach, where we bathed and lounged before dark. Susan rendered the humping hills along shore in charcoal on a rock. The sun set in a flaming ball, turning into a puddle that quickly dissipated on the flat line of the lake. Robert Barnwell Roosevelt camped in this same bay in 1862 and felt compelled to quote Longfellow:

> And the evening sun, descending,
> Set the clouds on fire with redness.

We might have been watching the same sunset, but for a single jet contrail.

If you are an angler, Roosevelt's *Superior Fishing* makes for good reading, not only because the fishing was so good, but also because he could make a hundred-mile canoe trip from the Sault to Batchawana and Agawa Bays sound like a full-fledged expedition. Roosevelt, uncle of our Rough Rider president, was part of the trickle of adventure tourists who traveled Superior during the early and middle nineteenth century. He had set out from Cleveland in 1862, traveling by boat to the Sault, "almost at the extreme northwest of American civilization," with his pal Don Pedro. Roosevelt, Don Pedro, and their Indian guides alternately paddled and sailed against the wind, west and north along the East Shore. As they sailed, they encountered a stream of Indians in canoes, paddling and sailing with their families as their dogs ran along shore. The adventurers struck their first fish, a four-and-a-half-pound lake trout, in Goulais Bay. Yet they hurried on, for Roosevelt's real interest lay in fly-fishing for brook trout at the mouths of Superior tributaries. Ascending the Harmony a short distance, they began casting with the sporting tackle of the day—"one-handed" trout rods about twelve feet long—and soon caught nearly a hundred one- to two-pound brook trout from the turbulent water below the falls, saving about two dozen to eat. Don Pedro caught a smallmouth bass of nearly four pounds. "The guides recognized him at once as an old acquaintance," Roosevelt reported, "and called him by the familiar name of *achigon*"—literally, in Algonquian, "ferocious." "Every river swarms, every bay is a reservoir of magnificent fish," Roosevelt wrote. "After having fished from Labrador to the Mississippi, and killed trout in every State where trout are to be killed, I am satisfied that the fishing of Lake Superior surpasses that of any other region on our continent, and is, as a natural consequence, the best in the world."

I had intended to follow in Roosevelt's wake and paddle into the deep bight of Batchawana Bay to the mouth of the Harmony River, where Roosevelt found the fishing to be "absolute perfection." The morning was ideal, warm and still. As we paddled, however, we realized we should take advantage of the calm conditions by traveling instead of fishing. We turned west toward Corbeil Point.

Our boats glided almost silently, the only sound the dripping of water from the paddle blade passing overhead. The reflection of shore and sky rippled on the gentle waves generated far out on the lake by yesterday's wind.

"The swells remind me of the silk sheets they use in Kabuki," Susan said.

It was not to last. By the time we approached the point, the wind had risen and a chop appeared. Once again the lake came alive with whitecaps, and we bucked the wind on the long shore past Corbeil Point before turning north and taking the two- to three-foot waves broadside. They were the largest waves in Susan's experience. To my relief she smiled and laughed as we bobbed, occasionally disappearing from one another behind a rolling wall of water. The wind and waves drove us into the mouth of the Pancake River, where we rested on a sandbar that all but blocked the river's mouth. After a half hour, we ventured again onto the lake, paddling into the wind more than an hour to make the far end of the two-mile-long beach.

Under normal conditions, Pancake Bay was an easy day's paddle from the Sault for voyageurs toting furs in thirty-six-foot birch-bark canoes. It was named, the story goes, because the voyageurs used the last of their flour in a feast of pancakes. Now the bay, ringed by pure sand, was the centerpiece of a small provincial park.

The beach was nearly deserted. We washed and laid out our paddling clothes to dry. We spread our inflatable mattresses on the sand and luxuriated in the radiated warmth of the beach, the soft lap of the water, and the hot sand on our heels. The afternoon was the definition of a pure northern summer, when days are so simple you can count things like shaving, bathing, eating, and smoking an evening cigar as important accomplishments.

Then a large man in a uniform walked up from the woods. With dark glasses and a mustache, he reminded me of a cop.

"You folks going to be staying with us for awhile?"

"We thought we'd spend the night."

He said he was the assistant superintendent of the park. "If you're going to camp overnight, it will cost seventeen dollars and seventy-five cents."

"Sure." I assumed he meant Canadian, but it still seemed high for a sand beach.

"You're on the group camping site, but we won't ask you to move."

Wonderful weather, I said, except for the wind.

"Yes," he said. "Unfortunately, it's not good for the forest. There's a provincial burning ban in effect. No fires, except in established campgrounds, and then only in the evening. I'll send a girl down. You can pay her by credit card or cash and she'll give you a receipt."

I was glad to see him go. He had nothing but bad news—seventeen dollars to camp and no fires.

Soon the "girl" arrived. She was blonde and pretty, muscular with icy blue eyes. She lived, it turned out, on Batchawana Bay.

"What does Batchawana mean?" I asked.

"Undertow," she said. "In the wintertime, where the mouth of the Batchawana comes out, where the narrows are—in the wintertime that never freezes because there's such a current. I think that's where they got the name *undertow* from. In the summertime, if there's any wind at all, that's where the waves will be. They're really choppy. We do a lot of fishing in that other bay called Harmony. You always end up going through a bit of a choppy wave before you get in there."

"What do you catch in there?"

"Lake trout and smallmouth bass and perch. Smallmouth are fun to catch."

"What's it like up the shore?"

"It gets quite rocky and craggy," she said. At Point aux Mines is the old shaft of a copper mine. "If you're close enough to shore, I don't think you can miss it," she said.

Over the years, I have learned to distrust that phrase.

We slept that night listening to the drone of cars on the highway and the occasional flatulence of an eighteen-wheeler coasting down the backside of Pancake Point.

The accumulating infirmities of age: All night long my right shoulder hurt, the result of a softball game nearly twenty years ago. I had caught a fly ball in center field, and the runner on third had tagged and broken for home. I threw toward the plate and heard a terrific tear in my joint. The catcher made the tag; the runner was out. I can't remember who we played or if we won, and I'm sure no one else remembers the play, not even the man on third, but all night I rolled from my right side to my left side to my right side again. My shoulder stopped hurting only when I lay on my back, but then I couldn't sleep. Finally, after seven hours of this, shortly after five, it was time to get up.

We wanted to clear Pancake, Coppermine, and Mamainse Points before the wind rose. The lake was calm and the sun still low over the hills when we shoved the boats into the water. We paddled in the cool shadow by shore, creeping along the building cliffs in near silence, as though privileged to enjoy such conditions. We passed rookeries of gulls, their nests situated on bare rocks. The birds flew out to meet us and made halfhearted passes at our boats.

At the tip of Coppermine Point, we looked out over more than a hundred miles of open water to the west and northwest. Twelve miles away, in 530 feet of water, lay the broken halves of the *Edmund Fitzgerald* and the remains—somewhere—of twenty-nine crewmen. The rock itself was stark, windswept, and mostly barren. We noticed a half-dozen small caves, just above water level. They appeared rather square, perhaps six feet high, wide and deep. Had they been excavated by the pounding surf? Or by men looking for copper?

Rounding Mamainse Point, we ducked between several small islands and shore. There we saw a collection of buildings, a house and a yard littered with piles of timber, abandoned boats, refrigerators, trailers, front-end loaders, and a crane. The highway ran nearby and at first we thought the place might be a truck stop where we could buy lunch. Instead, it was Ferroclad, a herring fishery still operating on the East Shore. Several commercial fishing boats sat quietly in the sheltered cove. No one seemed to be about and we continued up the shore.

Until this morning, much of the shoreline, with the exception of a few headlands, had been low and sandy. The forest had been leafy, primarily birch, maple, and other hardwoods. With Coppermine and Mamainse Points, the nature of the coast changed dramatically. The rolling hills of deciduous forest and beaches gave way to a craggy shore, with bare outcrops, rocky islands, and a boreal forest made up largely of spruce. Beyond the protection

North of Coppermine Point, the shore turns to cliffs and rocky headlands.

of Goulais and Batchawana Bays, the water turned suddenly colder. My
heels, resting on the hull of the kayak, turned to ice.

As we crossed Mica Bay on the flat water, the hazy horizon seemed to
disappear. I fell into a strange torpor and needed to concentrate simply to
keep from spilling over. At last we came to a small cove that ran along Point
aux Mines and immediately saw what appeared to be the old copper mine,
fifteen feet wide and twenty feet high. The point itself was a riot of pink,
green, and gray rock, twisted and tilted. The lake bed was carpeted with
pink and green stone, bathed in turquoise. The distorting lens of water
seemed to lift us over the rocks as if we flew, inducing a kind of vertigo,
and the bottom shifted as if it were a kaleidoscope.

Yet that was tame compared to Theano Point, which bulged from the

As we near the pictographs and the mythological retreat of Nanaboozhoo, hills rise along shore.

earth, bare and elemental, like an elbow of the old continent. Inside a cleft at water level, as if on an altar of rock, rested an offering of ice, unmelted even in June. Dikes of rock had eroded, leaving slots in the cliff. Along the crest of the point, several hundred feet above the lake, the stunted forest slanted from sustained lake winds.

Paddling this coast, you could write an essay on rocks: the crevices, the soaring heights, the color and texture, the shapes—like pachyderms, some of them; others angular and severe like blocks. It was magical to hear a brook trickling far back in a tiny crevice a hundred feet up the cliff—the *manidoog*, the spirit voices. It was awesome, in the original spirit of the word, to reach out and touch the core of the earth while dancing lightly on the water, poised on two elemental planes. At one point, Susan broke out in tears at the beauty of it.

The Ojibwa believed that magic, or spirits, concentrated in the massive headlands of the East Shore, not only because of their stark beauty and obvious connection to the inner body of the earth, one suspects, but also because they knew the rocks contained minerals, such as copper. For thousands of years, Indians had hammered at nuggets and veins of copper that appeared at the surface, pounding and annealing nearly pure metal into a variety of objects. Oddly, that copper long ago had been used for prosaic objects, such as knives and projectile points, but more recently it appeared only as ornaments and ceremonial objects, as though the pure metal had become exceedingly scarce. It has even been suggested that Indians feared verdigris poisoning from working with the material. Medicine men prescribed shavings of copper to the sick. One journal keeper wrote, "The chief who gave it said it would either cure or kill."

Because copper belonged to the mysterious domain of the Great Lynx, Mishi-bizheu, who lived in the depths of Superior, many Ojibwa feared they would die if the metal were found by whites. Yet find it they did, and by the 1840s mine shafts and head frames appeared along the shore, even though on paper, the land still belonged to the Ojibwa. Complaints that the miners were burning forests and driving away game—even an appeal made directly to the governor-general in Montreal—had no effect. In addition, modern mining may have offended the Indian mind because the shafts and drifts actually pierced the body of Mother Earth, a mortal wound compared to the minor abrasions the Indians had committed. Miners must have seemed like rapists. So in 1849, the Ojibwa chiefs Shingwauk and Kinebonegojing, with other Indians, two English adventurers, and, according to legend, a cannon, rousted the superintendent of the Point aux Mines operation from his sleep and drove away a hundred miners. For defending their rights, Shingwauk and Kinebonegojing were arrested and jailed for several weeks. A few years later, Roosevelt remarked, "The speculation never having been profitable, the company was only too glad to be captured."

Nonetheless, outcrops along the East Shore continued to attract speculators. Theano Point was named for the small boat of a uranium prospector that foundered and smashed against the rock in 1947. A head frame was erected and a shaft dug on the north face of the point. Though the mine was soon abandoned, about five thousand claims were filed in the area. One of those claims, near Montreal River Harbour, was held by Roy Ranwick. The mine played out quickly, so Roy and his wife, Dorothy, opened it as a tourist attraction. Each day up to a hundred people paid a dollar twenty-five apiece to walk five hundred feet along an abandoned drift that followed a seam of pitchblende. They listened to the frantic ticking of a Geiger counter and toured a display of fluorescent minerals. In the gift shop, they could buy radioactive ore samples.

So much for the heydays of Montreal River Harbour. These days it is a quiet place. We navigated the two rocky points protecting the river mouth and landed on the cobble beach along the river. The bog-stained water surged far out into the lake, but looked lifeless. I rigged up a rod and made several casts, with no success.

Across the river, a man cast a large plug into the air. He sat in a lawn chair and let the lure drift with the current far into the lake.

"What are you trying for?" I asked.

"Lake trout."

"What are your chances?"

"Not very good. Not this week. They haven't been biting all week. Water's too warm. Where you headed with your big kayaks?"

"Agawa Bay. Is there a town here?"

He shook his head. "No, there's a town at Sault Sainte Marie, and there's a town at Thunder Bay."

"Is there a grocery store?" Susan asked.

"You might be able to get something over there," he said, pointing to the hill behind us, "or over here," pointing to the hill behind him.

We walked up the grade, passing the fishermen's cabins of the Trail's End Resort, to the highway and over the bridge that spanned the Montreal River. The river was dry, blocked and diverted by the Great Lake Power Company dam. It once must have been a stunning sight, cascading through a red rock gorge. Now the dry chasm was filled with rock and the river emerged from the powerhouse at the base of the falls.

We crossed the bridge to the Twilight Resort, its cabins built to face not the spectacular lake, but the dirt road off the highway.

"Is there a restaurant here?" I asked the woman behind the cash register.

"Not yet. There will be. They're building an addition."

Her name was Sandy Steer. She was minding the store for the owners. Her husband, Don, was an amateur historian and had written a history of the East Shore. She pulled Don's book off a shelf. Twilight, we learned, had been built in 1935 as a camp for road crews building the highway along the East Shore. During World War II, it was converted to a work camp for conscientious objectors, primarily young Mennonites. Behind the counter was a picture of the falls before the dam. It ran full and sprayed into the plunge pool.

"It was really beautiful," Sandy Steer said. During the mid-1930s the power company built the first station at that location. Construction of other dams and generating stations continued for thirty years until the falls dried up. "It's too bad," she said. "It was a real tourist attraction."

What is the equation, I wondered, that expresses energy in terms of beauty? How many kilowatts justify killing a lovely river? How many dramatic cliffs are we willing to deface to feed a nuclear power plant or make a better bomb?

We bought pop and candy. Walking back to the boats, we looked again at the falls and read the graffiti on the cliff near the bridge: "Janet loves Fred" and "Don't eat yellow snow."

For several miles north of Montreal River Harbour, we paddled next to magnificent cliffs, mostly dark with patches of light, all enlivened by orange lichens. Eroded dikes formed soaring clefts that led deep into the rock. We saw patterns in the rock that looked like pictographs. But most likely they were not—just the red of the rock showing through the lichen. "If those aren't pictographs, they must have been an inspiration," Susan said. In fact, the Indians frequently made pictographs by scraping lichen away in patterns, like scratchboard art.

At the beginning of MacGregor Cove, we were bombarded by gulls. As we had noticed near other gull congregations, a single bird assumed the role of Stuka, diving toward our heads as less aggressive birds circled benignly. We passed between the two rock points guarding the mouth of Laughing Brook, a clear, bouldery stream that bespoke brook trout. A sign said: "Provincial fishing preserve; no fishing." Nearby was a cabin, with another sign "Private property—camping on beach only; shelter available on back porch." Leaving the cove, we passed Vrooman Island, its bowed trees trained by the wind.

Rock suddenly gave way to the low, gentle sweep of Agawa Bay. We had entered Lake Superior Provincial Park, one of the largest and most spectacular of the lake's wild lands. The beach, all seven miles of it, was nearly deserted, even though the highway ran close to the shore. The mouth of the Agawa River, near the end of the beach, was once the site of a Hudson's Bay Company fur trading post, a fishing lodge, and for thousands of years before that, a village site. Despite the long presence of humanity, the site was desolate. The mouth of the river spread wide in a peaceful estuary, reflecting the massive forested ridge that ran along the north edge of the river. The outwash of gravel and cobble suggested the river wasn't always so peaceful, at times flooding and sweeping debris down to the lake, including the uprooted, weathered trees, gray and barkless, on the gravel bars. The Agawa was beautiful for its starkness.

Ahead the shore once again erupted in rocky prominences, and the Agawa Islands rose bluish and preternaturally. In the afternoon haze, the horizon had disappeared and the islands seemed to float in the sky. The scene was glorious in its surrealism. And then we saw it.

Inscription Rock. Agawa Rock. It was a sheer, broad cliff that reminded me of nothing so much as a drive-in movie screen, but much, much larger, nearly a hundred feet tall. Indians and voyageurs would leave offerings of tobacco to the cliff. We paddled slowly until we saw the figures we had expected: two images of the horned sea dragon Mishi-bizheu, two large serpents, a horse and rider, four "suns," pairs of bears and caribou, many images of people in canoes. The images were the color of rust, painted within easy reach of the water. Most appeared above a sloping ledge, just above lake level, where the artist obviously stood. Around a break in the rock the ledge disappeared, yet there were more paintings: a fish, a canoe with two people, and the second image of Mishi-bizheu, which looked in profile like a bull, but with a long reptilian tail and spikes along its back. This last panel was inaccessible on foot. Did the artist stand in a canoe?

Susan said she was a bit disappointed. On the larger-than-life cliff, she had expected larger-than-life figures, she said, the Stone Age equivalent of the Stone Mountain light show in Georgia. No question the scale was wrong. The largest grouping would fit comfortably on your living room wall. They were man-scale paintings on a canvas of supernatural proportions.

Still, the Agawa pictographs are among the most spectacular of about four hundred groups of pictographs on the Canadian Shield, associated

Do the mysterious pictographs near Agawa Bay describe a pivotal battle or the sacred landscape of Superior, or both? (Photograph by Susan Binkley.)

with Algonquians such as the Ojibwa. Like nearly all the others, the Agawa images are the sacred red stain of red ochre, known scientifically as hematite or anhydrous ferric oxide. And like the others, they raise the questions: How old? Who made them? What do they mean? Why here and not a thousand other places along the shore?

The first printed reference to the Agawa pictographs is in Henry Schoolcraft's 1851 study of American Indians, accompanied by engravings of the images, based on drawings on birch-bark scrolls made by Shingwauk—the same Shingwauk, apparently, who led the charge on Point aux Mines. The pictographs, Shingwauk told Schoolcraft, recount the daring crossing of eastern Lake Superior by a fleet of war canoes led by the warrior and *Medae* medicine man Myeengun (the Wolf). Myeengun's warriors apparently paddled from the Keweenaw Peninsula across more than one hundred miles of open water to join the Agawa Ojibwa in battle against the Iroquois. Referring to specific icons on the rock, Shingwauk said the first of the five canoes were led by Kishkemunasee, the Kingfisher. The crossing took three days, represented by three suns. (There are four; Shingwauk's memory apparently lapsed on that point.) The rider on the horse was Myeengun. The men made the crossing with the blessing of Mishi-bizheu and the great serpent. Another pictograph site marks the point of Myeengun's departure, but that cliff, somewhere along the south shore of Superior, has never been found.

The pictographs are remarkably durable, but they are not indestructible. In the winter of 1877–78, a slab of rock bearing images of woodland caribou and other animals broke off and fell into Superior, its absence noted by fishermen the next summer. When Selwyn Dewdney, the pioneering Canadian student of rock art, first saw the Agawa pictographs in 1958, the message "K.D. 1937" had been painted in black over the central figure of Mishi-bizheu. This new "art," the work of the daughter of a nearby fisherman, was already beginning to fade. Today it cannot be seen.

Dewdney's attempt to describe the pictographs illustrates the limitations of science in dealing with such things. He laboriously recorded the pictographs, plastering wet rice paper over the images and tracing them with a Conté crayon. He concluded that the pictographs were made sometime after 1647, when the first horse arrived in Quebec, unless Myeengun had been to the plains and seen or obtained Spanish horses. (Indeed, the Jesuits'

21

journals cite a large battle between the Ojibwa and Iroquois in 1662.)
Dewdney was unable to find modern-day Ojibwa who could, or would,
interpret the symbols for him. In his book, *Indian Rock Paintings of the Great
Lakes,* Dewdney (with coauthor Kenneth E. Kidd) rejected a literal interpre-
tation of the images; nor, he said, were they art in a modern Western sense.
Their value lay not in the beauty and grace of form, but in their representa-
tion of the mystical. "To all appearances," Dewdney wrote, "the aboriginal
artist was groping toward the expression of the magical aspect of his life."

Anthropologist Thor Conway teased at the same puzzle. In 1981, when
Conway met Fred Pine, an Ojibwa elder and shaman, at the Garden River
Indian Reservation just east of Sault Sainte Marie, he had already studied
the rock art of various tribes for some twenty years. So he hardly felt pre-
sumptuous in asking Pine to tell what he knew of pictographs.

"The medicine people have been drumming longer than that," said Pine,
already in his eighties. Neither Fred, nor his uncle, Dan Pine, a healer, spiritual leader, and *Medae,* would confide in Conway. "They had to prepare me,
through a long apprenticeship, for an understanding of this enigmatic religious art," Conway wrote in *Painted Dreams.* Through long interviews and
stories, the story of the Agawa pictographs and rock art gradually emerged,
though in terms more abstract than Conway expected. "The soul speaks in
the language of images and symbols," he wrote.

First, Fred Pine revealed that ochre was mixed with binder made by boiling the cartilaginous spine of a sturgeon to a gluey consistency and adding
bear grease. This description is consistent with the observation of James
Isham in the 1740s: "The Glue the Natives saves out of the Sturgeon is very
strong and good, they use itt in mixing with their paint, which fixes the
Colours so they never Rub out &c." Conway even gathered rock chips that
had flaked from the face of the pictographs to analyze with an electron
microscope. No trace of the organic binder remained, but over time a veneer
of silica and other minerals had laminated the ochre to the cliff, explaining
the pigment's durability. Further, pictographs, including some at Agawa,
had been retouched or painted over. Conway discovered that under the
right conditions of light and dampness, a shadow of Mishi-bizheu emerges
beneath the later, bolder image. Conway even interviewed the author of the
black initials that once covered Mishi-bizheu. She explained that she had
thought the pictographs were mere graffiti. "There is a fundamental differ-

ence between aboriginal marks on stone and pioneer inscriptions, based on the separate philosophical relationships to the land evidenced by the two societies," Conway later wrote. "One regarded land as a spiritual source of identity; the other saw land as property." More succinctly, pictographs represent the shadowy world of the spirit; graffiti rarely does.

In a stroke of stunning good fortune for Conway, Dan Pine's grandfather and Fred Pine's great-grandfather turned out to be the same Shingwauk (the White Pine) who had informed Schoolcraft. In fact, said Fred Pine, Shingwauk painted the panel of the horse, rider, and four suns. Fred described to Conway the significance of the various elements of the pictograph, including a six-legged disc with a heart line. He identified the image as a louse, a favorite "spirit vehicle," a shape his great-grandfather assumed to travel in the feathers of a raven.

Even as Conway learned more of the icons and the narratives they illustrated, he remained puzzled by the location of the pictographs. Early explorers had noted only a few pictograph sites on Lake Superior, while thousands of suitable cliff faces remained unadorned. Over time, Conway came to realize that pictographs appeared only at sites associated with resident spirits. These "dreaming rocks," where spirits talked to men in dreams and visions, were only the portals to a complex landscape of spirits and myth that merged with the temporal world. Drawn at this raw spot on the shore, the Agawa pictographs proclaimed the exploits of one world and the mysteries of the other.

A cloud passed over; the wind rose. Susan became frightened because the sheer cliff offered no protection. We paddled quickly around the point and found shelter behind an island in Sinclair Cove. But once we landed, the sun came out. We set up camp and cooked dinner. In the waning light, we drank tea and shared a cigar, performing our own meditation on tobacco as the smoke wafted skyward and fog rolled over the lake.

The following day we crawled slowly past islands, river mouths, sand beaches, and abrupt headlands. The Sand River, in high water a paroxysm of rapids and falls in its final mile, trickled to the lake at a glorious sand beach, where Susan and I discovered the tracks of moose. Three miles offshore, the Lizard Islands lay low and green as lizards.

Up the shore, in Robertson Cove, we took shelter from sudden clouds and two-foot whitecaps. A gravel tombolo joined the mainland to a weatherbeaten rock. Ice had pushed boulders onto the slab, and recent waves or rain had left temporal pools. A Juneberry bush bloomed, and bird's-eye primrose and butterwort grew on the rock in a smudge of dirt. What is true of Lake Superior in general was certainly true of this tiny scene: elemental rock and water made a fundamental beauty. Susan was transfixed by the objects, which seemed arranged, she said, like a Japanese garden.

Afternoon grew colder. We paddled hard into the wind-whipped chop to a sheltered pocket in the lee of Bald Head. It was here that the highway angled inland. A hiking trail continued for a few miles but then ended. For the next thirty miles, we would be cut off from help in case of trouble. We rested and munched granola. On the lake, patches of shining water appeared and disappeared as clouds and patches of blue sky whipped overhead. "The funny thing about Lake Superior," Susan said, "is it looks like there must be good weather somewhere, and you're not in it."

We soon grew tired of trying to outwait the wind. We struggled around Bald Head and soon reached the mouth of the Bald Head River, where we paddled and then hiked upstream to a cascade. The river dropped perhaps thirty feet over tiers of gray and pink granite. I fished, flipping a small spinner in the deeper pools rimmed by alder. It *looked* good, like many of the streams in this country. But growing fish in these streams was like growing corn on rock, and for the same reason. The surficial rock and bogs and the cold climate made for infertile conditions for fish or crops, and the low, warm conditions in summer provided little to hold or sustain a trout. The agglomerations of trout that Roosevelt had encountered had rushed in from the lake. He had mistaken concentrations for abundance. Once the water dropped and warmed, the fish so evident in the springtime would retreat again into Superior.

Through the afternoon, we labored into the wind, slowly gaining shoreline. There are places you arrive at, sometimes by accident, that are so nearly perfect you start the impossible task of trying to rank your favorite places in the world. We came now to such a spot, a small cove and island. Sheltered from the wind, we thought the place was paradise. The beach, for the moment, was trackless sand. A small brook trickled from the cliffs behind us. Agawa's massive hills framed the view on our left. Center stage,

Leach Island rested on the sapphire lake. The sun emerged and warmed the little cove. I was glad I was not alone: I would hardly be able to contain myself. Our dilemma was this: If the wind were to subside, should we paddle on and leave this perfect spot?

The decision was made for us, and suddenly. In the perfect light of our perfect place, the sand flies come out in murderous force and devoured us as we devoured dinner. We threw the gear into the boats and fled up the shore.

We hadn't realized it, but the wind had been dying. The waves were rounding to swells, up to three feet high but easy to traverse. We paddled into a reddening sky past Beatty Cove, scouting the shore for a clearing as the swells sloshed into the cliffs. We found a camp in the woods just as the last light faded and the mosquitoes closed in like fog.

The next morning, Susan panicked. "My hand, it's numb. I can barely close it."

The last two days, we had been making up for our slow start. We were poised now to round Cape Gargantua, a pronounced beak of rock open to wind from the north, west, and south. With luck, we could clear it by late morning, while the lake was still calm. And with Gargantua behind us, we would be in striking distance of Michipicoten, where we had hoped to end our trip. At the very least, we could bail out where the road returned to the shore at Old Woman Bay.

But now this. She held out her hand; it was swollen. It had begun to hurt the first day out, but she had gamely continued to paddle.

"Let's go back to sleep. No need to get started right away."

We woke again at eight. "I have a plan," I said. "What if we paddle on to Gargantua? We can set up camp there, and I can hike to the highway and get the car." I would have to walk about nine miles down a dirt road and hitchhike about eighty.

"I don't like that plan. I don't like the idea of you having to hike like that."

"What are the alternatives?" I asked. To backtrack to Sand River? It was a longer paddle.

"We could press on to Old Woman Bay," Susan said. "How far is it?"

I flipped through the maps. A bit more than twenty miles. But what about her hand? I hadn't thought of things coming to a stop like this—the weather, sure, but not our own infirmities.

We took our time around camp. We fashioned a splint from a plastic food container and wrapped it with duct tape to limit the movement of her wrist. We pushed off about noon. We would limp to Gargantua Harbour and make our decision there.

The shore was steep and craggy, with several small skerries and sharp points of rock hooking into the lake. Rounding a massive bluff, we arrived in Gargantua Harbour, once the location of a village where fishermen packed lake trout and herring in ice to be shipped aboard the Booth Fisheries boats that traveled the shore. In the early 1900s, tourist cabins sprung up in the fishing village and cruising yachts moored in the harbor. Dances were held on the village dock. But with the demise of fishing in the 1950s, the village died and buildings now lay in ruin. As we landed at the old village site, several kids were playing on shore. Their parents, we learned, were ready to leave. Now would be the time to make our exit. I asked Susan about her hand. She could go on, she said.

"Are you sure?"

Yes, she said, she wanted to press on.

We looped through the harbor, looking for the wreck of the *Columbus*, a wooden steam tug that had caught fire. Cut from its moorings, it was pushed into the bay, where it burned brilliantly to the waterline and sank in thirty feet of water. "You can't miss it," we had been told, but of course we did.

We rounded the point guarding the north end of the bay. Ahead we saw Devil's Warehouse Island, so called because it was a source of the Ojibwa's sacred paints, in the form of a deep vein of hematite hidden in the treacherous depths of a cave. The island's caves and grottoes may also have hidden sacred *Medae* birch-bark scrolls. A sheer cliff of the island, in its various colors, suggested images, huge images, the shadows of pictographs.

"That's what you hoped the pictographs would be like," I suggested.

"Yes, like the light show on Stone Mountain."

The names of features around Gargantua suggest everything that is right and wrong with geographical names in the region. Gargantua and the nearby Pantagruel Bay were named by the French, perhaps the voyageurs, for the bawdy giant king Gargantua and his drunken son, created by the sixteenth-century French satirist François Rabelais. One can easily imagine that the voyageurs recognized kinship between their beloved giant king, with his bawdiness and insatiable appetites, and the Ojibwa demigod Nanaboozhoo. At times taking the form of a giant, Nanaboozhoo was the Ojibwa guardian, teacher, and trickster, a paradoxical character both powerful and fallible, wise and venal. He spent much time at Gargantua. Leaping once across Lake Superior, he oversaw the forests and lakes from a vantage point now called the Devil's Chair.

Devil's Chair, Devil's Warehouse, Devil's Frying Pan (a broad reef)—all at one time may have been named, if not for Nanaboozhoo, then for the many manitous, or spirits, that inhabited the Ojibwa world. To rename geographic features is the prerogative of the conqueror. But rather than simply renaming sacred features, the people who came to this country co-opted and subverted the names to demonize the very places that were once sacred. J. Elliot Cabot, the journal-keeper on Agassiz's expedition, observed that "the gods of the aborigines here as elsewhere are to their Christianized descendants nothing but the devil, the *elder* spirit of all mythologies."

John Ryerson, a Methodist missionary, passed Gargantua in the mid-1800s. Undoubtedly he surveyed the soaring cliffs and impenetrable forest of prickly black spruce. Perhaps for the thousandth time he heard the sing-song of the white-throated sparrow (*poor Canada Canada*). He may have thought of white men and Indians whose lives had ended in storms and shipwrecks and of the gnawing famine of a hard winter. Did he also reflect on his own religion's silence on the subject of dreaming rocks or the never-ending horizon? No, probably not. "A more sterile, dreary-looking region I never saw, one barren waste of rocks rising above the other," he wrote. How far is such a place from the Puritans' "waste and howling wilderness"? Or Cotton Mather's "Indian Wilderness," with its "horrid Sorcerers, and hellish Conjurers and such as conversed with Daemons." Could the gods of this place be anything but evil?

We paddled up Tugboat Channel. The channel, with a line of islands, skerries, and reefs to our left, gave the illusion of protection. The rock looked black against the water like sapphire. A light breeze nudged us along so that we made reasonable time, even though we paddled lightly to spare Susan's hand.

The channel delivered us to the very tip of Cape Gargantua. There our protection vanished. We were alone, surrounded by the thin horizon, as sharp as a razor. And directly ahead of us sat the Devil's Chair. It was indeed a throne of rock. Snow and ice hung in the crags, and tiny gnarled white cedars clung to the back. Portals that had eroded through the back of the "chair" looked out over more than a hundred miles of open water.

I told Susan I felt a chill.

Susan responded with a Japanese word: "*Sabishii*. It means lonely. It's a word you don't have to say with a subject or an object. It's just a feeling, an atmospheric word."

Sabishii. That was much better than *devil*. The Indians and the voyageurs left offerings of tobacco on the rock. I was neither an Indian, nor a voyageur, so I did not. Still, I wanted to move to a protected shore, to tiptoe out of here before the lake awakened.

A freshening west wind and growing waves washed us onto a long curved, cobble beach where we pitched our tent. We had paddled fifteen miles. Only a single point, Cap Chaillon, stood between us and a possible takeout at Old Woman Bay. On the map, Chaillon looked like a stone arrowhead. Once around the cape, we could glide eleven miles in the partial protection of Bushy and Old Woman Bays. With the aid of the splint and our easy pace, Susan's hand had fared tolerably well. We would get up early to get around Chaillon and would reach the highway by noon.

I woke at five with the best of intentions. But I had barely emerged from the tent when a sharp wind whipped in from the open lake. Whitecaps spread across our bay like a grass fire. I crawled back into the tent, hoping it would blow by. But it continued to build, and by the time Susan and I arose at six-thirty, the waves were growing larger. During breakfast, the tent stakes began to spring loose. We anchored the tent with rocks, driftwood, and bungee cords.

The wind increased throughout the morning and it began to rain. The tent shuddered; it began to leak, and then caved in as the right front pole bent like a bow. I scouted the woods for a sheltered tent site, but the black spruce formed an impenetrable wall. We would stand or fall on the beach. I straightened the pole, splinted the two windward poles with driftwood and duct tape, and then dragged the kayaks closer to the tent to anchor extra guy lines.

The foul weather had the heavy grayness and permanence of stone. I was anxious, but Susan recited things to be thankful for: it was Sunday, a day of rest, which we were getting in abundance. Her hand was feeling better. And we were, after all, safe.

We retreated to the tent and to our reading. Our choices seemed a little too queer to be real. Susan read Thomas Merton's *Thoughts in Solitude:*

> So the man who wanders into the desert to be himself must take care that he does not go mad and become the servant of the one who dwells there in a sterile paradise of emptiness and rage.

I read *The Manitous.* Basil Johnston's tellings of traditional Ojibwa stories of the supernatural are as lively, engaging, and earthy as Merton's philosophizing is abstract, stultifying, and ethereal. Soon we took turns reading of manitous; Merton was tucked safely in a dry pack.

The Ojibwa world was populated by *maemaegawaehnssiwuk* (fairies), *cheebyuk* (ghosts), *nebaunaubaewuk* (mermen), and the dreaded cannibals of the winter wind, the *weendigoes.* At the head of it all was the Kitchi-Manitou, the Great Mystery and creator, and Muzzu-Kummik-Quae, Mother Earth. Central in the pantheon of secondary spirits are the four sons of the human Winonah and the manitou Ae-pungishimook (The West), who raped her each time. Ae-pungishimook represented age and destiny and, as Johnston notes, age ravishes youth. The last son, immediately after birth, announced, "I am Nanaboozhoo!" Then his mother, Winonah, died.

In comparison to his brothers, Nanaboozhoo was only too human. While his brothers were the caricatures of human traits—the warrior, the mystic, the entertainer—Nanaboozhoo was the whole human, in all his frailty and faults and complexity. He has been described variously as the "prototype of humankind" and the "active quickening power of life." Though capable of superhuman feats, Nanaboozhoo was timid when he needed to be brave, vain when he should have been humble. He didn't pay attention as he should have to the wind, thunder, and waves, and he neglected rituals, ceremonies, and vision quests. He was the imperfect essence of the human character, capable of great things, but otherwise bumbling and struggling and failing to understand the world around him. Nanaboozhoo is the central and most beloved of the manitous. Stories of him are told in winter, when the animals are asleep, and the same story is told a different way each time. Despite his faults, he meant well, and that is the essential

meaning of the name the Ojibwa use for themselves and their allied tribes—
Anishinaubaek, the beings who derive their goodness from their intent.

As we read, each wave rolled down the beach with the sound of a jet.
The tent shook, filled with wind, billowed, lifted, and shuddered. The fabric
slapped and the poles flexed. Except to stroll the beach briefly, we stayed
inside all day. But for my watch, I had no sense of time.

At daybreak fog lay heavy on the water. The air was calm, but I could hear
the swells from yesterday roll along the beach. There's an old Finnish saying: "He who sleeps in a calm must row during a gale." We wanted to clear
Cap Chaillon before the lake took back the opportunity. We boiled water
for coffee, ate a cold breakfast, and packed up the gear.

On the lake, we bobbed in three-foot swells. Chaillon lay hidden by the
fog, but we could hear the crash of waves. We paddled on a compass bearing, keeping the surf to our right. (Merton: "We are like pilots of fog-bound
steamers, peering into the gloom in front of us, listening for the sounds of
other ships, and we can only reach our harbor if we keep alert.") I watched
the compass on my deck, knowing that once the sound of the surf faded in
the distance we would have cleared the point and could turn to the northeast. We paddled. We listened. We paddled. But the point seemed never to
end. I worried that beyond the point, large swells might come from a different direction, creating a weird mishmash of waves. What if Susan freaked
out? Yet each time she bobbed above a swell, she seemed calm and in control. Maybe I was the one who was freaking out.

"It's okay, we're doing fine," I said over and over. Susan said nothing.

The sound of waves fell away and we turned sharply northeast to find it
again. We had rounded the cape. At that moment, Susan's words began to
spill—about a book she had been reading, about the beauty of this place,
about the beauty of the fog, "like Chinese watercolors."

We ran with the gentle swells, gliding over water of the deepest teal.
The slosh of sidelong swells ran along the rock. Occasionally a freshet,
fed by yesterday's rain, would splash from the fog-bound cliffs to the lake
below. Entering Old Woman Bay, we paddled along the highest, sheerest
cliff of all. Did the face of an old woman really look out from the rock?
Maybe, but mainly I was impressed by the sheer mass, an unfathomable
weight held in judgment above me. What is a sacred place, except that

which makes you feel humble and insignificant in the face of Nature? And what is a manitou but the power of a place to move you to those thoughts? Such a thought may be too equivocating to pass muster with the Ojibwa, or even Thomas Merton. But, old agnostic that I am, it was good enough for me.

CHAPTER 2

Pukaskwa Peninsula: Michipicoten River to Hattie Cove

A S I HITCHHIKED BACK to our car at Goulais River, the first vehicle to give me a lift was a yellow pickup from the Ontario Ministry of Transportation. That seemed appropriate. The second was a Volvo that had passed me making vague grinding noises, but then doubled back two minutes later, turned around in front of me, and stopped.

"It's tough to get a good look at people at highway speeds," said the old man hunched over the wheel. "My wife said, 'It's an elderly gentleman. Maybe he's in trouble.' You have her to thank for getting a ride."

The woman moved to the backseat and let me sit in the front. Elderly indeed.

They were Joe and Marilyn Ueberschar. They lived in Michipicoten River and were visiting friends near the Sault. I said I had been kayaking. Joe seemed genuinely interested.

"Most people don't have much of an appreciation of nature," he said. "I like nature. More people should have an appreciation of nature."

"Do you hunt and fish?"

"No."

"Do you have a boat? Do you get out on the lake?"

"No, I've never liked water sports."

Joe Ueberschar spoke with an accent, a remnant of his life in a part of eastern Germany that later became Poland. He had emigrated to Canada after World War II. An electrician, he hired on as an electrician's apprentice in the iron mine in Wawa.

"Why did you come to Wawa?"

"There was only one other Jehovah's Witness in Wawa. I thought I might be able to do some good." It was then I noticed copies of the magazine *Awake* in the backseat. "What I like about *Awake* is that it always gives you the facts. You can trust that it will do a balanced job."

Marilyn said she had grown up "in the bush" near Timmins, two hundred miles northeast of the Sault. She had hitchhiked to school each day because there was no bus. She and Joe had married only seven years ago. Marilyn asked about my trip.

"How many people are with you?"

I realized Susan would be stuck at Old Woman Bay until I returned with the car. I didn't want anyone to know she was alone. I didn't know what I had to fear from a middle-aged couple in a middle-aged Volvo headed in the opposite direction, but I decided to lie.

"Four," I said. Joe and Marilyn quietly did the arithmetic, wondering how I, getting only a single car, would pick up four paddlers and four boats.

"How many people?"

"Four," I said, and changed the subject. "The trip was really beautiful," I said. "Stunning scenery."

We drove a bit in silence, over granite hills and down into wetlands and creeks. When he had arrived in Sault Sainte Marie, Joe said, he had traveled to Wawa on the Algoma Central Railway. The train had descended some five hundred feet into the canyon of the Agawa River. At that time, the road extended only as far as the Montreal River. Construction had been halted during World War II. Though Joe didn't say so, I had learned that Wawans, anxious for a road to their town, had marched in 1951 along the route to the Montreal River as a demonstration to restart construction. To dramatize their isolation, they covered the distance, less than seventy miles, in no less than seventeen days. The route, known notoriously as the Gap, wound inland, far from the lakeshore. It was, in the late 1950s, the only section of the Superior Circle Route yet unfinished. Highway surveyors built rafts to cross lakes and rivers. Construction of the roadway required three million pounds of explosives, the removal of ten billion tons of rock, and the building of twenty-five bridges. The highway opened 17 September 1960 with a parade of automobiles from the Sault to Wawa.

As we passed Pancake Bay, Joe asked, "Did you hear why they call it Pancake Bay?"

"Yes, I heard that story."

"What did you hear?"

"That the voyageurs were often low on provisions, except for flour. So they had pancakes before they went into the Sault."

"Well, here's what I heard. When they were building the railroad through here, they would leave from Sault Sainte Marie and arrive up here just about breakfast time, pancake time."

They turned at Goulais River and drove all the way to my car. As I stepped out, Joe gave me a couple copies of *Awake* magazines and invited me to visit.

The Pukaskwa Peninsula has the rounded but jagged contour of a flint scraper. The decision to locate the road in the interior to avoid the deeply furrowed shoreline was, in retrospect, remarkably good fortune. Elsewhere along Superior, roads penetrate to the lake. And with roads, come cabins and then homes and then gas stations, and motels, resorts, and restaurants. But along the Pukaskwa, the road lay, at its furthest extent, fifty miles inland. Except for a hiking trail along the western coast of the peninsula and some logging roads and jeep trails in the east, there are few incursions to the shore. In fact, there are few signs of human activity at all. The most pristine, rugged, and inaccessible portion of this wilderness is Pukaskwa National Park, the largest park along the lake. More than 95 percent of this vast park is classified as wilderness.

Oddly, there is little mention of the Pukaskwa in the journals of early explorers and traders. Cabot, the scribe of the Agassiz expedition, speeds from the Michipicoten River to the Nipigon region, his most telling description of the northeastern shore contained in this single paragraph: "Our little point was as silent as a piece of the primeval earth . . . as if no noise had been heard here since the woods grew, and all Nature seemed sunk in a dead, dreamless sleep." A century ago, loggers cut the best spruce along the major rivers and floated the pulpwood to the lake, where it was assembled in vast rafts and towed to mills elsewhere along the shore. Commercial fishermen operated in some of the small coves. But these activities died out long ago. Without a road to encourage and sustain new activity, the Pukaskwa slipped blissfully into the wilds until it was protected as a park in 1978.

In this unpeopled stretch of country survived unusual remnants of the Pukaskwa's forgotten lives: the so-called Pukaskwa pits, small but mysterious excavations of stones found along ancient beach ridges. Some of the pits appear to be simple foxholes, circular depressions several feet across and a couple of feet deep, where cobbles ranging in size from softballs to bowling balls have been removed. In some cases, rocks have been stacked around the perimeter of the depression—a snow fort in stone. No one knows why the pits were built or when they were constructed. Their locations aren't included on any general map I had seen. When I called Pukaskwa National Park to ask where I might look for pits, the young man on the phone declined to tell me because local Ojibwa considered them sacred sites and because the park was concerned about vandalism. I couldn't quibble, but his secretiveness annoyed me. Only after talking to several kayakers who had paddled the Pukaskwa shore did I come up with a list of locations where I might see the pits.

Susan and I decided to start our trip at the mouth of the Michipicoten River and paddle west and north around the peninsula to Hattie Cove, a little more than a hundred miles. The river mouth had a long history of human use. It was a strategic site during the fur trade because a sixteen-day journey up the Michipicoten, Missinaibi, and Moose Rivers led to James Bay. During the early 1700s, the French built a post at the river mouth to shortcut Lake Superior Ojibwa, who would bring furs to British traders. In later years, after the French had lost control of New France, the upstart North West Company established a post at the mouth of the Michipicoten to upstage the rival Hudson's Bay Company. The two companies merged in 1821, and Michipicoten River became the headquarters for the company's Lake Superior operations. That may sound impressive, but when Agassiz's party passed through in 1848, Cabot described a somnolent collection of whitewashed cabins and birch-bark Indian lodges. "The life at these posts," he wrote, "is a very quiet, and, doubtless, monotonous one. . . . An arrival from some other post, a straggling party of explorers for copper, and above all, an occasional packet of newspapers from below—these are the great events." Things picked up with the construction of the Canadian Pacific Railway in the early 1880s. Michipicoten was taken over by a mob of bootleggers led by the town sheriff. The location once again fell into disrepair. A caretaker at the post used records of the Hudson's Bay Company to light his fires. The Great Lakes Power Company, which built and operated several dams on the river, bought the property and, because it couldn't maintain what was left of the post, tore the buildings down.

When we arrived, foundations of the fort could still be seen, but the place wasn't much more energetic than when Cabot saw it. We drove across a sandy isthmus to what had once been a rocky island at the river's mouth. There we met David Wells, owner of Naturally Superior Adventures. That night we ate baked whitefish with him and several volunteers who had been helping to clear a trail. We had a sparkling view of the lakeshore, which stretched infinitely westward. Waves rolled up on the finger of sand at the river mouth.

I told Wells we had recently paddled the East Shore.

"Pukaskwa is a whole 'nother scale larger than the stretch you just came up," he said. He suggested things to look for as we paddled up the coast— Denison Falls, rocky niches to provide shelter if the weather turned bad as we approached Point Isacor, a shipwreck, the old logging village known as the Depot, the stunning entry of Cascade Falls into Lake Superior. He pointed out several good beaches and camps.

"Whether something is a good campsite or not has to do with a lot of things that don't have to do with the lake," he noted, rather enigmatically I thought. "Not only the wind direction, but things like, are you and your sweetie getting along right now? Are you not getting along, in which case they're all crappy sites. But you come back two weeks later and they might be great."

I didn't ask if his sweetie was still around. I did ask about the Pukaskwa pits.

He vaguely referred me to some locations. What were they for? I asked. He said he doubted they had been used as habitation, since they occupy the most inhospitable stretches of shore. He also doubted they had been blinds or lookouts. If they were blinds, he said, why are they arranged in patterns? If lookouts, why not simply wait in the trees? "I imagine some old Ojibwa somewhere has more thorough knowledge than he's telling."

When we awoke, the lake was flat but for gentle swells from yesterday's blow. We ate a cold breakfast and put on the lake quickly, clipping Perkwakwia Point, and passing Indian Beach, the small rocky islands in Doré Bay, and Doré Point. We landed on a gravel beach. The gravel came in all sizes, from pea to softball-sized, sorted by the waves and ice.

As we rested, eight kayaks rounded Minnekona Point from the north. To the best of my recollection, that was seven more than we saw during our previous trip. The paddlers said they had come around the Pukaskwa Peninsula from Hattie Cove, paddling south at first and then curving west. That was the usual way to make the trip and the direction that, at this time of year, most likely ensured favorable winds. We, for the sake of continuity, were determined to do the opposite.

Early in the afternoon, we stopped at the Makwa River. I cast a small spoon into a deep channel excavated by spring floods, but nothing followed. A gusher in spring, but slow, warm, dark, and stained by bog drainage in summer, the Makwa, like most of these northern streams, seemed to die during warm weather.

A couple of miles down the shore, the Mountain Ash River sneaked into the lake over a ledge of rock. The rocks looked like hippos, gray and deeply fissured. By afternoon, we reached the mouth of the Dog, also known as the University River. Once there had been a small commercial fishing operation here. When Agassiz visited *River a la Chienne*, he found a bear skull, two shoulder blades, and vertebrae stuck in the crotch of a tree. The jaws had been bound with spruce root and the bones painted with broad stripes of black and vermilion. Inside the skull was tobacco. The skull, Cabot wrote, signified the grave of a hunter.

We paddled up the broad estuary to see Denison Falls, but when we found a tent on the trail to the waterfall, we returned to the river mouth and pitched our tent on a broad sandbar. As we made camp, two men paddled into the bay. Doug and Phil were from Bayfield, Wisconsin. Doug, perhaps in his early thirties, had guided kayak trips on the lake and had a "winter number in Telluride," where he was a ski instructor. Phil, who was older, worked at a marina and served on the school board. Soon after, two other paddlers pulled into the estuary: Diane and Ricardo, both from Montreal. Like Doug and Phil, they had paddled down from the north and were headed to Michipicoten River. Put your tent anywhere, we told them.

"Geez, you guys might change my mind about Americans coming and wanting to take over Canada," Ricardo said.

"We'll let you know which part of Canada we want for this," Doug said.

Around the campfire, Doug told us about a previous trip to Michipicoten Island, a large island ten miles offshore. Indeed, we had seen it as we paddled today, floating on the dreamy mirage of the calm lake. As Doug and his party were returning to shore, the wind rose, kicking up six-foot waves. One of the paddlers became seasick. He was unable to paddle; so Doug towed him toward shore, the rope twanging and slackening as the boats heaved in the waves, until the surf pitched both boats onto the beach.

Doug had also traveled to Russia and paddled on Lake Baikal. It was the usual fiasco of traveling in Russia, he said, a trip marked by intransigence, drunkenness, and a rollicking and threatening kind of camaraderie. Nonetheless, the lake itself was stunning. Lying in a continental rift, it is surrounded by mountains. Though smaller than Superior, Baikal has by far the greater volume because of its depth, roughly five times that of Superior. More than anything, Doug said, he was astounded simply to be in Russia—the Russia of Dr. Zhivago, Stalin, and intercontinental ballistic missiles.

I gathered that he and Phil paddled together often. "I've boated on this lake for years," Phil said. "Sailboats. But once I got into a sea kayak and began paddling along its shore, I got an entirely different view of the lake."

Diane was a mathematician, Ricardo a physicist. She had traveled to Indonesia a year ago. He wanted to start his own business and be "a big capitalist." Diane said that when they had come to the Pukaskwa six years ago, they had seen no one. It had been like wilderness. But it had changed, she said. It had been discovered. That was the conundrum of a wilderness area, she said. You don't want to tell people about it.

During breakfast, a cold north wind poured down the Dog River valley. Susan and I bundled up and decided to try to push off before the weather worsened or the wind shifted. But as quickly as the wind rose, it died and the sun appeared. Soon we were stripping off clothes.

I fell into a comfortable groove, paddling smoothly and quickly, with little effort or the nagging pain I had often felt in my shoulder. Rocks rose up beneath us—gray, green, and rust, some jagged and veined with quartz. Then they dropped away as we glided out over a canyon of green water, as if flying.

Watching Susan's muscular back and shoulders and the glint of her earrings in the sun, I was struck by her confidence and toughness.

"You're a strong little shit," I said.

"I'm not so strong."

"Yes you are. If you were any stronger, you'd be better than me at everything."

"And what would be wrong with *that?*"

Off to our left lay Michipicoten Island. Yesterday, we could see only the highest point of the island. As we drew closer, two humps rose above the horizon, as if the island were a Bactrian camel walking over a rise. Throughout the morning, it had seemed to shift in the haze and shimmer of the lake. Now we saw it in its entirety. Seventeen miles from end to end, it appeared easy to hit on a compass bearing.

The Ojibwa believed Michipicoten floated on the lake, pushed this way and that by the wind so that sometimes it appeared close to shore and at others far off. They knew the island as the domain of Mishi-bizheu and as a source of minerals. Several legends discouraged visitors. Antoine Denis Raudot reported in the early eighteenth century that four Indians returning from the island had died of verdigris poisoning. Jonathan Carver told of Ojibwas who took gold from the island, but a giant waded after them and demanded they return it. In subsequent years, settlers mined meager deposits of copper ore, battling treacherous mine shafts, mud, bad air, poor light, and dangerous machinery. Michipicoten Island remained one of the most isolated and least visited places on the lake. To paddle across nine miles of open water to the hard, exposed shore of the island was an expedition in itself—one Susan and I were not prepared to undertake.

For the past two days our thoughts had been fixed not on Michipicoten, but on the sharp chin of rock known as Point Isacor. The coast broke sharply at this point, opening abruptly to a west wind. To make matters dicier, the four miles of shoreline preceding the point consisted of sheer cliffs vulnerable to a south wind. David Wells had said we could find shelter, but only in small nooks that would be uncomfortable in a storm.

As we approached Isacor, cliffs rose more than six hundred feet. Yet as high and as steep as they were, their faces were covered with trees, spruce and white cedar that started in the talus and shot up the cliffside. As we paddled, a bald eagle appeared.

Eagles have the uncanniest sense. In the Ojibwa world, they were intermediaries between the spirit and material worlds, messengers of the Kitchi Manitou. They were good omens. I am not inclined to believe (as we approached Isacor, I would have liked to), but eagles are damned impressive nonetheless, graceful, bold, and wide-winged.

The point was anticlimactic. No west wind waited for us—only more of the glassy lake. But the view was stunning: the rocks turned brick red and the lichens green. Dikes of black rock divided the cliffs. Cedars clung to the tiniest crevices, in hopes of becoming spirit trees. We landed at a cobble beach framed by cliffs and laid our stuff out to dry. As we dug out lunch, a family of mergansers swam in from the west. Three young otters swam in from the east. "Come here, come here," Susan called. Surprisingly, they came. She waded into the water toward them. They dove and popped again to the surface. With snakelike tails, they looked like serpents themselves, slithering through the water.

The shoreline gave way to more gradual, yet still rugged, country known as The Flats. I had no expectations of it, but was delighted. It was not a national park or a landmark. It was simply wild and seemingly endless. Floating Heart Bay, guarded by islands, ended in a long, sand beach. The Floating Heart River gushed over a thirty-foot waterfall to an inlet in the lake. The boulders were lively, electric green, like aftershave with golden flecks. Cormorants and gulls rested on a rock near the river's mouth.

But apparently we were not destined to stay here. "Let's go down to Le Petit Mort Rocks," Susan said. It was a name I could not pronounce, as I cannot pronounce anything in French. Susan said she wanted to go there because it was where Doug and Phil had begun the morning before. "I want to do it if those boys can do it in a day," she said.

We found a small beach set deep in a cove. A campsite lay just inside the fringe of woods. A trail led to a tall chimney and the ruins of a log cabin surrounded by old cans, pails, bottles, and slabs of concrete. The place had been thoroughly used. The cabin was poorly built with round logs held in place by nails. Black spruce closed in all around. How far did these trails go? For that matter, how far back in time had it been since this cabin was occupied? Not far, I thought, in either case.

When I read Pierre Esprit Radisson's account of his Lake Superior explorations, undertaken in about 1660, I was impressed by the remarkable number of people he encountered. Far from entering a trackless wilderness, Radisson and the Sieur des Groseilliers, with their band of Frenchmen and Huron "wildmen," fought and sneaked their way through a gauntlet of the feared Iroquois. Once on the Great Lakes, they regularly encountered Ojibwa, Cree, Huron, Dakota, Nipissing, Ottawa, and Assiniboine. Radisson wrote hardly at all about the land, but rather about the people he met.

By contrast, we had encountered only a smattering of boaters. Remnants such as the trashed cabin suggested that the people who had once lived here had packed up and vanished.

In the morning, gray clouds and choppy waves marched in from the southeast, where a weird pink light spread across the horizon. A flight of diving ducks sped as low as fighters flying under radar. It felt like the first look at fall. The radio reported one-meter waves and forecast waves of two meters this afternoon. Moving out of the protection of the rocks, we tossed among three-footers. Periodically, a four-footer ran beneath us and blocked the horizon. Susan appeared tense. I was on guard, though soon the waves rocked me into a kind of trance. We paddled beyond Ganley Harbor and then past a bay where, I was told, a ship lay in about fifteen feet of water. We would never see it through these waves. We ducked behind an island, and as waves crashed on either side, landed in a cove to rest.

The wind rose through the early afternoon, to the point where we put up the tent and prepared to camp. By late afternoon, however, it began to subside. We struck camp and paddled again into the waves. They were large, but with less wind, soft and friendly. We traveled quickly in the following seas. At Wheat Bin we saw a tent and a red canoe overturned on the beach. Two people walked the shore not far away. The Canadians have a custom, inherited surely from the Indians, of traveling by canoe along the Pukaskwa coast. I suspected these paddlers had been wind bound since morning, perhaps all day. I was glad to have the kayaks to avoid that frustration. We waved, they waved, and we pressed on by rock, bruise-colored and gray, rose and rust. The coast appeared especially craggy, topped by primeval forest. Waves had blasted out caves and overhangs in the cliffs. Pukaskwa Point made a dramatic statement. Rising two hundred feet, it made a face in profile. Misty opalescent light bathed water and sky. In front of me, Susan had her paddle across the deck and simply bounced in the waves as the water sloshed against the cliff. She looked at home.

Rounding the point, we looked for the Pukaskwa River. We saw no place to land, only a steep gravel bank under repeated assault by the waves. Then, as we moved closer, we saw that the gravel bar hid the narrow river mouth. On bounding waves, we surfed into a calm estuary flanked by dark cliffs. We set our tent on the sand. The location had been a seasonal camp for the

Ojibwa, probably for centuries. With several old campfires, it obviously remained a popular site.

The river reaches into the heart of the Pukaskwa Peninsula. Loggers on the tributaries would cut spruce and balsam fir during the winter and skid the logs to the riverside or onto frozen ponds behind makeshift logging dams. In spring, as the tributaries filled with snowmelt, the logs were rolled down the banks, the dams were opened, and the resulting flood of water flushed the pulpwood through rapids, falls, and canyons toward the lake.

In the morning, as the fog lifted from the river mouth, we paddled up the black cleft of the river. Cedar, spruce, and delicate brook lobelia clung to the cliffs. Finally we were stopped by a shelf of rock and a waterfall. It was a trickle; the whole river at this point necked down to a couple yards. In spring it would be a roaring torrent. As we eased back to the lake, Susan spotted a heavy iron ring hanging from a cliff, an anchoring point for a "boom" of huge logs that would stretch across the estuary and trap the accumulated bounty of pulpwood. As we paddled north along the coast, we passed short bolts of pulpwood the waves had thrown ashore in decades past.

As we rounded a point, the land disappeared into fog, as if we were paddling into a great white abyss. "Where now?" Susan asked. Indeed, where now? We followed a compass bearing into Imogene Cove. The bay was stunning, even in the fog—or perhaps because of it. As we neared cliffs, we could see that quartz veins shot like lightning across jagged red rock, suggesting bizarre figures. Were such patterns the origin of the thunderbird? Green water sloshed in grottoes and chinks blasted in the rock. As the sun burned through the fog, lighting the islands in the bay, we began to look for the old Depot.

At the mouth of the Imogene River, we spotted grassy fields and fireweed, sure signs of human disturbance in this northern forest. Log cribbing in the river suggested a wharf. At the edge of a clearing stood, just barely, a log cabin. The roof appeared to have collapsed long ago. Old tin cans surrounded the cabin and a wood stove lay in the woods. According to my reading, four hundred people lived here during the early 1900s, when the Depot served as the base for the Lake Superior Paper Company's pulp cutting operation on the Pukaskwa. During its heyday, on either side of the river sat a large bunkhouse, doctor's house, blacksmith's shop, harness maker's cabin, cook shack, warehouse, offices, cabins, stables, and hay sheds. A boom of

Little remains of the Depot, a bustling logging community that once existed in Imogene Cove.

logs contained pulpwood in the cove. When the season's logs had been collected, small tugs would gather the logs into a large raft, surrounded by a single boom up to two miles long. Large tugs snared the raft and towed it to the Abitibi Power and Paper Company mill at Sault Sainte Marie.

Whole families lived at the Depot. Ships visited the community during the summer, but in the winter the Depot settled into deep isolation. The only way out was the seventy-mile White River Trail. When a logging sleigh smacked Joe Lefebvre in the chest and broke his jaw, he stayed in camp eighteen days, his jaw wired shut, until he was hauled out by dogsled to White River. The trip took thirty hours each way.

The inhabitants of the Depot were French, Scottish, Scandinavian, and Ojibwa. Finns unfailingly built saunas near their homes. Many lived here year-round. According to a display we found near shore, the cabin we saw had once been inhabited by Gord and Lee Fletcher. One poster showed a decorative iron cross. It was made for Raymond Lafleur, whose photo was shown with a caption explaining that he had died in a house fire eight days after the photo was taken.

The Depression killed the Depot. Loggers left in the spring of 1930 and never returned. An Ojibwa family lived on the site for many years. Today fireweed and raspberries grew in profusion; lichens covered the droughty openings and crunched underfoot. Late blueberries were shriveled and dry. We found the remnants of an old road, logs (perhaps the remnant of an old building), and a porcelain vessel of some kind. I surveyed a half mile of beach, the islands, and the lake to the horizon. The only person I saw was Susan, bent over, botanizing. In fact, we had seen no one for some time. Despite the evidence of people, even the spirits seemed to have left this place. To me it was, simply, empty.

The wind was up again, and we fought with every stroke around Davis Island toward Pointe LaCanadienne. Paddling around Superior had made me infinitely more aware of the wind than I ever had been—its direction, its speed, its gusts and variability, whether it was stiffening or flagging. This morning it blew strong from the west-northwest. We paddled hard into peaked waves up to three feet high. Pointe LaCanadienne was a massive headland, elemental, exposed and raw. Just rock and water that, in the wind, seemed infinitely cold, deep and blue. Rounding the point, we turned broadside to the waves. The wind put Susan in a foul mood, as though it were a personal affront. We decided to put ashore at Richardson Island.

Old beach lines, or terraces, mark much of the Superior shore. Agassiz, the earliest and most forceful proponent of glacial Ice Ages, noticed these terraces and wondered if they were evidence of higher lake levels or rising land. In the years since, geologists have concluded that they are both. As glaciers receded from the Great Lakes basin, the melting ice opened lower outlets to the glacial predecessors of Superior, dropping the water level in stages. Today's Lake Superior, for example, may be nearly six hundred feet lower than Glacial Lake Duluth.

Despite the evidence of the old beach ridges, the exact level at each stage has been difficult to determine because as the water dropped, the land rose. With the retreat of the ice, a mile deep in places, the stubbornly elastic

45

bedrock rebounded, rising at glacial speed, in some cases more than three hundred feet. Since the glaciers retreated to the northeast, the southwest was the first portion of the basin to begin to rise. Rebound continues today and is most significant in the northeast (near the Pukaskwa, in fact), which rises nearly twenty inches per century, relative to the southwest shore. To confuse matters, the rebound of land near the lake's present outlet has again *raised* levels in the past three thousand years. Around much of the Lake Superior shore, especially in the northeastern end of the lake, old strand lines sit several hundred feet above the present lake level. They are simply beaches of rocks, sorted by size, much like any other beach except that they are now encrusted with lichens. From the water, old beach ridges appear as gray-green plateaus.

It is on just such abandoned beaches that Pukaskwa pits are found. We knew that a concentration of pits occurred somewhere near Richardson Island. As we approached, we spotted an old beach ridge, weathered gray-green, perched twenty to thirty feet above the lake. *Ah, a perfect place for a Pukaskwa pit.* We landed on boulders below the beach ridge and spread our clothes out to dry. Then I walked up the slope and poked through a fringe of spruce separating the active beach from the old beach. And there they were, right at my feet—two Pukaskwa pits.

One was shallow, as though it had caved in on itself. The other was in better shape, about three feet deep and six across, as if someone had lifted rocks out and carelessly stacked them on the perimeter to make a foxhole or fort. The rocks were encrusted with bright green and pale gray lichen. The boulders, which ranged in size from bricks to concrete blocks, were far more angular than the boulders on the present beach, suggesting that the old beach had not been active for long. Scanning around I saw one other pit and perhaps another. Had they been made simultaneously? And why? I eased into one to see what I could see. I had no illusions that I would be blessed with sudden insight or transported through the millennia to see as the makers of these pits might have seen. The pit did provide a good view of the water—but not as good as if I simply sat on the beach. I had heard that Pukaskwa pits provided a view of an island, and sure enough, out in front of us sat a rocky island.

Could the pit have been a blind from which to hunt caribou? You'd be hidden, but not as well as if you simply stood behind a tree. Perhaps it was a fortification for battle. The sharp loose boulders would make it difficult for

The puzzle of the Pukaskwa pits: were they sacred sites or something more prosaic?

someone to run up on your position without twisting an ankle. On the other hand, your enemy could land two hundred yards away and avoid you altogether. Then, as you looked out to the island, he could sneak through the woods and shoot you in the back. Maybe they were storage pits. In preparation for traveling, Ojibwa could have stored inessentials in under-ground caches until they returned. Unfortunately, as my own experience demonstrated, these pits were rather easy to find.

The Pukaskwa pits first came to the attention of the archeological world just over a half century ago. In 1949, Colin MacMillan, a paper mill employee on an autumn boat trip, was hunting for grouse near Richardson Harbor when he nearly stumbled over a shallow pit surrounded by a rock wall. In the summers that followed, he showed the structure and others like it to two advisors to the Royal Ontario Museum and to Tom McIlwraith, head of the anthropology department at the University of Toronto. McIlwraith and MacMillan, searching the shore between Pic Island and Ganley Harbour, found 180 pits, though none were as well preserved as the first. Their location ranged from the first abandoned strand line near the water to very old beaches 150 feet above the present lake level. McIlwraith asked local Ojibwa if they knew what the pits were for. The Ojibwa told McIlwraith they knew nothing about them. Indeed, they hadn't even known they existed.

In 1960, J. Norman Emerson, writing in *Ontario History*, suggested the pits were religious sites, where young men maintained lonely vigils, fasting for days and waiting for the vision that would define their lives. He came to this conclusion, he wrote, for the simple reason that he could think of no other. In the 1970s, Ken C. A. Dawson, chairman of the anthropology department at Lakehead University in Thunder Bay, surveyed pits along the Canadian shore. In 1979 he published "The Pukaskwa Religious Stone Features of Lake Superior." Citing Emerson, he concluded that the pits were religious sites. In fact, he went so far as to distinguish, on the basis of their shape and configuration, "oracle grots," "vision quest pits," and "conjurers lodges," among others. Since Dawson's paper, the belief has become widespread that the pits served various ceremonial or sacred purposes. The evidence? None, unless your idea of evidence is the lack of a better explanation.

Researchers have had trouble enough with the more prosaic mysteries of the pits, such as their age. Scientists knew the approximate ages of various beach lines, but the pits might have been built long after the beaches rose above lake level. Early excavations of several pits turned up a smattering of broken pottery and projectile points. These items, too, could be dated with some accuracy, but since they fell freely through the cobbles, their depth and position said almost nothing about their relationship to other found objects or to the age of the pits. Conceivably, a brand new penny could fall from a researcher's pocket and clatter between the cobbles until it came to rest next to a three-thousand-year-old spear point.

Brian Ross, an archeologist for Parks Canada, and Matthew Betts, an archaeology undergraduate at the University of Toronto, have attempted to date the pits according to the tendency of rock to soften with exposure to the elements. The two men examined about two dozen pits at two sites along the Pukaskwa coast, using a device called a Schmidt hammer to compare the hardness of rock at the bottom of each pit (exposed to weathering when the pit was constructed) to the hardness of cobbles elsewhere on the beach terrace. Knowing the rate at which rock softens with exposure to the elements, Betts was able to estimate when the cobbles were excavated. In a paper published in *Archaeometry*, he concluded that the pits were constructed by the Blackduck culture (quite likely Cree) between four hundred and nine hundred years ago. Pits built on old beach ridges far from the lake gave evidence of being even younger than pits found nearer the water.

When I talked to Ross, I mentioned that I was skeptical about the religious origins of the pits; I was especially suspicious of a scheme that distinguished invocation structures from oracle grots. Ross said he was, too. He suspected most pits, if not all, were built for utilitarian purposes. Imagine the Indians of an earlier era, he said, traveling the hard coast in bark canoes, dugouts, or skin boats in pursuit of fish. Lake trout and whitefish were most accessible in spring and fall, when the weather on the lake was unpredictable and severe. They needed to build shelters near shore to wait out seasonal storms. Perhaps they excavated pits, stacked the rocks in the form of walls, and stretched hide or lashed birch-bark to a sapling frame to form a roof. Pits without walls might have been used as caches for property or food.

If nothing else, Ross said, the sheer concentration of pits in places argued against their use in vision quests, which, after all, required solitude. The old beach line that Susan and I now explored seemed just such a place. Within minutes we spotted at least a dozen pits. Several were fairly distinct. Others were invisible up close, but as I stepped back, I could see a pattern to the rocks suggesting that sometime in the past they had been arranged— the shadow of human endeavor.

We ate lunch and idled on the beach until late in the afternoon, when we pushed off to make a few miles before evening. But the sky suddenly turned gray and a gust of wind funneled up the backside of Richardson Island with such force we could barely make headway. We landed on a gravel tombolo and hiked up to another old beach ridge to look for a campsite.

Breasting the rise, we confronted another Pukaskwa pit. It was magnificent in comparison to the others, perhaps eight by ten feet and surrounded by a wall fully two feet high, with a small break or "doorway" opposite the lake. This, judging by the location and appearance, must have been the very pit MacMillan discovered a half century ago.

We found a tent site nearby and returned to the pit after dinner to drink tea and smoke a cigar in contemplation of the waning day. Perched about thirty feet above the lake, we faced the setting sun with a long view down a line of cliffs running toward the northwest. Behind us, a mountain of rock rose several hundred feet. I felt as though we rested on an altar.

I sat inside the pit and studied the lichen-encrusted rocks. Whose hands laid these? How long ago? And for what purpose? As I stood back to take a photograph, a single beam of crepuscular light streamed eerily into the pit.

"Don't we always like to think it's ceremonial?" Susan remarked.

Yes. As Jake Barnes might have said, isn't it pretty to think so? If we once called spirits devils and denigrated what Indians thought holy, we now seem to insist on the opposite—that all they touched is worthy of veneration. In this spirit of political correctness and romanticism, a crude rock structure can no longer be a food cache or a leaky shelter. It must be a vision quest pit, an oracle grot. As I looked at the pit, I thought it was most interesting not for what it revealed (or failed to reveal) of early inhabitants, but for what it said of modern sensibilities.

Skeptic that I am, I entertained an image of Ojibwa teenagers on a vision quest. The spirits are slow to speak. Getting bored, the kids build forts on an old beach and fling rocks at one another.

Something about the morning made it unappealing. It was a day without character. The sun appeared, but intermittently. The wind blew from the north, but not hard. Waves danced on the lake, but without force. I arose with aches and pains, the infirmities of age multiplied. Thank God I had Susan to buoy my spirits.

"Bah, humbug," she said.

We pulled on our wetsuits, still wet. And they smelled bad. "I'm imagining I'm climbing into a warm sleeping bag instead, with the smell of spring air," Susan said. "This is the real Pukaskwa pits." I pulled on mine as if it were someone else's cold dead skin.

We paddled without ambition, landing at Otter Island for lunch. A screech high up in the cliffs called our attention to a nest of peregrine falcons. Up on the first beach ridge we found more Pukaskwa pits, all small and caved in, without walls. We continued along the outside edge of Otter Island, hugging the cliffs to avoid the rising wind. At the northern tip, sunlight brightened the red and white lighthouse. Through a narrow channel, sheltered by a small island lying next to Otter, we paddled into Old Daves

The Otter Island Lighthouse: the cheery red and white exterior belies a grim past.

Harbour, named for a commercial fisherman nearly a century ago. Across the channel sat the red and white residence of the lighthouse keeper, with perky dormers on the second story and flowers outside. Its cheery appearance belied its history: during a late November snowstorm in 1930, assistant keeper John Moore bled to death on the doorstep. The keeper, Gilbert MacLachlan, remained with the body nearly two weeks, eating the last of the season's supplies of crackers and water, until a boat hauled MacLachlan and Moore's corpse to the Sault.

We crossed to the mainland, rolling over the sidelong waves, to Cascade Falls. With low water, four gentle braids fell directly to the lake. As we landed, a canoe approached from the north. The two young canoeists were Canadian. The men had put in near the headwaters of the White River. For eight days they had run rapids and portaged falls through the wild back

These young Canadians, whom we met at Cascade Falls, were undertaking a bold adventure.

country. Three days ago they reached Superior and began following the
Pukaskwa coast, eventually to reach Michipicoten River. Yesterday they had
paddled down from Oiseau Bay, which struck me as remarkable, given the
strong wind and unprotected shore. Their canoe was lovely wood and canvas, with rich wood gunwales and ribs. "I built it at a canoe shop I worked at
in Maine," said the fellow in the stern.

"We're just staying for lunch," I said. "If you want to stay here, you're welcome to it."

"Good, we're awfully tired," the sternman said.

"We've been up since five," said the bowman.

One had curly blonde hair; the other the beginnings of a neat beard.
They looked as though they might have stepped out of a magazine story
from the forties. I admired them. I thought that a man who takes such a trip
in a wood and canvas canoe not only likes canoeing, but he must also love
canoes, and he must be a romantic.

The following morning, we reached Grandma Stevens Pond, separated
from Superior by a strand of rock and fringe of woods. Susan spotted three
otters and paddled off to make friends, leaving me to hike into the pond
with a fishing rod. The lake was named, the story goes, in the early 1900s,
when the Stevens family sailed the shore in their yacht *Cambria*. The grandmother insisted that she be put ashore in her wheelchair to fish the pond
for trout.

These days, Grandma would need an airlift. The boardwalk for her
wheelchair was long rotted away, and I clambered over rocks, roots, alder,
and blow-downs. After a hundred yards, I reached a bog-stained pond. I
began casting a small spoon halfway to the far shore. Soon, a strike. Then,
a fish, a twisting, squirming brook trout of about nine inches. Within a half
hour I had caught many more, including several that measured a full foot.
They were stunning, already in their spawning colors, as dark as ripe olives,
like the water, with bellies like fire and pectoral fins trimmed with pure
white lines. They were, perhaps, the most beautiful freshwater fish I had ever
seen. I called for Susan. No answer, so I hiked back to the big lake to find her.

Susan, just pulling up to shore, reported on the otters. An adult and two
kits swam to her kayak, growling and hissing. They dove and cavorted. One
of the kits skedaddled, but the other alternately swam alongside the boat
and rode on the mother's back. Susan didn't know if they were playing or

defending territory. They would not leave her until she paddled away to re-join me.

The remainder of the day we followed the gray shore. The land was ut-terly elemental. Indeed, it appeared as though the vegetation had simply been peeled back from the shore, leaving long tapered outcrops. English Fishery Harbour, backed by dark mountains, framed a stunning sweep of rocky islands. Mammoth rocks, pink, gray, and green, breached the surface like whales. Spruce and cedar, like bonsai, clung to the tiniest perches. The most subtle line separated the calm gray water from the calm gray sky, as though one reflected the other endlessly. At that moment, I thought it was the most beautiful stretch of shore I had ever seen.

We swung perhaps a half mile from shore, paddling through islands and skerries scattered across the lake like crumbs fallen from the mainland. They were nearly bare, except for lichens, though one supported a forest of double-crested cormorants, standing, hooked beaks tilted upward. Though we approached no closer than a couple of hundred yards, they leaped off the rock, nearly belly flopping on the water before their wings bore them up. In flight, their wing beats appeared double-jointed and flappy, unlike the stiff whistling strokes of a loon.

We passed through Oiseau Bay—"bird bay." Stretching more than a mile back into the land, it enclosed at least two dozen island. The rocks rippled with veins of quartz and intrusions of various colors. Finally, in the last hour of light, we landed at Fish Harbour, where a beach of sugar sand stretched nearly a mile. We set our tent on an established site. The Coastal Hiking Trail followed this section of shore, bringing hikers carrying a steady supply of food, which, we were warned, attracted black bears. After dinner, we cleaned up scrupulously. As always, we packed the food in the front holds and wiped all traces of food from the boats.

The quiet of the evening amplified the call of a distant loon. The hum of a nighthawk's wings sounded like jets. I listened for sounds of metal dishes and the dull thud of a plastic boat. I was troubled by thoughts of waking to find a kayak perforated by tooth holes and claw marks. Gradually these pre-occupations fell away and I slept.

From Fish Harbour it was an easy paddle to to Hattie Cove, where David Wells was to have dropped our car. With only eleven miles ahead of us and a south breeze behind us, we should be on the road by midday.

We ducked behind a string of islands. For two miles they blocked the wind. Beyond Shot Watch Cove (named for a pocket watch found with a bullet hole—no explanatory circumstances known), we ran out of islands and angled into the lake. An eagle flew overhead. "Bald eagle!" I shouted over the wind. Good omen.

Soon we were bounding in waves up to five feet high. They came from behind, raised our boats, and then dropped us into a deep valley where the horizon disappeared. The waves raced ahead of us with dizzying speed. Two hundred yards ahead they hit the cliffs and exploded. I looked over my shoulder with the vague notion of turning back. But that would have involved turning around, broaching to the waves.

Up ahead, the rock jutted out directly into our path. "Let's move out a little, Susan," I said. She kept her head straight ahead and continued to bear toward the cliff. I could see she was struggling to control the boat. "Let's move out a little! Follow me!" Her boat turned toward the open lake.

We looked down a long jagged shore. Landing was impossible. Another point appeared ahead, with breakers exploding. We moved farther into the lake. The largest waves collapsed in foam with the sound of ripping canvas, the wind whipping the spray down the lake. As our boats surfed on the face of the waves, I reached out with my paddle to steady myself. I wondered how Susan, who didn't know a low brace from her foot brace, would handle this. As each wave passed beneath my boat, I looked around to spot Susan and scan the shore. She seemed to be doing a marvelous job, though I didn't know how.

I spotted a small cove in the rock. We could land. But then what? Waiting out the wind in a cove so small we couldn't even take a walk would be intolerable. And if we had to stay the night, where would we sleep? Better to risk going around the next point. I knew the mouth of the Willow River would offer shelter and a good camp.

If the phrase *sitting duck* ever had meaning, it was now, as a five-foot wave rose up at Susan's back, curled, ripped, and broke over her shoulders. Her kayak surfed across the wave. The pile of water buried her paddle. I watched with helpless detachment and was stunned to see that she did not flip over.

She blew water out of her face. "That's enough!" she said.

I paddled to her boat and we rafted up, grasping each other's boats. The stability was immediate. Together we rode the waves toward the bay at the mouth of the Willow.

"It will be like glass," I said.

"Yes, and the check's in the mail."

As Susan held my boat, I stroked slowly toward shore to put us in the lee of the point guarding the river mouth. The waves dropped suddenly from feet to inches.

"Okay," Susan said. "It's like broken glass."

We set up camp on a beach near the mouth of the placid sandy Willow, where we could rest against driftwood logs and watch whitecaps march across the opening of the bay. We dried clothes, drank tea, hiked the trail behind camp, picked a quart of ripe blueberries, watched a porcupine chew on the wall of an old outhouse, and listened to the forecast (strong winds for the rest of the day, diminishing toward evening, and then building overnight from the west).

I watched the lake for any indication that the wind had dropped. Finally, the whitecaps seemed to wink out, like city lights late at night, until I could see only a few. The horizon, once scalloped, now seemed dark and quiet. But the light plays tricks in the late afternoon. From a quarter mile away, with the light oblique, anything seems small and manageable. Only as you venture into it do you realize how large and tumultuous the waves really are. Stay or go? I suggested to Susan that it might be time to leave. She was reluctant.

Then the thunder began, ending the debate. We made dinner: Japanese curry and canned chicken over Cuban black beans and rice. For dessert, we ate blueberries, bountiful, large, luxuriant, ripe. With our evening tea and cigar we admired our bright boats on the beach as geese flew over the lake and diving ducks paddled in the bay.

Things could have been worse.

Even though the hiking trail ran behind us and crossed the Willow less than a quarter mile away, our camp was less like Radisson's and Grosseilliers' hurly-burly of human traffic and more like Cabot's "dead, dreamless sleep." During the night rain fell and the wind died. Fog closed upon the lake. A tent sat on the point just north of the Willow, but its occupants had kept quiet and to themselves; we didn't notice them until we paddled out of the bay, past wet rocks and weary swells sloshing against the cliffs.

At Picture Rock Harbour, named for the pictographs the Ojibwa created by scraping lichen from the rocks, a shape seemed to rise out of the water, like a whale in the fog. The whale turned into a canoe, paddled solo, with a kayak right behind. As we passed about a hundred yards distant I called, "You just starting out?" One of them said something indistinguishable over the sound of the waves. But then he added: "We only made a mile the first day." I imagined that they had left Hattie Cove and sneaked around the long finger of Campbell Point, only to be chased back by the high seas.

Campbell was our only remaining concern. It jutted into the lake nearly a mile. Yesterday's waves would have piled directly into it. If the point were at all sheer, the waves would have created a confusing tumult of waves and reflection waves that might have persisted through the night. As we approached the point, the fog closed in. We continued blindly on a compass bearing. After nearly a mile we heard surf and then saw the waves beating the dark rock. The water was confused, and we kept our distance as we rounded the point into the shelter of Hattie Cove and the landing at Pukaskwa National Park headquarters.

We found our car. As we unloaded our boats, a man and woman prepared to launch a red canoe. She wore a sweatshirt that said Ontario Provincial Police.

"Did you hear the news?" she asked. She paused, as if for effect. I always suspect when I have been in the woods a long time that something of earthshaking importance has happened, that I will come back to find that the president has died or war has broken out. I've come, in fact, to measure the wildness of country by my degree of isolation from daily events and news.

"No, what?" I said.

"Princess Diana died."

CHAPTER 3

Coldwell Peninsula: Little Pic River
to Port Coldwell

From the steep bank along Jellicoe Cove, look out over Peninsula Harbour to the end of a club-shaped point, where Peninsula Hill rises five hundred feet above the lake. Far off in the other direction, the gnarly arm of Ypres Point cradles Hawkins, Skin, and Blondin Islands. The view is wooded, rocky, primeval. On a clear day it may extend twenty miles or more. Surely it occupies the pantheon of Superior's grand views. Or it would. Drop your eyes from the far distance of the horizon, through the middle distance of Hawkins Island, and turn your attention to the beach at the base of Peninsula Hill. There, belching steam and smoke and fumes, sits the James River Marathon pulp mill. One look at the mill was enough to convince me I didn't want to paddle in the bay; I imagined my kayak melting beneath me. So I decided to skip the town of Marathon and its pulp mill and resume my travels a few miles to the east, at Neys Provincial Park on the Coldwell Peninsula.

It was late September and I was alone. The leaves were well along. On the northern shore, autumn colors are singular and somber, primarily the yellow of birch, the dark green of spruce and fir, and the occasional deep gold of tamaracks. September brings a profound change in the prevailing winds. Shifting from the southwest to the north, they blow harder and last longer. The lake, a reservoir of cold in summer, becomes a source of comparative warmth, fueling storms that whip across the lake. I hoped to make one last trip before the fabled storms of fall put an end to my season.

The provincial parks were closed for the year, but I managed to reach Ross Hart, the park manager at Neys, on the phone. Come down to the park office, he said; they were just cleaning up for the season. Hart was young and strongly built with close-cropped hair, a one-time wrestler. As we drove down to the interpretive center, he told me about the park. A herd of about a dozen woodland caribou lived in the park, he explained. Another small herd occupied Pic Island, about a mile offshore. To see them was rare, he said. He had worked in the park eight years and never had. Then, just two weeks ago, a visitor told Hart that he had photographed "an elk" with his video camera. That, Hart knew, would be extremely unlikely. Elk most likely had not walked this ground since the Ice Age. "No, I've got a video," the man insisted. It wasn't an elk he showed Hart, but something nearly as remarkable: a woodland caribou. "I don't think he realized how lucky he was to see it," Hart said.

The interpretive center was closed for the season, most of the exhibits packed away. Hart pulled a sheet of plastic off a table, revealing a model of a prisoner-of-war camp, painstakingly built to scale by Ryan S. Thom of Thunder Bay. The camp stood where the park campground sits today. The one foundation that remained allowed park historians to determine the locations of the buildings, including several barracks for prisoners inside a perimeter of triple barbed wire.

Neys was one of Canada's nine "black" camps, reserved for German officers and avowed Nazis. Prisoners wore a bull's-eye on their backs. It provided a target in the event of an escape and perhaps a powerful psychological deterrent. The prisoners, by several accounts, were an industrious and creative group. One sketched scenes from the bush camps where the prisoners cut pulpwood for the logging companies. Heinz Leischnig built a detailed clipper ship in a screw-cap bottle that turned up at a garage sale in Bracebridge, Ontario, in 1983. Prisoners laid cobblestone walks of Lake Superior rocks between the barracks. Others distilled and hid more than forty gallons of homemade whiskey. Two prisoners carved, but apparently never used, a kayak they intended to paddle to the United States (neutral territory before America entered the war).

Neys was one of three prisoner-of-war compounds along the Canadian shore. The others were at Red Rock (on Nipigon Bay) and Angler (about five miles west of Nipigon). In April 1941 twenty-eight noncommissioned Luftwaffe officers and U-boat veterans at the Angler camp escaped through a network of tunnels excavated beneath the barracks. One tunnel, extended 150 feet long, was ventilated by a fan that forced air through pipes constructed of empty milk cans and papier-mâché made of toilet paper, flour, and water. Another tunnel led to a six-by-nine-foot "work room" tall enough to stand in. A radio, blackmailed from one of the guards, had been rebuilt inside a model of

the battleship *Bismarck;* the swiveling gun turrets controlled the radio tuner
and volume.

Escaping the Angler camp was one thing; escaping the Canadian wilds
was quite another. The escapees soon realized, if they hadn't known already,
the genius of locating prisons in the Lake Superior country. Quite simply,
with the lake on one side and forest, bogs, lakes, and cliffs on all others,
where could they go? In the days before a highway crossed the top of the
lake, there was no escape. The country itself was prison. During the next few
days, as a blizzard blew in from the lake, most of the men were rounded up in
the woods near camp. Five prisoners were flushed from a railroad shack; four
were shot, and two died. Only two prisoners managed to put distance between themselves and Angler. Horst Liebek and Karl Heinz-Grund managed
to jump aboard a Canadian Pacific Railway train as it slowly chugged up a
steep hill. As searchlights swept through the woods behind them, they disappeared around a bend and headed west along the north shore of the lake.
They hid in, of all things, a refrigerator car. Afraid they would freeze, they
hopped off the train near Kenora, built a fire, and warmed up before catching
another train west. In Winnipeg, they bought a paper announcing their own
escape. As they traveled, they told people they were Dutch coal miners. In
Medicine Hat, Alberta, a railroad policeman didn't buy their line, and they
were arrested. To their astonishment, on their return, they were treated as
celebrities by locals who wanted to see "the Nazis."

In addition to German prisoners of war, Canadians of Japanese descent
were imprisoned at both Angler and Neys, the result of the same paranoia that
led to the internment of Japanese-Americans in the United States. After the
war the camps were bulldozed. Hart said he still found chunks of concrete and
barbed wire, along with the odd pot or pan, back in the woods. Occasionally,
a former prisoner would visit the park. One, a prisoner of Angler camp, settled
in Longlac, seventy-five miles north. A prisoner of Neys returned to Germany
but then brought his wife and daughter to live in Manitouwadge.

Hart said I could leave my car in the park and camp by the mouth of the Little
Pic River. Many years ago on a car trip around Lake Superior, I had crossed
the bridge over the Little Pic and glanced in astonishment into a slit canyon
more than one hundred feet deep. I never forgot that view. The campground
lay near the river's mouth, with black cliffs looming above. Periodically
through the night, the Canadian Pacific girdled the cliff like a snake. I felt the

vibrations of the diesels; the beam of the headlight swept through the tent. There was something rugged and exciting about the trains, and I did not mind that they woke me.

Morning broke gray and cold. A stiff breeze whipped in from the south. The waves were small but according to the radio would build to one to two meters by evening. If I wanted to paddle around the peninsula, I shouldn't dawdle. I packed and launched on the Little Pic. The river opened onto a sand beach more than a mile long. I paddled beyond the surf zone and bucked wind toward Prisoner Cove. From there I could follow the shore and dodge the head wind.

Still several hundred yards from shore, I saw something that seemed portentous, if only because it was so odd. A small songbird bobbed and flitted on the wind. What was it doing alone and so far from shore? From nowhere, a small falcon, most likely a merlin, dove on it and missed. The raptor circled, dove, and missed again. This happened several times, the songbird dodging the falcon's talons until it reached the safety of the woods.

Beyond Prisoner Cove, the shoreline turned to dark rock and bright lichen. The soaring hills of the peninsula crowded the shoreline, getting closer and closer, until they formed cliffs and the stark headland of Guse Point. I crossed Thompson Channel to the sheltered shoreline of Pic Island.

The island was gnarly and lumpy like a ginger root, with two deep bays. Its highest hills soared more than six hundred feet above the lake. *Pic Island*, a painting by Lawren Harris, is a study in the island's bold forms and contrasts. The area was a favorite destination of the Group of Seven, one-time commercial artists from Toronto who set out to transform the conservative and European-dependent character of Canadian art and define an independent national style by painting, in Harris's words, the "wild richness and clarity of colour" in the Canadian landscape. The seven, including Harris and A. Y. Jackson, traveled north on the Algoma Central Railway and worked out of Coldwell, the Slate Islands, and Jackfish. They became known for their bold forms and pure colors. Harris, a poet, was transfixed by the luminance of the landscape:

> And light has no weight,
> Yet one is lifted on its flood.

Today's light had purity of its own: the wind whipped the lake into hard-edged scallops that reflected the bright gray of the sky and the dark gray of rock. I followed Windy Bay toward the western tip of Pic Island. A century ago, one of the radical ore boats called "whalebacks"—known as "floating steel cigars" for their shape or "pig boats" for their blunt bows—broke loose from its tow line and drifted for five days on storm-tossed waters until it fetched up just around the point, on the southwest shore of the island. The crew escaped, barely, but *Barge 115* was hammered by surf. Hart had told me that a part of the hull remained visible in shallow water and pieces of the boat lay on shore. As I approached the point to search for the wreck, a bald eagle flew over the water.

Clearing the point, I was whipped by the roaring wind. Waves struck the cliffs and danced around me. I grew dizzy looking at them. The shore ahead offered no protection. Within a minute I was completely unnerved and retreated to the lee of the island, rather than to share the fate of the whaleback. The good augured by the eagle's appearance apparently was this: I had the good sense to chicken out.

Back in the shelter of the island, I watched a loon and grebe and admired the red rock in the cliffs. I stopped for a bite and spotted several iron rings set in the rock, undoubtedly to anchor booms of pulpwood. Moss grew in mounds on the fringe of the forest; I reached into one up to my elbow without feeling rock or ground. I scanned the hills and shores for caribou, but saw none.

Beautiful though the island was, I didn't want to get stuck out here in bad weather. I listened to the radio again: a small craft wind advisory had been issued for western Lake Superior. Surely it would come this way. I shoved off and glided by dark rock and dark water, the subdued colors of the trees and the deep folds of the hills. I decided to head east toward the McDonald Islands, a cluster of rocks across a half mile of open water. As I emerged from the shelter of Pic Island, the waves began to build. I pulled into the McDonalds on the crests of three- and four-foot rollers. I glanced at my map, took a bearing for Johnson Harbour on the mainland and set out across the mile-wide channel, open to the southeast wind.

The bounding waves cut off the horizon as I dove into the troughs. As one large wave passed beneath me, I felt my heart in my throat—the sensation of weightlessness? Or fear? I overreacted, and braced clumsily. I didn't like being alone, and I hated the idea of dying anonymously and mysteriously. To settle my nerves, I took slow easy strokes and tapped the tops of the largest waves with my paddle. I looked anxiously toward shore for the opening to

Johnson Harbour. As I drew closer, a gap appeared behind Foster Island. As waves crashed on reefs and skerries around me, I eased into the sandy bay.

Imagine the Coldwell Peninsula as a dark fist thrust into Lake Superior, a good five miles across, with blunt rocky fingers. On the ring finger is a big stone, Foster Island. I was sitting between the fist and the stone (a mere hundred feet away), watching out one side of the island and then the other as the steadily rising wind whipped the lake into a frenzy of whitecaps. South of me, beyond the flyspeck of rock that gave me shelter, lay 150 miles of open lake—open lake clear to Munising, Michigan. According to the radio, all stations—Stannard Rock, Copper Harbor, Whitefish Bay—reported south winds. All that wind and all those waves ran across uninterrupted water, blocked by nothing until they hit Foster Island and died in an explosion of

The Coldwell Peninsula harbored prisoners—in more ways than one. The beach behind Foster Island (in the distance on the right) provides a snug camp in gale-force winds.

foam and spray. Maybe this evening. Maybe tomorrow morning. Sooner or later, the wind would die or shift. Depending on the direction it moved, I could return west to the Little Pic River or continue east, through Devils Gap, past Detention Island, and into Port Coldwell.

Meanwhile, it was a good spot to be stuck, with a sand beach perfectly sheltered from any waves. There was a large fire ring and a wooden tripod covered with nails for hanging clothes. A trail led back to a plywood toilet seat lashed between two spruce trees.

With high hills and cliffs on three sides, I could get the Thunder Bay marine station only by walking around the beach, holding the radio above my head and tilting it just so. According to the 4 P.M. report, the wind had died and waves were a half meter or less. Yet that contradicted the evidence at hand. I could see that whitecaps still ran beyond the island. The forecast said the wind would stay in the south and build through the night and tomorrow, with waves growing to two meters.

When I paddled with Susan or my daughter, Kate, we would stay ashore because of their limitations, not mine. So I didn't take being wind bound personally, a reflection on my own frailty as a paddler. Now, it was my limit that was exposed. It was my uneasiness in the channel, my fear of paddling through Devils Gap. I didn't like it. Responsibility for someone else had made me feel stronger, if only because my own weaknesses remained hidden.

The day grew grayer and grayer until it disappeared into evening. Fog—inexplicable in such windy weather—hung on the highest peaks of Pic Island until I could no longer see.

The next morning broke sunny with strong winds forecast. Already whitecaps beat the reefs on the far side of Foster Island. Still, I could hope. I ate breakfast, struck the tent, and packed the boat with the intention of paddling out from behind Foster and sneaking around the point through Devils Gap if I had the chance.

I wedged into the boat and stretched the spray skirt over the cockpit. I was acutely aware of my unease in the waves yesterday. I'd feel better, I thought, if I flipped over and righted myself with an Eskimo roll. I had never rolled this kayak with this paddle with all my gear aboard and all the clothes I wear in late September. A roll would be good. It would build my confidence.

I pushed off and paddled into the sheltered bay. Before I gave it another thought, before I had a moment to reconsider, my face hit the cold water and a second later I hung upside down in disbelief, staring upward through the clear water at the deck of my boat and the refracted silver sky. Cold water trickled through the neck of my rain jacket and underneath my wetsuit.

What had I done? Fail to roll now—what would happen to my confidence then? I imagined myself completely unnerved, sitting on this beach until the lake turned flat calm. That might be December. Mostly it annoyed me that I was I suffering this crisis. How often had I failed to roll a kayak, even when it counted? Once in twenty years perhaps, on a raging river, under conditions much worse than this. But I had never been completely alone. That was the difference.

I reached toward the surface with my paddle, swept slowly in a large arc, snapped my hips, and popped to the surface. It was that easy. Now I was ready. But as I paddled from behind Foster Island, a large swell rolled beneath the boat and the horizon disappeared behind a wall of water. Two more large waves followed. Approaching the point, I looked out on a lake in pandemonium and retreated to the shelter of the bay.

I set my tent again and made lunch. There wasn't much to do. The hiking was miserable—nothing but hills and cliffs covered with thickets of black spruce, downed trees, and pockets of bog. I recalled that Paul Theroux, camping by himself for several days on a small island in the South Seas, kept a rigorous schedule to buoy up his spirits. I brewed tea. I read. I watched bumblebees work over the last of the summer's goldenrod and pearly everlasting. I paced from one end of my beach to the other. It was 160 yards long; five laps equaled a mile. I made a habit of walking a mile, counting each lap. If I felt anxious, I walked another mile.

Every four hours I listened to the new forecast. The announcer reiterated the stations in a voice rough enough to open the hull of a freighter: *Thunder Bay, Sault Sainte Marie, Killarney.* I loved that voice. I usually listened twice, to detect subtle changes in wind direction and speed, as though I were a Cold War Sovietologist, studying the faces along the Kremlin wall for the appearance of a new one, the disappearance of an old one, anything that would suggest a seismic shift in power. The 4 P.M. forecast had wind switching to the northwest in western Lake Superior. Should that front move in my direction, I would be able to slide through Devils Gap. There was also a chance of thunderstorms tomorrow morning. Meanwhile, winds in eastern Superior registered twenty-five knots from the south-southeast. Whitecaps danced on the reefs near Foster Island, occasionally exploding in geysers of froth.

For dinner I cooked sausage, rice, and black beans. Then I smoked a cigar. In the gloaming I noticed a light—I thought it was a light—far out on the lake. A boat? I was a long way from shipping lanes, and I couldn't imagine a small craft out on a night like this. I consulted a map: it must be the Otter Island Light along the Pukaskwa Peninsula. I listened again to the new forecast: bad news. The wind would continue through tomorrow, with waves building from two to three meters—six to ten feet.

When I was a teenager, I fancied myself a rugged loner. I read Jack London and books about camping and woodcraft. I imagined myself exploring wild country for days or weeks on end. Then one summer, after a weekend at the lake cabin, my parents drove home to work, leaving me to fend for myself for the week. Almost immediately, a black anxiety descended, giving the lie to my sense of myself. I remembered that so well because I felt something so very similar now.

I gathered some clothes I had hung on the tripod. In the sand, I noticed an arrow, about a foot long, whittled from a stick. One end was sharpened; the other end was decorated with three feathers, held on with duct tape.

Clearly, this was the work of the wind bound.

The next morning, a switchy wind cut through my sheltered bay. The radio report: waves of two to three meters. Wind still from the south. Thunderstorms likely. There was no decision to be made—no decision except what to have for breakfast.

I began walking the beach early, startling a merganser near shore. It ran across the water like a lizard, never opening its wings. It must have wondered, *What is he doing here?* My beach seemed to have shrunk. What had been a wide sandy path was now covered with bushes down to the water. Minutes later, the beach reappeared, ten feet wide. I realized the wind had blown so hard for so long, it had created a seiche, raising the water in places and lowering it in others so that now it sloshed back and forth as if in a bathtub. I marked the low water with a stick and, out of curiosity and boredom, began timing the fluctuations.

11:40 Current runs through the bay, water level rising.

11:43 Water rises a foot high on stick. Waves lap at grass on shore.

11:44 Current switches direction as water runs out of bay.

11:47 Waves stop; bay is calm. Water at full ebb.

I talked to myself, at length and with vigor. I made lunch, boiled tea, and read travel stories. Gretel Ehrlich wrote that the Chumash Indians of California faced long waits for the weather to break before crossing to the Channel Islands in small boats. They sang of their crossings: "I make a big step. I am always going over to the other side."

Through the day, I took pains to camp well. I was especially careful with the food. I had about a week's worth; losing some to dampness or a bear would be one of the few things that would force me to move prematurely. (This seemed an unlikely place for a bear, since there appeared to be few berries and few human visitors, and I had seen no tracks.) Above all, I wanted to avoid anything that would narrow my options: burns, scalds, or broken bones. When I idly whittled a kayak and a fish from driftwood, I never cut toward myself as I normally would.

The 4 P.M. report: more bad news. A gale warning had been issued for western Lake Superior; winds of forty knots or more. I pulled the kayak nearer the tent. I cut up a long rope to better anchor the tent fly. I guyed one peak of the tent to a tree and the other to the boat. The physical preparation was easier than the mental preparation. When would this end?

I decided to walk a mile. Then I walked a second mile. Then a third mile. And a fourth and a fifth. This was the Prisoners Peninsula. Susan and Kate would be worried, but they would be fine. Worry is not fatal or even harmful. But I had to keep my mind on the tasks at hand: monitor food and look for an opportunity, a good opportunity. That perhaps was the greatest danger: to give in to anxiety and impatience. Nothing, after all, was wrong. If I had to, I could walk out, over to the east shore of the peninsula and then north to Coldwell, about five miles in all.

Modern life had poorly prepared me for sitting in one place and keeping my own company. No radio. No television. No distractions to anesthetize me to my private thoughts. I imagined an Ojibwa holed up in a small cove with a birch-bark canoe, waiting for the chance to move. I suspect that having lived with the lake all his life he had a keen intuition about winds, light, the meaning of seiches. Would he have looked for guidance in dreams and omens, signs I would consider coincidental, such as the appearance of an eagle? But what might one recognize by *how* an eagle appears, how it flies in a particular wind? When is an omen a subtle indicator? I wondered if the Ojibwa, like the Chumash, danced to prepare for a crossing—to invoke the spirits and, perhaps more important, to instill patience. Patience. Preparation and patience.

Drizzle fell through the night. I slept as late as I could, but by seven, I was slept out. I couldn't rest anymore.

The eight o'clock forecast: gale warnings in effect for all the Great Lakes. An intense low-pressure cell sat on northern Ontario. When it moved eastward toward Quebec, the wind would switch to the northwest and diminish. But that would not happen until tomorrow. In the meantime, winds ran to forty knots this morning and waves to four meters on the open lake. Four meters, my god, nearly the length of my kayak.

Some stations reported winds had shifted to the southwest—that was good news. Waves continued to explode on the reefs beyond Foster Island. But something was different. I ran down to the other end of my little beach and looked to the gap between Foster and Pic Islands. The wind seemed to have switched toward the southwest. If so, I might be able to dodge to the inside of the waves as I sneaked into Devils Gap. I couldn't tell. I decided to paddle out and look.

My hands trembled as I cooked breakfast and struck the tent. The morning flew by. Gusts of wind blew across the beach, but they came from the west. Yes—blow, blow all you want. The wester the better.

I loaded up the boat. I took firewood from the cockpit, where I had kept it dry, and stacked it beneath a fir. I thought I might need it if I returned. I looked around camp—I would say fondly, but my fondness was predicated on not returning anytime soon. I hopped into the kayak and pushed off. The water ahead appeared calm. As I neared the point and moved out of the shelter of Foster Island, I began to feel the southwest wind. The largest waves ran far out on the lake. An eagle soared out of the trees. That seemed too good to be true.

Rounding the point, I felt the waves from the day before, about a yard high, surfing my kayak through Devils Gap. The waves were round and friendly. The more dangerous waves were still a long way off. After a half mile, I passed Detention Island; the waves diminished and the wind fell to nearly nothing. It was quintessential kayaking weather: gray fog draped the black rocks and soaring hills. Devils Cove seemed not the least bit devilish— just gorgeous wet rocks and the solid colors of creation. I saw another eagle and thought, *This is the most beautiful place on earth.*

I glided along a black cliff into Port Coldwell. It seemed the kind of rock the Ojibwa might have decorated with pictographs, though I saw none. Inside the harbor along shore sat rusted machinery, wooden beams, pieces of iron, and huge bolts, all gray, black, and rust, the color of wet rock, lichen, and water. Across the channel, two people were casting. As I crossed the channel, I could see it was an old man and woman.

I landed near them and stepped from the kayak. As though I lived outside my body, I heard a man jabbering about being wind bound, sitting alone for three days behind Foster Island, pacing the beach, looking for the slightest break in the weather. I could have talked all day. I imagine they looked at me as though I had just landed in a flying saucer.

"We were here Saturday and it was really whipping up in here," the woman said.

"Waves were going up over the rocks," the man said.

"We were catching fish," she said. "Today's the last day of fishing, so we said we're going to come out anyway."

They were Miriam and Gene Mosindy. They had lived in Marathon since 1933. He had worked for the pulp mill since 1946. She had been a secretary.

I asked about the scrap and docks across the channel. It had been a fish-processing plant, Gene said. Men would toss fish from the boats onto a conveyor belt that ran to the fish house.

"This used to be a thriving fishing village," Miriam said. "The Canadian Pacific Railway had a station here."

"There's an old cemetery there, too," Gene said. "There's a fellow—the town was named after him—Coldwell."

"He was an engineer and he came here and was instrumental in developing this fishing plant," Miriam said. "He also had something to do with the railroad. The railroad was being built through here. When he died his remains were sent to England, but in his will he wished to be buried here. And so they brought him back here."

"They sent him back?"

"Yeah."

"When did this go under?"

"When the lake trout went," Gene said. "When the deep seaway came in, the lampreys came in." He pointed to the wrecks of old boats along shore. "There was a big dock here. A hundred years old those things are."

Thirty years ago, Gene said, he used to catch brook trout—"speckled trout," as Canadians say—of two to three pounds. Some were even larger. "But they're not there anymore," he said. "The lampreys got them. It's changing, like everything else. Time marches on."

Then he added: "Believe it or not, I'll be eighty-four October the second."

I believed it, though he surely looked healthy, especially to have walked down here and fished from these slick rocks.

I left them and paddled past the rotting boats. I landed where a rutted dirt road led up the hill. Before reaching the railroad tracks and the highway, the road curved around the cemetery. The verdant grass and clover were mowed short. Centermost was a dark granite obelisk: "Erected in memory of R. W. Coldwell. C.E. 1860–1914." Apart from the cemetery, the town site had grown up in aspens and grass, raspberries and willows.

I listened one more time to the weather: the gale warning was still in effect. Waves ran three to four meters on the open lake. But Port Coldwell was calm, a world apart. The view from the graveyard was lovely—overlooking a lonely fjord in a lonely season, with yellow birch and dark spruce, all shrouded in gray. I saw that the two tiny figures on the distant point had built a fire.

The deep cove at Coldwell once sheltered a thriving fishing community served by the Canadian Pacific.

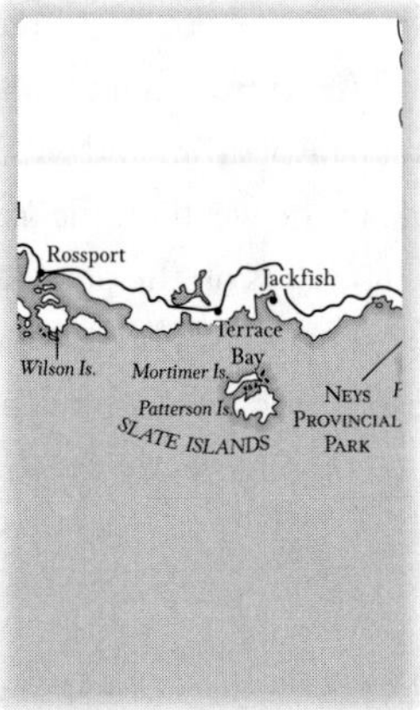
Rossport
Jackfish
Terrace Bay
Wilson Is.
Mortimer Is.
Patterson Is.
SLATE ISLANDS
NEYS PROVINCIAL PARK

CHAPTER 4

Slate Islands

O F THE MANY ANIMALS that symbolize the Superior country and wilderness—the loon, the gray wolf, the moose—one stands out for its rarity
and utter failure to survive where civilization has encroached. The woodland
caribou, with its short legs, long back, magnificent rack, and Frisbee feet, is
an emblem of the time when the Ojibwa and Cree ruled the forest primeval.

Two hundred years ago, as journals of early explorers make clear, woodland caribou roamed the shores of Lake Superior and its major islands. It is a
pair of woodland caribou, after all, that run across the face of Agawa Rock.
In the time since, however, the caribou has all but disappeared. In the isolated, nearly untouched wilderness of Pukaskwa National Park, caribou total
only about a dozen. Similar numbers populate the Coldwell Peninsula and
Pic Island. Along the great wild shore of Superior live gray wolves, moose,
and even lynx, but only a handful of caribou are to be found over hundreds
of square miles.

The glaring exception to this pattern is Slate Islands Provincial Park.
Here, on a knot of islands measuring only six miles across, lives a thriving
herd of caribou that numbers in the hundreds. Not only is the Slate Island
population the largest herd of caribou on Superior's shores; it is also the
densest concentration of woodland caribou living anywhere in North
America. Their existence raises two questions: Why did caribou, once so
prevalent, all but disappear from Superior's shoreline? And why do they
flourish on the Slate Islands, in habitat that, according to conventional wisdom, is entirely unsuitable for them? To better understand both the questions and their answers, I paddled to the Slate Islands to talk with Tom
Bergerud, who had studied this particular herd for twenty-five years.

From the town of Terrace Bay, where we launched our boats at the mouth of the Aguasabon River, the Slates float dreamy and purple eight miles distant. The air was hazy and acrid from forest fires, one near Marathon to the east, the other on St. Ignace Island to the west, where a plume of smoke rose in the form of a thunderhead.

There were four of us. Susan paddled a new boat, which took getting used to in the two-foot chop and sideways wind. Layne Kennedy, an old friend and freelance photographer, had a new kayak, too, a big-volume boat to hold his camera gear. Layne's friend, Bill Brent, a whitewater rafter from Portland, Oregon, paddled a rental. It had no rudder and the stiff wind kept the boat weathercocked. To compensate, Bill paddled furiously on one side. We waited for him to catch up, but just as he approached, we cruelly continued on toward the dark shapes of the islands.

The Slates are unusual for reasons that have nothing to do with caribou. The presence in the islands' bedrock of so-called shattercones, resembling small pointed ice-cream cones, suggests to some scientists that the area was struck by a large meteorite, which vaporized and liquified the crust. Imagine a pebble dropping in the water: by the prevailing (though not unanimous) theory, the Slates are the hardened *bloop*. The lakeshore environment and the isolation of the islands have provided a refugium for several disjunct populations of arctic-alpine plants, such as the Alpine bistort (*Polygonum viviparum*) usually found along the tree line, where Inuits ate it with seal oil as a source of vitamins A and C. The Slates possess a streamlined fauna. Red fox have somehow found their way to the islands. Larger predators, such as bears, lynx, coyotes, and wolves (until very recently), have not. Snowshoe hares live on the islands. So do some of the boldest beavers in existence. Having lost their fear of predators, since there have been none of a size to worry about, beavers have fearlessly waddled more than a mile from water to find suitable trees for food. Puzzled researchers have found trees chewed off five feet above the ground, as though Ice Age beavers the size of black bears had managed to survive on the Slates. Only with time did they realize the beavers had been standing on three feet of snow.

Two hours after we launched, we reached the north side of Mortimer Island. The rock was dark and textured like the skin of a rhino. We paddled east to the lee of a tombolo joining Mortimer to what had once been a smaller island. Layne immediately spotted tracks on the beach. In the gravel, they were indistinct, but given their size they could have been made by nothing other than caribou.

The next morning we packed up camp and paddled into the protected channels that run between the islands. Several small cabins sit along shore, most built by locals before the islands became a provincial park and still maintained by them for use on a first-come-first-served basis, with the re-signed tolerance of park officials. Just offshore from one of these cabins, we met two kayakers. The man had a weathered face and an intense gaze. The woman was agitated. They had camped on a grassy clearing next to a cabin, the interior of which was covered with mouse droppings and graffiti. The messages were more disgusting, she said, than what the mice had left. A motorboat and some jet-skiers had roared up. The boaters sat on the dock and then moved into the site for a couple of hours. "It's the first time in a wilderness setting that I've felt uneasy," she said.

But caribou had walked by their tent, and they had spotted more just south in McGreevy Harbour. The man pointed to a grassy clearing about a mile away.

Next to the clearing sat a scuttled barge. As we inspected the old hull from our kayaks, Layne spotted two caribou, browsing by the edge of the clearing. As we drew closer, the caribou faded into the woods.

We landed to look around. The barge, I learned, had been outfitted with a steam-powered crane to load pulpwood cut from the islands. After its hull was damaged by a dropped log, it was pulled ashore and used as an office and dock. On shore lay remnants of heavy machinery, slabs of iron, hardware, and piles of cans and broken china. Up to sixty men once lived and worked here, loading pulpwood onto freighters for shipment to Detroit. Susan and I walked past the clearing and up the hill and found a dilapidated cabin. All around, the ground was trampled, the underbrush browsed down. The crush of forest duff betrayed the presence of a caribou one hundred feet off. We sneaked closer. Despite our presence, it lay down. It had mere nubs for antlers. We spotted a second caribou deeper in the woods.

We set camp nearby in Fisherman's Harbour. Old-man's beard hung so thick from the trees it colored the canopy light green. But below a razor-sharp line five feet from the ground there was no lichen at all. Wherever there was sand or fine gravel, we saw caribou tracks.

These were woodland caribou (*Rangifer tarandus caribou*), a different sub-species from the more familiar barren ground caribou of Canada's tundra. The woodland variety is larger, averaging four hundred pounds for bulls, three hundred for cows. Large sharp hooves carry the caribou over boggy ground and snow, and give it purchase on ice and a means to paw through crusted snow to eat lichens, the primary winter food. The caribou is unique among large mammals in feeding on the lichens that grow on trees and rocks (called reindeer moss for this fact).

Though caribou once lived on every shore of Lake Superior, they were most common along the northern shore. "Caribous are found all through this region, but not in great abundance," wrote J. Elliot Cabot, who traveled the Canadian shore in 1848. "An Indian who passed last winter on Isle St. Ignace, killed twenty-five caribous in the course of the winter, and was thought to have done very well." They also lived on the major islands, including Isle Royale and Michipicoten, where wolves eventually followed. In 1771 Alexander Henry found them on Caribou Island. Lying thirty-eight miles from Gargantua Point, Caribou is the most isolated of Superior's islands. Henry speculated that the caribou were carried out on floating ice. They might have crossed during one of the rare winters when the lake virtually freezes over. With their large hooves and buoyant, hollow body hair, they might even have swum. The Nipigon Museum has a photo of a canoe on an inland lake, towed on a rope tied fast to the antlers of a swimming caribou.

At one time, woodland caribou were the only hoofed animals to live in the spruce and fir forest at the apex of Superior. Moose lived along Minnesota's North Shore and the lake's southern shore. White-tailed deer lived only along the south shore or, according to some observers, were not seen near the lake at all. The 1800s brought a warmer climate. At the same time, loggers invaded the shoreline forests, claiming first the valuable pine and then the less valuable pulpwood along the Canadian shore. White settlers moved into cutovers. Caribou, like their boreal cohorts, the wolverines and lynx, retreated northward. Permanent populations of woodland caribou disappeared from Wisconsin in the late 1800s and from Minnesota in the 1930s (though a rare migrant still sneaks across the border from Ontario). By the mid-1900s, caribou had vanished from all but the northernmost shore, from Thunder Bay on the west to Michipicoten River on the east. Conventional wisdom held that caribou depended on old-growth forests with plentiful old-man's beard in the conifers and reindeer moss in the small openings. As these forests were logged, the lichen and caribou disappeared. Hunting by settlers hastened the process.

The retreat continues. Before pushing off for the Slate Islands, I visited Linda Melnyk-Ferguson, a wildlife biologist with the Ontario Ministry of Natural Resources in Terrace Bay. She referred to a big wall map of recent and current clear-cutting north of Superior. "Caribou have been sighted up here," she said, tracing areas near Geraldton, sixty miles from the lake, and northward. As the forest is divvied up into smaller uncut islands, caribou retreat, while moose and deer advance.

Ironically, when caribou were common along the shore, they apparently did not inhabit the Slate Islands. They arrived only in 1907, the year that Dolf King, keeper of the Slate Island Light, saw the tracks of seven animals crossing from the mainland over the snow-covered ice.

That evening, Susan and I paddled across McGreevy Harbour to the tip of McColl Island. There we found a woman, in her forties, pretty, with dark hair, hauling luggage into the old fisherman's cabin. She introduced herself as Heather Butler, Tom Bergerud's wife, and invited us in for tea. She was nursing her seven-year-old son, who had an earache. Tom was still out on the lake with their nine-year-old boy. "This is kind of a sentimental journey for us," she said.

When they first came to the islands in 1974, Bergerud was an associate professor of ecology at the University of Victoria, British Columbia; Butler was his graduate student. She was studying the breeding behavior of caribou in North America for her thesis. Bergerud was testing a controversial hypothesis that wolves, not loss of habitat, were responsible for the disappearance of woodland caribou through much of their range. The Slates fit his needs perfectly. Cut-over and frequently burned, they appeared to be the antithesis of classic caribou habitat.

Bergerud and Butler ran transects through the interior of the islands to determine the abundance of caribou sign. They also set about to tag caribou and estimate the total number of animals by the frequency with which tagged caribou were recaptured. That presented a difficulty: how does one catch a strong, vigorous, panicked four-hundred-pound animal with hooves and antlers?

They devised a trap of saplings, logs, and wire, baited with a salt lick.

Butler and Bergerud also discovered they could herd solitary caribou swimming the channels between islands. One of them, perched on an outcrop, would give a signal as a caribou appeared. They would jump in a small outboard and give chase, pulling alongside the caribou before it reached shallow water. They would grab it, drag it into the boat, hogtie it, and then race to shore, where they would weigh and measure it, take a blood sample, and tag it before setting it free. One caribou, Butler said, sprang free and ran through the back wall of the tent. Another leaped back into the boat. "I got kicked a few times but I always had my life jacket on and that helped," she said. Soon they learned to use two boats: the first to buzz around the caribou to keep it swimming in the channel and the second to help herd the animal into a funnel and corral built on shore. "Seeing those first few tagged animals was so exciting," Butler recalled.

A fence built of saplings guides swimming woodland caribou into a corral to be tagged.

Soon Bergerud returned. Long gray hair curled from under his baseball cap. He hadn't shaved for days. As his son scrambled around the beach, we sat and discussed the things he had learned about the Slate Islands herd.

First, he said, there were far more caribou than anyone had realized. Instead of fewer than fifty, the estimate when he began his research, there appeared to be more than two hundred. In the twenty-five years that followed, they traced a population that oscillated between boom and bust, once growing to more than six hundred only to succumb to mass starvation and drop to fewer than one hundred.

A measure of their desperation is their most common cause of death— tumbling over cliffs as they reach for scarce lichens. They also die in birch trees, hanging themselves by the legs, neck, or midsection as they leap for lichens. "March and April are the big months to die," Bergerud said.

In less than a century, the Slate Island herd seems to have adapted to this major theme of its existence. To get by with less, they are smaller than their mainland counterparts. Mothers separate from their young at an earlier age to tend to their own nourishment. An extraordinarily large proportion of females, nearly half, are barren. Unlike mainland caribou, few Slate Island females have antlers. Bulls delay growing antlers until as old as four. (Mainland bulls begin growing antlers their first fall.) When antlers do grow, they are smaller than those of mainland caribou. The antlers are also smaller than the antlers of the founders, a fact Bergerud established by digging up large, fifty-year-old antlers on Edmonds Island.

The Slates are severely overgrazed. Caribou have killed all the ground hemlock. For a quarter century, at least, there have been no new sprouts of aspen, no new birch, no new mountain ash or mountain maple. The caribou eat tree lichens from blow-downs. "When a beaver cuts a tree down, the rabbits are waiting for it, the caribou are waiting for this stuff," Bergerud said. "It's an interesting interaction between rabbits, caribou, and beaver."

Their habitat has been logged, burned, and grazed to the nubs, yet Slate Island caribou live at a higher density than any other herd on earth. What about the traditional notion that logging, fire, and lichen destruction are responsible for the demise of caribou? "That's a completely wrong idea," said Bergerud.

If caribou can thrive in the logged, burned-over forest that more and more typifies the Lake Superior country, why have they disappeared? The answer is more complicated than the change in habitat, Bergerud said. Caribou have been done in by their two close relatives—white-tailed deer and moose.

As loggers felled the old conifers and forest fires opened the canopy, aspen, birch, and other fast-growing deciduous plants sprouted in the openings, providing excellent forage for deer and moose, which followed logging north into caribou range. Whitetails harbor a parasite, a contagious roundworm that in its adult stage lodges in or near the deer's brain. Apparently benign in deer, the brain worm impairs moose, eventually causing a kind of delirium, and is deadly to caribou. Along the south shore, where whitetails flourished after logging and fires, the mere presence of the deer and their parasite probably eliminated caribou.

Deer were much less successful along the north shore, where bitter winters made survival difficult and deep snow made them easy marks for wolves. But moose, with greater body mass and longer legs, flourished in the young forest left by logging and fire. By 1895, only twenty years after logging began along the Canadian shore, moose were found everywhere except the Nipigon region and what would later become Pukaskwa National Park. Moose, in effect, brought their own deadly pest—not a parasite, but wolves.

The complicated relationship between moose, wolves, and caribou begins with the caribou's calving strategy. The Ojibwa called the woodland caribou *ah-dik*, "he that goes." To survive, caribou "space out," Bergerud said. "They make it a searching contest for the wolf." Pregnant cows scatter along shorelines and swim to offshore islands—one here, a couple there—creating a near vacuum of caribou. Fifteen minutes after birth the calf can run and swim, and mother and offspring are ready to evacuate the calving ground. With caribou so scarce and the chances of finding a vulnerable calf so slight, wolves can't expend the energy to search for them. Wolves cannot risk building a den and giving birth to pups in a location where all available prey ups and leaves. As a result, caribou and wolves coexist in low, scattered numbers.

Enter the moose. Unlike caribou, moose don't move to remote calving grounds; they stay put. Once moose occupy an area, wolves are able to follow and find food year-round, killing the smaller, more vulnerable caribou as they find them. Once moose reach a density of about one per square mile, Bergerud has calculated, wolves exist in numbers great enough that caribou disappear. "They want to live in a simple system where there is no alternative prey," he said. Woodland caribou survive only on islands without moose and, as a consequence, without wolves.

Tom Bergerud's journal for 7 June 1994 contained an ominous portent for the Slate Island caribou: a wolf track. It was the first sign of wolves Bergerud had noted. Soon, he and his assistants were seeing tracks on the sand beach in Sunday Harbour and scat at the fox den near Horace Cove. In fact, there appeared to be evidence of two wolves, one large and one small, though the smaller one was never seen. Bergerud assumed they walked out on the ice during the cold winter in early 1994. Soon there were signs that the pair had given birth to a single pup.

Immediately, it seemed to Bergerud, the caribou were more skittish than usual. A sudden move by a caribou approaching a salt lick could trigger a stampede. Furthermore, hardly any calves survived. Before the wolves arrived, calves made up 10 to 20 percent of the herd. But a year after the wolves appeared, fewer than 5 percent of the herd were calves.

Bergerud predicted that if a wolf pack became established in the confines of the islands, they could kill caribou down to the last one. Wolves will kill in surplus when they find calves in great numbers, he said. They will eat only the best parts, the milk curds and soft tissue, before looking for the next. The notion that wolves are prudent predators, that they will not destroy their food supply, he said, is the result of "so much Walt Disney."

But then something happened—something for which Bergerud had no explanation. All signs of the pup disappeared. Then the large wolf seemed to vanish as well; only the small wolf remained. The next spring more calves appeared. "This wolf apparently was not capable of killing adults," Bergerud concluded. "They were back to the old days of lying down and relaxing around the lick."

The following morning, as Layne and Bill headed into the forest to photograph caribou, Susan and I paddled west out of the protected channels between the islands into the wide blue yonder of the open lake. The very sight of the wide horizon chilled us. We landed on a gravel beach to pull on more clothes. This beach, like any other square foot of land that would hold a track, showed signs of caribou. A series of beach ridges rose about forty feet above lake level. I climbed the ridges, thinking this would be a perfect place for a Pukaskwa pit. Sure enough, on one of the highest beach lines I saw a pit in the brick-sized cobble, about two feet deep and five across. Might someone have hidden here in wait of caribou?

Through the day we paddled counterclockwise around Patterson Island, the largest of the Slates. In contrast to the forested shores of the protected channels, the lakeward shores appeared blasted by wind, waves, and ice, the veneer of forest peeled back to reveal cliffs and jagged points. In Sunday Harbour, we wandered around the grounds of a two-story, red and white clapboard house. Once the lighthouse keeper's residence, it was now used by fishermen. The yard was covered with hoof prints and caribou scat. Red-osier dogwood and rose bushes were browsed to sticks, and the branches of the mountain ash were pruned from the bottom to the height of a caribou.

It was midafternoon. Smoke from distant forest fires had settled over the islands. As we launched, we could barely see a mile across the harbor. We

The Sunday Harbour Light has been automated, but the former keeper's residence still stands near the bay.

paddled up the east side of Patterson, behind Pearl, Shell, and Cove Islands. Then, rounding a large point, we met a northeast wind head on. Soon white-caps danced all around us and we surfed onto a gravel beach. As we built a fire from driftwood in the protection of an outcrop, Susan looked to the ground.

"That's wolf scat!" she exclaimed. Indeed, it seemed to be—big and hairy, but dried out and possibly quite old. "Don't leave me here. I hear they go after the old and the weak," Susan said.

We had no cook kit, but we scrounged in the holds of the kayaks for turkey sausage to roast on a stick. By nine o'clock, the lake had flattened. We navigated by the black outline of the trees and arrived at our camp well after dark.

There is nothing worse than following serious photographers. Next morning, as Layne and Bill spent an hour taking pictures of beach cobbles, Susan and I grew bored and split off to explore. In Copper Harbour, on the protected side of Mortimer Island, we spotted the black entrance to a mining adit in a cliff just off the beach. We ducked inside and followed it back about sixty feet until it ended in a pool of water of indeterminate depth.

We paddled down Lawrence Bay. Narrow like a fjord, it was one of the most beautiful passages among the islands. We flushed three caribou on a hillside. Reaching the end of the bay, we hiked along a small stream, terraced by beaver dams, into Hart Lake, where we surprised a bull in a grassy clearing. Tracks and droppings were everywhere. Returning to the boats, we sneaked to within ten yards of a caribou in a thicket of alder.

On another island, we walked into the black spruce, balsam, and old birch, where the ground was crisscrossed with caribou tracks, caribou paths, caribou highways. We discovered a skeleton, largely intact. The backbone lay in two pieces. We found a hip bone, ribs, and leg bones. We located the lower mandibles and then, about ten feet away, the skull, with an idiotic grin and empty eyes. A symbol in life of the Superior country as it once existed. A symbol in death of a hard life, the changing forest, the dynamic of nature. The bones were clean and mostly white, without obvious tooth marks. Was it an old wolf kill? It didn't seem so to me, but I was no expert.

What about the wolves? I had asked Bergerud. If a wolf pack took hold, should the wolves be trapped to save the caribou? Or should nature be allowed to take its course and perhaps destroy the herd? He had rambled in

The adit of an old mine opens, appropriately, to Copper Harbour, on Mortimer Island, one of the Slate Islands.

his answer. He explained that the Ontario Ministry of Natural Resources had transplanted caribou to other islands: Michipicoten, Montreal, and Leach. So if wolves, starvation, or disease were to exterminate the Slate Island herd, this island genotype would survive. Only in a later conversation was I able to coax a more direct response: "To answer your question," he said, "we've gone through this wonderful twenty years of seeing this laboratory and this place chewed to pieces, and I would like to see the herd managed, either by wolves or by people. I'd like to see the wolves. It would be another experiment."

The conventional telling of the Slate Island story has the caribou first appearing in 1907. But who is to say they hadn't lived here many times before? In the thousands of years since the glacial ice retreated from Superior, caribou had many opportunities to reach the Slates. Perhaps this scenario had already played itself out many times. Caribou arrive. They flourish. Wolves follow. Caribou disappear. The forest heals. Decades later, centuries later, caribou reappear.

Nature, after all, is never really in balance. The balance of nature is simply one catastrophe offsetting another.

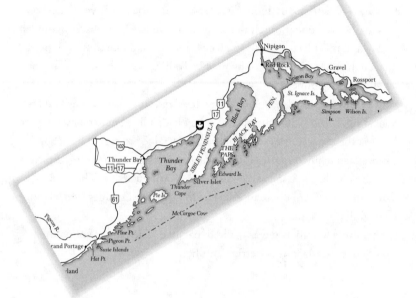

CHAPTER 5

Nipigon Islands: Rossport to Pigeon River

THE ANNALS OF Lake Superior shipping are filled with tales that illumi-
nate the valiant side of the human character: Captain William E. Morse
evacuated his crew but refused a lifeline himself with the words "Not by a
damn sight" before the foundering *William F. Sauber* exploded and sank near
Whitefish Bay. Seaman Fred Benson leaped from the deck of the grounded
Madeira, scaled Gold Rock Point, and dropped a line by which eight of the
nine remaining crew climbed to safety.

Other disasters expose our vices and foibles. Such is the tale of the
Gunilda, a testament—at least as it has been handed down over generations—
to parsimony, arrogance, and impatience.

The steel yacht, nearly two hundred feet long with twin masts and a
stack amidships, was built in Scotland in 1897 and sailed across the Atlantic. In 1911 its owner, New Yorker William L. Harkness, an original investor
in Standard Oil, embarked on a long cruise on Lake Superior with his family, two guests, and a crew of twenty, including Captain Alexander Corkum.
The *Gunilda* dropped anchor in the Canadian harbors of Port Coldwell and
Jackfish, where the fishermen and railroad workers marveled at a boat of
such opulence.

Harkness next set sail for Rossport, even then a quaint fishing and railroad village. The approach to its harbor is protected by a string of islands
that, taken as a whole, stretches more than one hundred miles across the
crown of Superior. By custom, a local pilot would board large incoming vessels to guide them safely through the archipelago. Harkness thought the
fifteen-dollar fee was extortionary; so he directed Corkum to take the wheel
himself—and to hurry to try to get the best dockage available. Unfortunately
for Harkness, his U.S. charts lacked critical details about Canadian waters.

About six miles from harbor, Corkum drove hard up onto McGarvey Shoal. Harkness rode a motorized lifeboat into Rossport to telegraph his insurance company, while the crew and guests remained on board the *Gunilda*, whose graceful bow angled helplessly above the water.

When the tug *James Whalen* arrived, the passengers left the stricken yacht. But as the *Whalen* fastened a line to the *Gunilda*'s stern and pulled her from the shoal, the *Gunilda* took on water and slid backward, coming to rest 240 feet beneath the surface. But more on that later.

Over the years, various efforts have been made to salvage the luxury yacht and its rumored treasure of jewels. Two men have died in dives on the wreck. One attempt to seize the boat with a grappling hook disturbed the hull, which slid fifty feet deeper.

Among the scant treasures to have come from these efforts are a part of one mast, which stands as the flagpole outside the Rossport Inn, and a small lantern, which hangs on a wall in the hotel lobby. Built in 1884 to serve passengers of the new Canadian Pacific Railway, the two-story inn, called the Oriental Hotel until 1910, fell into disuse and disrepair during the 1970s. Ned Basher, a jet fighter pilot stationed in Duluth, discovered the inn while sailing among the Rossport islands. He bought the building in 1982 and refurbished it in time to open on the inn's centennial. He met Shelagh, a Canadian, in the Bahamas in 1986, and they have worked summers at the inn ever since. These days, Ned, with a thick knot of gray hair, is an ambling and soft-spoken presence in the lobby and around the grounds. Shelagh, trim and brunette, waits tables and runs the kitchen.

The inn's old, small rooms have the cozy charm of a nest, and after our long drive from the Cities, Susan and I immediately set about to nesting. After our nap, we walked the streets of town. Rossport remains a quaint village, though the fishing nowadays is strictly for sport and the Canadian Pacific no longer stops. Slow, heavy freights snake along the twisting cliffs by the lake and roar into town. I put pennies on the track and waited with childish glee as a train rumbled by less than one hundred feet from the front door of the inn and set the windows to rattling.

The northern bluebells were in bloom. So were the apple trees, a full month later than my tree at home. Sailors tended to two motorboats down at the government dock. The town has the slapdash look of the Canadian north and appears to have grown organically in the complete absence of zoning—a mix of large homes with grand windows, small houses with compulsively tended yards, and tarpaper shacks in various states of decay surrounded by firewood, welding tanks, lumber, plywood, and re-bar. The Forget-Me-Not Gift Shop, a wood-slab building facing the waterfront and filled with tourist trinkets, began life in 1936 as Molinski's Garage. We visited the town's two churches, one Catholic and the other Protestant, standing side by side on the ridge overlooking the lake. In the cemetery that stretches behind them, we read the names of the one-time parishioners and townsfolk, including the Molinskis.

After dinner—grilled chicken and fresh trout at the inn—Ned stoked the log sauna out back. We sweated in the dim glow of a lantern. The sauna wasn't hot, but I liked the lantern light and the gloom of the sauna. I especially liked the idea of a sauna on the shore of the largest lake in the world.

We cooled off on the wood deck, warmed up one last time, and rinsed off in the trickling wisp of a creek that ran nearby. We retired to the second-floor deck of the inn to smoke a Cuban cigar we bought in Thunder Bay. Well, it was reputed to be Cuban, but it smoked exceedingly hot and dry. Served us right, I suppose, for breaking the trade boycott in spirit, if not in law.

Ned stopped by, and we all looked out over the dark outline of Quarry Island just beyond the harbor, with occasional interruptions from the Canadian Pacific. Ned said he had been stationed in Duluth and had flown F-4s, the muscular twin-engine fighter-bombers used in Vietnam. I asked if he was one of the guys who thundered barely above the treetops and nearly made me jump from the top of a granite overlook while hiking the North Shore.

"Yep, I'm one of those guys," he said. "I apologize. I apologize for all the rest of them."

Ned said he detected a whiff of prosperity in the air. The development boom was on in northeastern Minnesota: land prices were soaring and houses and condos were sprouting like mushrooms along the Superior shore. It would be a long time before such development would reach Rossport— Lord knows, the Trans-Canada Highway connecting Thunder Bay to Sault Sainte Marie wasn't completed until 1960—but people were hungry for a taste of the old-time North Shore, as yet untainted by condos and golf courses. He talked about fixing up the broken-down general store on the main street "downtown." He suggested I buy it.

"Fix it up, sell high-end stuff," Ned advised. "You know, we've got guys who'll come through here who'll pay a hundred dollars for a shirt. People like you. You've got good gear. You're not going to make it selling milk and bread. It needs someone with some imagination."

A train rumbled by, shaking the inn, and filling my heart with glee.

Morning broke gray and cool, the hump of Quarry Island shrouded in fog. Susan and I launched our kayaks, packed with lunch along with extra food, warm clothes, and a tarp in case the weather turned and forced us to spend the night among the islands.

We paddled past the small island guarding the harbor, where we watched a raven dive repeatedly on a bald eagle, until the larger bird abandoned its perch at the top of a conifer and disappeared into the distance. We continued to the east, between Quarry Island, where light-colored sandstone was mined for buildings and bridges, and Nicol Island, where two operators named Smith and Mitchell butchered cattle to feed Canadian Pacific crews. Past Healey Island, we crossed to Channel Island, named, perhaps, for the clear view down the Schreiber Channel to the blue mounds of the Slate Islands in the far distance.

Our kayaks moved as serenely as loons. Cobbles and outcrops, sharply outlined in the clear water, passed beneath us, as though we flew over rough terrain. Occasionally, we heard the distant throb of the Canadian Pacific, so distant and diffuse that it seemed completely unrelated to the colorful cars inching along the gray-green cliffs.

We explored the nooks and hidey-holes in the marbled cliffs of Channel Island. "It looks like beef," Susan exclaimed. It did, with green-white marbling throughout the bent and folded layers of red rock. A profusion of cedars, deep beds of moss, and a sprinkling of birch and spruce covered much of the shore. I enjoyed paddling these sheltered areas, getting a glimpse of the open lake without having to be out on it. We crossed the narrow channel to Wilson Island, and then across Swedes Gap to Copper Island, within two miles of the resting place of the *Gunilda*, covered now by impenetrable gray.

Circling the south shore of Wilson Island, we burst upon the full expanse of Lake Superior—or rather, it burst upon us, an unblinking flat line, an open fetch of more than one hundred miles. Within minutes, the wind came from nowhere, honing the waves to a sharp scalloped edge. Dark cliffs, looking toward the open lake, stood barren and grim. Battle Island and its lighthouse, where we had hoped to paddle, suddenly seemed far away. We landed on a beach in a cove, where a small stream ran to the lake, to pull on warmer clothes. On the sand, we spotted a wolfy scat. I teased it with a stick and it fell apart into hair and bones.

Ned Basher had told me that the keeper at Battle Island Light would row to the Sault for Christmas. I imagined sitting in the boat alone, pulling at the oars by day, camping along shore by night, for 250 miles, fresh snow on the land, a rim of clear ice along shore, clear days of subzero weather giving way to sudden storms.

I was, I had learned, only as calm as the weather. I contemplated the days ahead, paddling down the long finger of Thunder Cape, across the open water and shipping lanes outside of Thunder Bay, in and out of the long string of small islands to the Minnesota shore. I reminded myself that the vagaries and dangers of Lake Superior can be sidestepped with time—if only one gives oneself time, if one is willing to spend extra days on an isolated beach, waiting for the weather to clear. The challenge is not only weather, but also loneliness. Any change in the weather, the slightest ruffle on a previously calm surface, raises the question—Go? Or hold tight? Paddle on? Or take shelter? The decision must be made. And therein lies the anxiety: I like neither risking my life, nor spending long days alone.

In *Superior: The Haunted Shore*, Wayland Drew referred to the lake's commercial fishermen, saying, "No Europeans have lived more respectfully of the lake or with a more acute sense of vulnerability." They lived with this decision and no doubt felt the same anxiety—no one, perhaps, more than Adolph King of Rossport, who over nine seasons would pilot his fishing boat almost daily to the unexploited fishery of Superior Shoal, nearly forty miles from the nearest sheltering land.

By contrast, I thought of William L. Harkness and his apparent impatience and arrogance—poor lubricants in any decision. But Harkness had made the same mistake a second time. Local salvagers warned that the *Gunilda* was unstable and would list dangerously if she were simply towed off the reef. But Harkness, again suspecting he was being ripped off, would spend neither the time nor the money to hire and wait for additional assistance. Instead, he ordered the *Gunilda* removed. She slid off the reef, rolled hard to starboard, filled, and sank, lost forever into Superior's depths.

And so I resolved that as I continued in my travels around Superior, I, too, would live respectfully and not give in to arrogance or pride, or to let anything other than the lake determine my schedule.

That evening, back at the Rossport Inn, Susan and I waited for my friend Jim Weseloh and his son, Ben. Susan would go home tomorrow, but Jim and Ben would join me for the next five days, as far as Silver Islet.

I had known Jim for more than twenty years, since we worked together at the Minnesota Department of Natural Resources. I had known Ben since he was a baby. He was only four months old when his parents first brought him on one of our canoe trips. I remember him covered by blackfly bites. As a child, Ben could be willful, and the more he rebelled, the more Jim nagged. Some days I found it hard to be around the two of them together.

As Jim's truck pulled up to the inn, I was astounded to see that Ben was driving. It had been four years since I had seen him. He stepped from the car, tall and handsome. I shook hands with him, looking eye to eye. I would put those other memories away for now.

Jim and Ben were renting gear from Superior Outfitters in town. The owner, Dave Tamblyn, soon joined us in the lobby of the Rossport. We spread out Tamblyn's navigation charts and plotted the days ahead. Before us lay a trip of about seventy miles. Our route wound along a crenulated shore including more than seven hundred islands, by far the most complex shoreline on Superior. The archipelago promised to be wild country, far from help, with no permanent settlements or year-round residents among the islands. At the same time, the islands and channels would provide protection from strong winds off the lake. That was important because Jim and Ben, though experienced in canoes, had rarely paddled kayaks and never on water as formidable as Superior. On the sixth day, Tamblyn would meet us at the old mining town of Silver Islet at the tip of the Sibley Peninsula, better known as the Sleeping Giant for its resemblance to a recumbent human. Tamblyn would bring Jim and Ben back to Rossport and I would continue alone along the string of islands that leads past Thunder Bay to the Minnesota shore and—who knows?—perhaps as far as Duluth.

That evening, as we ate at the inn and the Canadian Pacific rattled the picture windows, an older man and woman pulled in with a trailer carrying a black wood-and-fabric kayak, built in the style of the Inuit *baidarka*. I recognized the boat from television: it belonged to a woman—the woman stepping out of the car—who had been paddling around the lake last year. She had traveled by herself, even though she was about sixty. And the man—I recognized him, too, from the small world of Lake Superior kayaking. He was one of the guests present when Susan and I had had dinner with David Wells at Michipicoten River the previous summer. I remembered the man had been looking wistfully over Superior and explaining that he had just watched his wife paddle from sight on an excursion around the lake. So I left my dinner and went out to meet them. She was Mary Jo Cullen and he was Torfinn Hansen.

As we talked, Mary Jo's story unfolded. She had started her trip in late August, far later than she had wanted. She had headed south from Michipicoten to the Sault and then west along the south shore. In Duluth, she had made the evening news (which was when I saw her). But by then, she was well into the fall storm season. Strong winds kept her several days in the public campground in Grand Marais, where she shopped and talked to folks as she waited. As the weather abated, she continued up the shore. At Pigeon Point, on the international border, she was caught in a sudden storm. She took shelter in Hole in the Rock and waited out the storm alone in this mere grotto of rock two hundred yards across. When the weather broke, she continued to the northeast but soon had second thoughts. She was already deep into October with more than two hundred miles to go. She didn't care for the almost certain prospect of being wind bound for several days so close to winter. So she pulled out at Silver Islet and called for a ride. Now, she and Torfinn were driving back to Silver Islet, where she would resume the last leg of her trip. She was only mildly disappointed, she said, that she had to complete her trip in a second stage. What was more important to her, she added, was that she do it alone.

We talked excitedly in the dining room. I told her what we were up to and she produced her navigational charts, sealed in a clear, waterproof envelope. She pointed out campsites and places of interest she had heard about. We would be paddling in opposite directions, and we said we would look for each other in passing.

That night Susan, Jim, Ben and I took a sauna behind the hotel.

"Goddammit, Jim, I'm going to die," Ben gasped.

"Get back in here," Jim snapped.

"You're crazy," Ben said, flying out the door.
"Get back in here!"

Ben would paddle Susan's boat; Jim would use the larger rented kayak. For
the first-time kayaker, loading a kayak for a long trip is a daunting task. The
big cook kit, used countless years for canoe camping, doesn't fit through the
hatch. Neither does the large sleeping bag, the large tent, the large dry-bag
of food, the large dry-bag of clothes. Nothing fits until you pull it apart and
jam it piece by piece into the hold. As Jim and I dithered over a large pile of
camping gear, clothes, packaged food, paddles, and life vests, Ben appeared
defeated by the task and constructed a melodrama. "We're all going to die,"
he proclaimed. "This will never fit." And it didn't; we left the most dispen-
sable of their gear in their truck. We launched our boats, so heavy they
scraped along the bottom until the water was several inches deep.

We could have followed the shore to the west, past the town of Gravel
and Kama Bay to the Nipigon River before emerging through the Nipigon
Channel to the exposed shore of Black Bay Peninsula. And there would
have been a certain historical interest in doing so: between 1684 and 1924,
eighteen fur trade posts had occupied the shore of Nipigon Bay. Furthermore, on the cliffs at the mouth of the Nipigon River, Indians had painted
a pictograph. Ostensibly a leaping human figure with buffalo horns, it was
said to be the Ojibwa's water spirit, a *maemaegawauhnse*, which had the ability
to vanish into solid rock and follow the subterranean passageways leading
to Lake Nipigon. The Nipigon River was famous in more recent times for
more tangible reasons. "Gentlemen anglers" began arriving at Nipigon for
brook trout fishing in the 1860s. In *Superior Fishing*, Robert Barnwell Roosevelt wrote that on the Nipigon, "barrels of trout, averaging four pounds,
have been taken in one day." Even the Prince of Wales showed up with a
rod. One angler wrote that the Nipigon had been "popularized and com-
mercialized . . . crowding portages with fellow tourists bumping canoes
continuously." In 1916 Rabbit Rapids, just below Lake Nipigon, produced
the current world record for brook trout at fourteen and a half pounds. As
popular as it was, such fishing couldn't last; anglers eventually skimmed the
largest fish from the Nipigon fishery. Despite the overharvest and construction of dams along much of the river, the Nipigon and its estuary provide
one of the last refuges for the two- to four-pound lake-run brook trout
known as "coasters."

We, however, had bigger fish to fry. We intended to get as far from the highway and traffic as possible and follow the more interesting shoreline among the islands that form the long archipelago that runs all the way to the Minnesota shore. We crossed Wilson Channel to Vein Island, ducked behind Minnie and Harry Islands, crossed Simpson Channel, and rounded Morn Point to enjoy the full effect of Superior's power: the sharp blue line on our left and the ravaged shoreline rock to our immediate right. Of course, by the time we had accomplished this, the midday wind had risen from the west and we battled for every bit of forward progress, at the rate, it seemed, of a yard for every stroke of the paddle. With this wind behind her, Mary Jo must have been flying.

Jim and Ben knew little about kayaking, but their years in canoes served them well. They were a bit stunned by the ferocity of the wind, but paddled well enough and certainly weren't timid. In fact, I called to Ben to keep him near shore, both for safety, should he flip, but also so we could find what meager shelter there was along the craggy shore. Cliffs were pitted and gray, twisted and turned like hemp rope, and stripped bare of anything more recent than Precambrian.

We ducked behind Raymond Island, rounded Beetle Point, and tucked in behind several small skerries. The wind began to flag, and by the time we rounded Grebe Point, in the hazy light of late afternoon, the water had turned to mercury, all silver and rolling smooth. As we paddled into Woodbine Harbour, cliffs to our right and a smattering of islands to our left, even Jim, with whom I had shared many wilderness scenes, marveled at the beauty of it.

Twenty years ago, a group from Thunder Bay claimed the many islands at the mouth of Nipigon Bay in the name of Nirivia, a combination of Nipigon and Nirvana—also the name of the Thunder Bay bike shop belonging to Nirivian Grand Admiral Dave "Zeus" Krujzewski, whose old cabin cruiser served as flagship of the Royal Nirivian Navy. The islands, by the founders' reckoning, had never been claimed on paper by Canada, Ontario, or any of the First Nations along the shore, and they were proclaiming it a "place of exquisite beauty" that should be protected from development forever. Aside from some travel and nature writers, who have suggested the Nirivians are a movement of some kind, I've never seen that anyone takes the Nirivians seriously, except for the province, which took

An inexplicable marker—the border of Nirivia?

them to task for building their geodesic domes on crown land at Armour
Harbour.

Paddling along the crenulations of St. Ignace Island, we were approaching the heartland of Nirivia.

"That boat up ahead—is it a Nirivian patrol?"

"Watch out for the Nirivian black helicopters."

Atop a tiny island near Armour Island, we spotted a four-by-four post,
two feet high, supported by a cairn of rocks. We landed and scrambled out
to explore, displacing the gulls. The post, encrusted with lichen, bore no
writing, no clue to its origin or meaning. A boat approached from the distance. Nirivians? No. As we returned to the kayaks, the boat revved up and
the three anglers turned into Armour Harbour.

We lunched on Armour Island, on a steep gravel beach, where we sat on

a boom log. Thirty feet long and nearly three feet in diameter, it was probably Douglas fir or Sitka spruce, imported from the West Coast for this specific purpose owing to its size, toughness, buoyancy, and resistance to rot.
Large holes, bored through each end so a cable could pass through, were
reinforced with a wooden cap and rubber bumpers to withstand the stress
of towing ten thousand cords of wood across the tempestuous lake. The
islands had many such reminders of human industry.

The islands were being studied as a future national marine conservation
area. Over the years, I had developed a kind of suspicious ambivalence toward such things. The islands, mostly crown land, were not the managed
wilderness of a park. They were instead a kind of neglected wilderness of
thick second-growth forest, otters, bears, wolves, and moose. Designation
as a national conservation area would protect the islands and mainland
shore from mining. Logging would probably be more highly regulated.
Areas of special ecological concern, such as rare plant communities and
nesting sites of colonial water birds, would receive special protection. On
the other hand, designation would bring more visitors. And more pesky
regulations. But those were petty concerns. Designation as a park of some
kind was perhaps the only way to ensure the land remained natural.

We put to the water once again. Trolling a plug, I caught a sleek lake
trout, about three pounds. It was beautiful: thin and silvery with a dark back.
We had no easy way to keep it for dinner, so I returned it to the water, where
it sped away into the clear water like a torpedo.

To the west, a finger of land extended from St. Ignace, giving the impression of a long peninsula, but as we drew closer, it broke apart into islands: Bowman, Paradise, Raven, Talbot. At the southeast end of Bowman
we landed at a weathered boathouse flying a Canadian flag. A log house sat
just up the hill. The site, according to a guide I had read, had been a fishing
camp, in use from the early 1880s until the widespread decline of the lake
trout fishery in the 1950s. I peeked in a window: pots sat on the stove. Someone had snuffed a cigarette directly on the stove top. A sign on the wall said
"Kemp Fisheries Ltd., Thunder Bay." In the yard sat a wooden boat, gaping
spaces in its hull. Up a well-graveled trail was another boat (smaller and
even more dilapidated) and an old cast-iron stove. And finally, down a
wooded path in a tiny sunlit clearing, covered by the white blossoms of
bunchberries, was a grave. A rusted Campbell's soup can held dried flowers.
A plaque on a white cross said: "In memory of Thomas Lampshire, Talbot

On Bowman Island stands an old fishery, as well as the most evocative reminder of the Lighthouse of Doom.

Island lightkeeper, died 1869." The lives of Lake Superior lighthouse keepers were renowned for hardship, isolation, and loneliness, but none, I had learned, were so ill-fated as those who manned Talbot Island.

Thomas Lamphier and his wife moved to the Talbot Island Lighthouse in 1869. Built just two years earlier, it was Canada's first station on Lake Superior. The Lamphiers were not its first occupants. William Perry manned the light in the first season. In those days, keepers had to find their own way to the mainland at the end of the shipping season. Perry closed for the year and set sail in his open boat for the Hudson's Bay Company post at the mouth of the Nipigon River. He never arrived. His body and boat were found the following spring in Nipigon Bay.

Thomas Lamphier knew of the lake's tantrums and dangers. For nearly twenty years he had sailed a schooner out of Fort William. He and his wife decided not to tempt fate by sailing to the mainland at the end of the season. Instead they would winter on the island. The keeper's residence had been remodeled and enlarged to make it more comfortable. The Lamphiers were hardy, familiar with the severity of Superior's weather and the length of its winters. Mrs. Lamphier was a native of the far north, near Hudson Bay. A Lake Superior winter would hold few surprises for either of them.

During the Lamphiers' first months on Talbot, ships navigated the confusing knot of islands at the entrance to the Nipigon Straight by the lighthouse beacon. Then, as shipping ceased and winter descended on Superior, Thomas Lamphier fell ill and died. With no boats passing, Mrs. Lamphier could not get off the island. Indeed, she couldn't even get her husband's body off the island. Talbot Island is solid rock and there was no way to bury it. Mrs. Lamphier wrapped her husband's corpse in canvas and dragged it outside.

Through the winter the body lay behind the house in a rocky crevice, as Mrs. Lamphier, we are to assume, ate at the table where she had dined with her husband, slept in the bed she had shared with him, and lived the winter life they had planned together. Months passed in the grip of the snow and ice. Finally, spring arrived—late, as it always does on Superior, where the cold body of the lake delays the onset of warm weather. Thawing and melting occur at a glacial pace; the season turns with agonizing slowness. Was Mrs. Lamphier frantic for her own survival? Did she miss her husband terribly? Did she simply want to be rid of the body? All we know is that she was forced to live with the physical evidence of her husband's death for months until one spring day, when she spied a small boat on the lake and flagged down its occupants, a small party of Ojibwa, who carried her husband's body to Bowman Island and buried it, marking the grave with a simple cross. By the time the government supply ship arrived, according to one account, Mrs. Lamphier's hair, glistening and black as a raven when she arrived at Talbot Island, had turned snow white.

If anything, the Lamphiers' tragedy seemed only to solidify the curse of the Talbot Island light. At the end of the season in 1872, the third keeper, Andrew Hynes, closed the lighthouse, loaded his supplies and gear on a small boat and, on a clear day, set off for Fort William. The weather turned suddenly and persistently stormy. A trip of eighty miles that should have taken three to four days lasted eighteen. At that time of year, the storm most likely poured out of the northwest. We can imagine Hynes beating against the wind, cresting mammoth waves and dropping into deep troughs, as he tried to keep from being blown into the open lake. Perhaps he took shelter on shore, pacing the beach for days, without food, sufficient clothing, or adequate shelter. We shall never know what happened, for when Hynes finally struggled ashore at Silver Islet, he was barely coherent. Hypothermic and exhausted, he soon died.

Hynes was the last keeper at Talbot Island. The light was abandoned and fell into ruin. In 1964 a local man, Jim Sigurdson, located plaster lath, nails, and fireplace bricks from the structure. In the late 1970s, the priest from Rossport and Bill Schelling, a commercial fisherman who lived on Bowman Island, placed a new white cross and bronze plate, with Lamphier's anglicized name, on the grave. For years commercial fishermen talked of a woman with flowing white hair walking the shore of Talbot Island, near what had become known as the Lighthouse of Doom.

Skipping among islands, we reached a tight little cove formed by a crooked finger reaching from shore. It was known as Squaw Harbour or CPR Slip, for the Canadian Pacific Railway, which built small cabins on the cove in the 1920s for company guests on fishing trips. When we arrived, two large boats were tied to the dock. A cabin sat in the woods. Three fishermen were cooking potatoes and trout in a big black wok over an open fire.

The real attraction of CPR Slip was its wood-fired sauna, with two capacious changing rooms. It was built by a group of pleasure boaters, primarily from Nipigon. After years of visiting the site and cleaning up garbage left by other boaters, they wrote the landowners (no longer the Canadian Pacific) and explained they would like to build a sauna on the property: "Enclosed please find a copy of a blueprint for a steambath which we would like to erect." A few days later, a letter went out from H. F. (Fraser) Dougall of Thunder Bay: "Go ahead. Glad to hear of your efforts."

That, in a nutshell, is the difference between us nonmotorized types and the motorheads. We are nomads; the yachtsmen and fishermen are builders, planners, improvers. We would as soon hang a 200-horsepower Yamaha on the back of a kayak as truck in the materials necessary to build a sauna. We envision a primeval Nature; the motorheads seek to change Nature into a garden. We are examples of Aldo Leopold's "A-B cleavage: man the conqueror versus man the biotic citizen."

Not that I minded the builders—at least not a few of them, and for now. I was happy to use their sauna. We stoked the stove and split extra wood for the three fishermen to use after us. When we hopped into the sauna, it was 70 degrees Celsius (about 160 degrees Fahrenheit) and climbing. Pails of hot water warmed above the stove. We perched on the steep benches, scrunching in the corner between the back wall and the ceiling, where the greatest heat collected. Ben was dubious: "We're going to die." Then Jim plastered the rocks with cold water and we fled the sauna to avoid the scalding steam. In a few moments the worst of it had cleared and we took our spots again, basking in the heat.

Nothing seemed more natural than a sauna on the shores of cold Superior. The Finns who settled this country must have thought the same. With its boreal forest and clear lakes, the Superior country was the mirror image of their homeland. For the Finns, the sauna (pronounced *sa-oo-na*, not *saw-na*) was not an endurance test, but a place for renewal. In fact, there is a saying that a person should behave in the sauna as he would in church. Indeed, the Finnish sauna, with a tradition of at least two thousand years, embodies much the same spirit as the Native American sweat lodge. The Finnish *Kalevala*, a collection of ancient legends and songs woven into an epic poem, contains imagery that would have been familiar to the Ojibwa:

> Then the aged Väinämöinen
> Spoke aloud his songs of magic,
> And a flower-crowned birch grew upward,
> Crowned with flowers, and leaves all golden,
> And its summit reached to heaven,
> To the very clouds uprising.
> Then he sang his songs of magic,
> And he sang a moon all shining,
> Sang he moon to shine forever
> In the pine-tree's emerald summit,
> Sang the Great Bear in its branches.

Jim and I would race to the lake by turns and cool off in the shallows. Ben simply toweled off. He didn't know what he was missing—the exhilaration of the cold water and the rush of warmth and relaxation that followed. But then came an insult to this rejuvenating process: pulling on our wetsuits, all because Jim wanted to get a few miles down the shore before evening.

We glided on a calm lake over shallow-lying boulders. The evening was magical and conducive to making miles. I had been down this road with Jim before, so to speak. As a rule, he did not push hard during the day; he simply never wanted to stop. We would pass up perfectly good campsites in the hopes of finding another before dark.

We paddled along the southern tip of St. Ignace before crossing Blind Channel. As the sun neared the treetops, we still had not found a suitable camp. Finally we landed on a hump of gravel. We graded the rocks with a driftwood log until we had room for the tent and then cooked dinner in the shadows cast by the full moon.

The next two days we followed the islands that fringe the lakeward shore of Black Bay Peninsula. Soaring hills, humping hills, sloping hills, weird hills of all shapes rose on the peninsula. Hills shaped like Diamondhead, hills like the Rock of Gibraltar, hills like the back of a dromedary, of a Bactrian, hills like elephants. Adding to the strangeness of the landscape, two loons sailed by as we neared Otter Island. They flew low over the water, split around our boats and then, at sixty miles an hour, circled us in opposite directions. Cabot wrote that whenever loons flew by, the "men began to shout 'oory, oory,' which seems to be the Indian 'hurrah,' whereupon the bird would usually fly in circles round the boat." I had called out "oory" on earlier occasions with no effect at all. A third loon joined in. They all circled our boats twice more and then shot off over the open lake.

The weather deteriorated during the afternoon. We found shelter that night in a bay behind Shesheeb Point, on the site, according to one guidebook, of an old hunting and fishing camp. Logs of an old wharf remained in the lake. An iron ring was embedded in an outcrop. We camped amid various debris, including a fifty-five-gallon drum, several feet of stovepipe, rusted cans, and hard ground encrusted with lichens. In its favor, there was space for the tent, and a fringe of trees broke the wind.

The next morning we found more signs of humanity. At Black's Wharf were the remains of an old commercial fishing station, with a cabin of particle board. At the south end of Lasher Island we climbed a sloping gray point to inspect another four-by-four marker carved with initials now illegible. By chance we chose the channel into Loon Harbour, so thoroughly surrounded by Lasher, Borden, and Spain Islands that it appeared landlocked. There, along the shore of Spain Island, we found timbers, gears, a flywheel, and two boilers. It was, I learned from Barbara Chisholm and Andrea Gutsche's *Superior: Under the Shadow of the Gods*, the remains of a pulpwood loader, used to hoist logs from Black Bay Peninsula onto boats in the early 1900s. Campfires had been built on a rock nearby, as though people liked camping by the ruins of their own civilization.

We continued southeast through a long rocky gap, riverine in appearance, toward Swede Island. Ben did not know it, but Jim and I were navigating toward another sauna. Ben, to his credit, was becoming adept at map reading. With his nose in his charts and his hands held high as he paddled, he ripped big holes in the surface of the lake.

"Sound of power," he would say.

"Sound of wasted energy," I would reply.

Why were we headed into the deep bay on Swede Island? he asked.

Another sauna beckoned, I said. As Ben complained, Jim and I turned toward the dock, where a large runabout and a small fishing boat were tied.

Outside a small cabin we met a couple from Thunder Bay. Russ, in his mid-forties, was soft-spoken with eyes the color of the lake on a sunny day. "We're sort of the caretakers," he said in a noncommittal way.

"Do you get here often?" I asked.

"Not often enough—maybe once a year," he said. They mostly fished and relaxed. "If we don't keep the garbage cleaned up, the Ministry of Natural Resources says it will burn the place down." He invited us to chop wood and take a sauna.

Russ and his wife had talked to Mary Jo Cullen the night before. She had intended to follow the channel between Loon and Borden and camp in Loon Harbour. Somehow we had missed her. "She's such a small woman," Russ said. I found the remark ironic, as though anyone's size matches up favorably to the task of wrestling Superior's waves. "I think you guys are crazy for being out there like that," he added.

Since we had put in at Rossport, the Chicago Bulls and the Utah Jazz had played the National Basketball Association championship game. We were eager to know who had won.

"Yeah, I was watching it last night," Russ said.

"How did it turn out?"

"Oh, I fell asleep. I was looking for the hockey game."

The sauna was much smaller than the one at CPR Slip. It was darker, hotter, more ramshackle, too, and for all those reasons seemed even more like a rural Finnish sauna. The temperature, after we stuffed several birch logs into the hearth, soared to 175 degrees Fahrenheit, not hot by Finnish standards, but the hottest I had experienced in some time. The *löyly*, the burst of heat that washed over us when we threw a dipper of water on the superheated rocks, was much more intense as well. The word is impossible for a non-Finn to pronounce and nearly as difficult to translate. *Löyly* is really part scalding water vapor, part metaphysics:

> Come now, God, into sauna
> to the warmth, heavenly Father
> healthfulness to bring to us,
> and the peace secure to us.

At one point, Ben and I both both burst from the sauna, seriously worried our skins would blister. Jim, inexplicably, stayed behind. To cool off, we stood out on the windy point and looked through the sauna's guest register.

This from Rick, Sandy, and Barb, July 1994: "Good to be back at Swede's. It's been a couple of years. On our way to Rossport. Hope to bump into you sometime."

A sailor on a nineteen-foot catamaran: "Sailed in from Silver Islet. Slept out under the stars on sandy spit. Full moon and beautiful sunrise. No bugs. Most memorable moment: a heated debate with a stubborn Irishman, Tom, over depth of water in shoal areas on chart."

April 1998: "Got here Easter Sunday and stuck out a gale until Easter Monday afternoon. First time I've ever kayaked on Superior in April. It's wild!"

The last entry: "Many thanks to Sally and Russ Jackson for throwing a few more sticks on the sauna stove and firing it up. Felt wonderful to these old bones after a long cool day on the water. . . . Am completing a circumnavigation of Lake Superior. I started last August at the Michipicoten River and got as far as Silver Islet last October. Hoping to have a leisurely trip to the starting point by end of June. Mary Jo Cullen, Wawa."

Ben made a melodrama of the sauna.

"I'm going to die!"

"Get in here! It's good for you!"

Which was entirely indefensible.

"You should get cleaned up."

Which was entirely defensible, since we were all sleeping in the same tent.

We finished the sauna and dressed. The wind was raw and fog had moved in. This had always baffled me. How could it be both windy and foggy? We hoped to proceed southwest to Macoun Island, a spit of rock that lay, invisible, two miles away. I took a bearing from the map, double checked, and we paddled off into the fog, as though off the end of the earth. As we rounded the craggy shore of Swede and lost the protection of several islands to the east, the wind suddenly hit us hard. It was cold, and we still could not see a trace of Macoun.

"Are you sure we should do this?" Jim asked.

"Sure," I said, not at all sure.

But as we continued into the great unknown, the wind and waves building, Jim's doubts prevailed. We backtracked to the shelter of Swede Island and listened again to the weather report: small craft wind and thunderstorm advisories. We decided to head north in the lee of Swede and follow a more protected route. Reaching Gourdeau Island, we set off for Stanton and Hanbury Islands, two miles away. The fog had lifted a bit now, and we could see the islands clearly. We expected that the islands behind us would provide shelter from the wind and waves. For the first mile, we paddled briskly through small waves that quartered from the rear, but as we reached the halfway point, the waves began to build. Our boats twisted and surfed as the waves passed beneath us.

"Why am I getting nervous about this?" Ben asked.

"Well, because we're a half mile from shore, we're in the middle of Lake Superior, and the waves are getting kind of big," I replied. I didn't want to sound alarmed, but I sounded less sympathetic than I meant to. As the waves sloshed around us, I pulled in close to Ben. At the moment, with the brashness scared out of him, I felt downright compassionate.

Jim paddled twenty feet ahead. "What's going on back there?" he hollered, a bit nervously I thought.

"Paddle easily and relax," I told Ben. "We'll be fine." With the wind from behind, we soon made the gap between the two islands. The waves dropped immediately. We paddled up the protected side of Hanbury in an intense but brief cloudburst. I felt like a duck. We found a long beach in a cove on the island. Unfortunately, there was no obvious place to camp, so we pitched the tent in the dripping woods and made dinner.

"Don't want to do that again," Jim said.

"No," I agreed.

Because of our maneuvering to avoid the wind and waves, we were no closer to Silver Islet now than when we finished our sauna. Ben looked at the map. "You mean that's all the farther we've gone today? We'll never make it!"

As I planned this trip, I had hoped that several weeks in the wilderness would reveal secrets unlikely to unfold on mere day trips and weekends. The howl of wolves. Perhaps even the fleeting sight of bobcat or lynx. What I did not anticipate was the confounding ineptitude of our national symbol.

While writing a book about bald eagles a few years ago, I uncovered some amazing tales of their proficiency as hunters. Eagles have been observed taking geese on the wing. They have formed a squadron to take geese on the water. They have hunted in packs for rabbits, even walking through underbrush to flush prey for waiting comrades. An eagle was even seen diving beneath the surface of the water like a kingfisher to snare a particularly elusive coot, popping to the surface and then using its wings to swim to shore. So when I saw a confrontation shaping up between an eagle and a swimming merganser, I watched raptly.

About a quarter mile away, an eagle had sailed from a tree near shore and, with a few slow beats of its wings, had drawn close to two mergansers swimming in the open lake. One merganser dove and did not reappear, leaving the other swimming on the surface and grunting at the eagle, which wheeled above it. Perhaps the merganser was injured and could neither swim underwater nor fly. Or perhaps, with the eagle in control of the sky, it preferred to remain on the water. At any rate, the eagle dove, and the merganser, grunting vigorously, dove momentarily and bobbed to the surface seconds after the eagle had passed. And so it went. The eagle would dive and the merganser would duck beneath the surface or dodge to the side at the last split second. The eagle would flap to gain altitude, wheel around, and try again. This happened perhaps a dozen times. With each pass, the eagle tired until it could barely stay out of the water. It labored heavily to shore, where it perched in the low branches of a dead tree.

"Let's yell at the eagle," Ben said.

"The merganser's hurt," Jim said. "It's going to die anyway."

"I want to see what happens," I said. I wanted blood.

The eagle flew out again, making three or four passes. Each time the merganser dodged; each time the eagle missed and seemed to have greater difficulty regaining altitude. The eagle returned to its tree and stayed there until we grew impatient and paddled off.

Down the rocky shore we landed for a snack. I got out of the boat and popped the front hatch for some food.

"You're going to open your hatch?" Ben asked. Actually, it was more of an assertion, or even an accusation. "You're going to open your *hatch?!*"

"No, I've already opened my hatch." I dug for some gorp.

"What are you *doing?*"

"Oh, it's some ancient ritual I do," I replied sarcastically. Now that we had stopped paddling, I pulled on a jacket.

"Aren't you *hot?*"

"You know, Ben, what you've got to learn is that people are different. No, I'm not hot. Your questions are accusatory and rude."

"All I did is ask you if you're hot."

"No, you asked something different and it would be good for you to learn the difference."

Quiet settled over everything.

Then Jim said, "Well, where are we?"

We paddled down the last of Black Bay Peninsula, passing the Paps, breast-shaped hills the men of the canoe brigades called *Les Mamelles*. On a little island near Magnet Island we passed a commercial fisherman's place, with a bunch of blue barrels and ramshackle buildings along shore and up on a small ridge. The boat was gone; I think we had heard it earlier in the day. In Indonesia, where I had recently stayed along a sparsely settled coast, a whole village would cluster around a fishery. There would be hustle and bustle, people talking and spreading fish out to dry. Here it was quiet, gray, deserted.

We argued a bit over the route around Edward Island, a stony Rorschach of points and bays. (Edward was the site of silver exploration in the 1870s. Prospectors eventually gave up, but not before filling ten thousand boxes with core samples.) Ben wanted to round the north side of the island, a microscopically shorter route, but one that would expose us to the full force of wind pouring out of Black Bay. We stuck instead to the south shore.

On the west shore of Edward Island, we debated whether to cross the four miles to the Sibley Peninsula. But since the sun was setting and we didn't know if we could find a camp there, we decided to use our remaining daylight to look on our side of the channel. But campsites were hard to come

A pocket beach of cobble provides a campsite on Edward Island.

by; the shore was solid rock and in the bays, forest crowded nearly to the water's edge. We settled, finally, for a notch in the cliffs, probably where a dike of soft rock had eroded away, leaving a steep-walled slot forty feet wide, extending back about sixty feet. It was filled with stairsteps of cobble, sorted by millennia of sou'westers. We pitched the tent on the highest terrace, where the cliffs framed a perfect view of Nanaboozhoo, the Sleeping Giant. In the setting sun, he lay in stony repose, four miles long, hands folded on his chest, his feet disappearing in the low mist.

According to Charles Lanman, who traveled the Lake Superior country in 1846, Nanaboozhoo died in battle with the "Evil One," struck dead by an immense club. More often I have heard the story that the protector of the Ojibwa lived through a time of terrible famine and scarcity of game. Nanaboozhoo's wife nagged him for his ineptitude as a hunter and provider. Finally, in a rage, he struck her and killed her. Looking at her body, he was instantly remorseful. He ran in panic until he fell dead from exhaustion and grief. The Great Spirit mercifully turned Nanaboozhoo to stone to survive for eternity.

But the story that follows is the one I like best because it tells not only of the death of Nanaboozhoo, but also, figuratively, of the Ojibwas' reign in Lake Superior country. One day, as Nanaboozhoo sat on the shore of the lake, he idly scratched earth and discovered a vein of silver. Alarmed because white men coveted the stuff and would drive the Ojibwa from the land if they learned of it, Nanaboozhoo gathered up all the silver he could find and hid it on a tiny island. One Ojibwa chief watched him, and after Nanaboozhoo had left, he sneaked back to the island to take some silver to make weapons. Later, the chief was killed by Dakota. Seeing his silver weapons, the Dakota realized the silver must have come from Ojibwa land. The Dakota devised a scheme: they would brag of their discovery to the whites, who would drive off the Ojibwa, take the silver, and then leave the land for the Dakota. As the Dakota led two white men to the island, Nanaboozhoo discovered them and caused a big storm that drowned them all. As punishment for killing the white men, the Great Spirit turned Nanaboozhoo to stone. But more white men came, and they discovered the silver, buried on the small island, only ninety feet across. Once known as Skull Rock, it is known now as Silver Islet.

The next morning, with plenty of time before we were to meet Dave Tamblyn, we decided to paddle to Silver Islet to explore. Lying a mile from

Jim and Ben approach Silver Islet, once the site of one of the richest silver mines in the world.

the town of the same name, it could easily be called Gull Islet. Perhaps three hundred screaming gulls covered a speck of rock the size of a football field. Once the rock was much smaller, but it had been reinforced with gravel and rock fill. Still, it rose a mere five feet above lake level.

We landed among the wheeling gulls. As we walked, however, we soon discovered gray fuzz balls, the gull chicks, stumbling over the rough rock. One scampered off into territory of another gull and was grabbed roughly and thrown aside. Watching carefully for chicks, we avoided what appeared to be the nesting area.

We looked over the timbers and concrete foundations of the old Silver Islet Mine. Silver was discovered here in 1868. Within two years, mining began. Breakwaters and a coffer dam, built on the rock's perimeter to allow excavation, were soon destroyed by fall storms and rebuilt at double the thickness. Eventually a shaft extended nearly a quarter mile below the surface of the lake. Four hundred eighty men worked sixty hours a week under dangerous conditions, with the constant threat of flooding. Large waves occasionally breached the breakwater and crashed over the shaft. Men who had other options took them. Workers quit, struck, or threatened to strike for reasons "as many and as opposed to compromise as Quills on a porcupine," wrote mine captain W. B. Frue. Silver Islet was Canada's first successful silver mine and, for a while, one of the richest in the world. But during the winter of 1883–84, the lake froze early, preventing the shipment of coal to power the mine's pumps. The shaft flooded and was abandoned. In thirteen years of operation, Silver Islet had shipped more than three million dollars worth of ore.

We left the island to the scolding gulls and paddled into town, once home to miners and then loggers. The town library was located in the saloon; the librarian was the bartender. Today, Silver Islet is made up largely of summer homes, which stretch a mile along Sibley Cove and Camp Bay. The centerpiece of town, sitting at the base of the dock, is the old general store, a three-story structure built during the mine's heyday and recently refurbished with a cafe. We stripped off our wetsuits, unpacked, sorted our gear at the landing, and walked up to the store. Inside were the old wood floor and high shelves. The young woman behind the cash register said she grew up in Thunder Bay but spent summers in Silver Islet. She and her parents were just "weekenders," she said.

Jim, Ben, and I ordered ice cream. We hung around the dock until Dave Tamblyn pulled up with a trailer. I helped them load boats and gear. And then they left. Just like that.

Suddenly I felt very much alone. I might have even been willing to argue with Ben.

As I killed time on the Silver Islet dock, a large boat throwing a mountainous wake motored up the channel toward town. It was the *Westfort* of the Canadian Coast Guard. As it pulled into the dock, the deckhand threw me a hawser. Seconds later, the captain emerged from the cabin. He had the shiny black pompadour and the swollen, sleepy good looks of a young Robert Mitchum. He wore aviator sunglasses and two gold chains, one with two Coast Guard insignias and the other with a cross. He wore his shirt open two buttons and talked to everyone who came down to the dock. He handed me a card: Robert King, commanding officer, rescue and environmental response. I introduced myself, and that was the last I had to say for awhile.

"A couple of weeks ago we got a report four days after a guy left not in a sea kayak like you have, but in an ordinary kayak with a spray skirt. It didn't have none of the straps—I see you got a little tiller on there—none of that stuff. Something you'd probably put in a bathtub. He went out, he told nobody where he was going. He was only two weeks in town from British Columbia. Four days later, one of the people he was working for called and said he was missing. He left in gale force winds to go from Chippewa Park to Pie Island, and the winds were out of the south, so he had to go right across that. I found his kayak three days later and his body nine days later. Yeah, he ended up over off of Sawyer Bay on the other side of the peninsula."

"Did he have a wetsuit?"

"No, no, no. Just skinny little shiny shorts, a T-shirt, and a purple and black life jacket. We had two Hercules aircraft, two Labrador Coast Guard military rescue helicopters, boats crisscrossing the area for four days. Searched as far away as the Keweenaw Peninsula in Michigan and all the way down to Marathon."

"How often do you get stuff like that?"

"Not too often. Probably about thirty calls a year. That's not too much. But that one was a recipe for, uh—bad weather, gale warning, doesn't tell anybody where he's going, when he's coming back. I don't know what the hell. You guys are probably equipped for ocean going. Using all that common sense you have, eh?"

"I hope so."

"I'm the guy who had to bring that guy back to his family. We were all crying, I was crying. What they say about fish food is true. Once you fall in, you're just another piece of floating stuff."

I asked him to describe his boat. The *Westfort* was forty-four feet six inches long, he said, designed to weather the heaviest seas and to right itself if it capsizes. "It's not built in any way for pleasure. Yeah, yeah, you get the shit beat right out of you. Two years ago we were on a rescue with an American cruise boat called the *Grampa Woo*. Just off of that island, Trowbridge Island. About four miles sou'east of that island. That's where the whole thing took place. We were out there in twenty-plus-foot waves. The boat can take the big sea, but it's really hard on the crew. I've broken bones. It's pretty claustrophobic when you close everything up. If you're running in a following sea with a lot of wind, eh? The diesel fumes come right inside the thing there, and if you lock it up it's like being in a coffin. You get sick on diesel fumes. The good thing about this boat is that no one has ever been killed in it on our base. I've gotten the most broken bones on it because I've been on it the longest. One of my guys, Billy, rescued these people. In the meantime he cut his leg open like that [drawing his finger across his leg]. He got back to the boat and there were pretty good waves. He sewed himself up right in the wheelhouse. 'Just keep her steady, Bob!' He just chewed on a pencil, I guess. He was half frozen anyway. He was in the water for a long time. So he didn't notice it too much except that the blood was gushing all over when he came out. They were taking people off of that island. Their boat was up in the rocks."

He started with the Coast Guard in 1976 on the Great Lakes on buoy tenders and icebreakers. He grew up on a small Indian reserve named Gull Bay, on the west side of Lake Nipigon. "For me, a big trip out was to go to Armstrong and watch the train come in. I'd get all dressed up and stand on the platform. Have the old Ford pickup running there and wave at the girls on the train. I got one one time. One came off. For two days. I put her on the train two days later. She went to Winnipeg. She liked me. She wanted to be with a real Indian. I said, 'I'm about as real as you can get, eh?'"

"Is that Ojibwa or Cree?"

"That's Ojibwa. Cree's a little bit more north. We kicked their ass out of there. I grew up with no electricity and we still had dog teams when I was a kid, eh? My dad never drove a car, but he had a boat. He was a commercial fisherman. My grandfather was a boat builder on Lake Nipigon. He had dog teams in the winter and boats in the summer. I used to let the dogs go in the summer because I would feel sorry for them. And then you'd have to chase them down, eh? The only reason you get a dog to pull is you tie them on a short chain. I used to feel sorry for them. When somebody tells you— nowadays they don't use dogs commercially no more, they just run the shit out of them till they die, I guess—but when they say the dogs love to run, wouldn't you if you were tied to a three-foot chain your whole life? They just want to get the hell away. They don't want to pull that sleigh, they just want to get away. When I look at it now, it was a necessity. But for pleasure, it is something that would turn our people off. Our dogs died trying to save my dad one time. My dad tried to push the dogs, and the dogs said no no no, and finally they went through the ice. He lost his whole dog team. He made it okay. He got out, but the dogs went down. If he had listened to his dogs, it wouldn't have happened."

"Did they tell Nanaboozhoo stories at all?"

"A lot of the stories were always told by the older people. My dad told me stories. They're much like any other story you'd hear in your own grow-ing up. Why things happen. There was a little mischievous creature of the lake called *maemaegawaehnse*. He'd say, 'Don't go to the lake or *maemaegawaehnse* is going to get you,' eh? That's what the old people tell you. That's what it was—a funny little guy who would grab kids and take them down. So the kid wouldn't go there. Little things like that. How the birch bark got the black marks on it. Things like that."

"How did the birch bark get the black marks on it?"

"Well some Indian was by the fire and he burned his ass. Caught on fire. And he went around putting the fire out on the birch trees and left little black marks from the charcoal. Funny stories like that."

I wanted to hear more about the *Grampa Woo*. When the well-known Min-nesota tour boat, which operated along the North Shore as far as Thunder Bay, went down in a late fall storm in 1996, it was the talk of the lakes. It had been moored to a two-ton block of pig iron and concrete in Grand Portage, awaiting new propellers, when near-hurricane winds blew the ship and its makeshift anchor into the lake. Its owner and captain, Dana Kollars, and his mate, Robin Sivill, raced to the drifting *Woo* in a motorized raft, hoping to somehow get the *Woo* to safe harbor. The U.S. Coast Guard had no large boats in the area. A passing freighter, the *Walter J. McCarthy Jr.*, was nearby. It drew alongside the *Woo* to bring the men aboard. But Kollars hoped to save his boat as well as his skin. He refused to come aboard, but persuaded the crew to throw down a three-inch hawser to tow the disabled ship.

"The *McCarthy* was towing this thing into Thunder Bay. It was blowing, blowing, blowing really hard. Hurricane winds, 170 kilometers, that would be like eighty, ninety knots. The lowest barometric pressure ever in the state of Michigan. The idea was Gerry [Dawson] was to go out there with the *Glenada*, his tug, and relieve on the tow for that big ship. We were tasked by our rescue coordination to go out there and stand by with Gerry in case he needed a hand and so on like that. So we went out there and of course everything happened the way we knew it would happen. As soon as they made the turn, that's when the wind would be the worst and the rope would break. So here we are: the rope breaks, the thousand-foot ship takes off, and here are these two in the boat. What are you going to do? You can't leave the guys. So you got to try everything you can. You can't leave. We knew if we left, they're going to be dead. We knew if we stayed, they would probably be dead anyhow and we'd all be dead, but you got to stay. That's what you do, you stay right to the end. I could never leave them. Neither could Gerry. So we're trying everything we thought of. Gerry's got the best shot because he's got the seventy-foot tug. All he does for a living is run into boats with the damn thing. Big tires on the front. The idea was just to nose into the beam on it somehow. I think he put the nose to the beam and just rolled it in there like that. He had a great big deckhand, Jim Harding, and Jim was a big, tall guy, arms down to the floor, eh, and somehow he reached these two men and because of his strength and his size he got these guys off this damn boat onto the bow of the *Glenada*. But during the whole rescue everything was moving at about four and one-half knots. That was the drift rate of the *Grampa Woo*. It's not like everything is stationary. Everything is moving. There's movement everywhere—up, down. You can imagine.

"Then we had to make our way into that Tee Harbour. We were gone for three days before we could come home. The wind finally died down to about forty knots and we came home. We didn't just sit in there. The wind was even increasing, coming over the cliffs there so it was just terrible. We sat for two days with the engines running. Beach right up on the rocks with the engines running, and both boats lashed together really tight, eh? Really, the worst storm I had ever seen in my life. I never seen nothing like it. It was just terrible. There were hundreds of—they call them waterspouts, but they're just like mini tornadoes. It was like ballerinas everywhere. Hundreds of them. High—fifty to a hundred feet with the water spinning like that, eh? Oooo. The hell with that, eh? Never mind, Gerry, we're going to stay here now. That's too crazy, eh? So the second or third day we were getting fed up with it, eh? We were all stinking, eating two-year-old hot dogs. We had no food. I had a helicopter fly in stuff the first day. They couldn't get in anymore after that because the winds were too bad.

"The idea was that if it [the drifting *Grampa Woo*] missed Passage, it might sneak through the gap there, then maybe the wind would have died down in a couple days and maybe it wouldn't have. After it calmed down the Americans could have picked it up on the other side. [But it didn't sneak through the gap. It missed by a couple hundred yards.] It's still piled up on Passage Island. It wrecked quick. It actually drifted on there and just smashed up. That storm went on for two days, pounding and pounding and pounding."

King invited me aboard the *Westfort* for a tour. Then he asked, "Do you want to put your kayak on board and ride to Pie Island?"

I was tempted. The paddle to Pie Island, across the shipping lanes into Thunder Bay, was the trickiest part of the trip ahead. I could be stuck as I waited for favorable winds. But I decided I would rather make the crossing on my own.

Then he said, "If you run into trouble, give me a call anytime. Call collect if you need to." I don't know where he thought I was going to find a phone, but I was touched by the offer.

Walking around town, I discovered my kayak was beached on private property, and the owner told me to move it. Feeling lonely and unwelcome, I loaded up, pulled on my wetsuit and spray jacket, climbed in the boat, and pushed off. I paddled into a wind ripping out of the southwest, kicking up small whitecaps. The wind seemed to be rising. Rather than make the six-mile crossing to Pie Island, I decided to lay in at Tee Harbour, at least until late afternoon, to wait for the wind to drop.

Tee Harbour was the site of a fishing village until residents decided they should move to the road and floated their buildings to Silver Islet. No buildings stand there now, but Tee Harbour had a settled appearance nonetheless, with a long, curving beach where families played. Compared with the hard, boreal shoreline I was used to, the forest seemed suddenly more deciduous, with big birches. The harbor sits beneath the towering cliffs of the Sleeping Giant, the highest cliffs along Superior. Thunder Mountain, nearly one thousand feet higher than the lake, was the home of thunderbirds (*animikeek* in Ojibwa), which ruled the skies, in opposition to Mishi-bizheu, lord of the lake. The thunderbirds would make war on Mishi-bizheu, shooting lightning from their eyes.

I made an early dinner to prepare for paddling that night. I could walk across the narrow harbor peninsula and periodically check the wind. Through the afternoon it showed no signs of abating. I would need an hour to reach the end of Thunder Cape, another two hours to make the crossing, and perhaps an hour or more to find a campsite on Pie Island. I checked the weather again: small craft wind advisory with winds of twenty knots. I began to wonder if I would regret turning down Bob King's offer of a ride. By six o'clock I decided to wait until morning—the only reason to move on was my own anxiousness—and hiked several miles to kill time until dark. I kicked up a snowshoe hare, a porcupine, and a white-tailed deer that did not want to leave the campground. A band of gulls mobbed two eagles, driving one eagle two to three miles offshore, where they continued to harass it.

That evening, two sailboats and a runabout motored into Tee Harbour. The wind had finally died, and I could hear voices over the water as they set anchor. Already I felt less lonely. One of the sailors saw my camp and yelled ashore, "You got that fire going? We're going to be over in about a half hour!"

"C'mon over. I'll put the brats on."

"I've got a match." I saw a small flame in the near dark.

Soon, they rowed ashore in small rafts: three men, two women, and a large dog. They were from Thunder Bay. The man with the lighter had a tanned, creased face, big teeth, and an anxious grin. Quick with jokes, he smiled and laughed conspicuously. His eyes darted around the group and his hair seemed windblown, though at the moment there was no wind.

They tried to start a fire, but I soon realized they were getting nowhere. I set out into the darkness to round up kindling and dry curls of birch bark, which immediately carried a flame to the rest of the fuel. Around the fire, we talked in amazement about the kayaker whose body Bob King had found. No one could understand why he would head out in such ferocious weather unless he simply underestimated the water because he came from the West Coast and thought Superior, after all, was merely a lake.

One of the men, Paul, seemed quite serious. His eyes looked at you and did not turn away. He said he had sailed among the islands. He talked knowledgeably about the water between here and Sault Sainte Marie. I felt much less lonely than I had earlier in the evening. At 11:30, I stood up to go to my tent. The anxious man asked, "Were you at Silver Islet about eight hours ago?"

"Yes."

"We heard there was a kayaker headed for Duluth. Is that you?"

"Yeah," I said with secret satisfaction. "That's me."

Through the evening a big freighter, lights ablaze like a city afloat, motored through the gap into Thunder Bay. The throaty engines sounded like a freight train that labored heavily, but never went away.

The sailors were asleep aboard their boats when I struck camp and paddled down the long finger of Thunder Cape, where red cliffs illuminated by the rising sun rose steeply from the lake. I had worried about this crossing for several days, weighed contingencies with the better part of my psychic energy, and considered the dangers of encountering large boats in the ship-ping lanes. But as you get down to it, it is all anticlimactic. If the weather is good, off you go.

The weather was good.

Thunder Bay formed an enormous gulf, the city lying far away in the hazy distance. I stopped only once, to look back at Nanaboozhoo. Within two hours, I reached Pie Island, which was no cheap piece of work, with gray cliffs rising three hundred feet from the water. I landed amid the blocks of talus at the base of the cliffs for a snack amid a cacophony of bird song and clouds of midges, stuck by the thousands to the tacky basal leaves of butterwort. The bladderwort's secretion of mucus and enzymes digest the prey, fortifying the plant with nitrogen, which is lacking in the meager soil.

Precipitous Thunder Cape, which lies at the feet of the giant Nanaboozhoo, points across the shipping lanes of Thunder Bay and down the long archipelago that leads to Minnesota.

At Pie Island, where a voyageur once reported seeing a merman, the rocks announce their presence.

After a brief morning wind, the lake had turned again to mercury. As I paddled down the exposed cliffs of Pie Island, the low morning sun and sharp shadows made faces in the rocks. I saw faces looking down from the cliffs, faces looking up, long faces with long Roman noses and heavy brows, faces that screamed. In 1782 a voyageur named Venant St. Germain, an Indian woman, and three other voyageurs made camp on Pie Island. At sundown, as St. Germain set nets near shore, he saw a human form with the torso of a child, a small handsome head with eyes "extremely brilliant." It held one arm in the air, the other on its hip. In testimony some thirty years later, he suggested it might be a *nebaunaubae*, a merman or water manitou. No wonder the Ojibwa painted rocks. If it is possible to speak silently, the rocks shout.

Through the day, across the dead calm of Superior, I followed the narrow archipelago that runs from Pie Island to the southwest. Many of the islands were prospected in hopes of discovering another mine like Silver Islet. In the early 1870s, an Ojibwa woman showed friends a piece of silver ore. She refused to reveal the source until a group of Americans paid her twenty dollars. She found it, she said, on Pie Island. She promised to take them to the site, but before she could, she died, reinforcing the Ojibwas' belief that leading whites to minerals brings bad luck, sickness, or death. By 1875, a shaft had been sunk on Pie Island. A flurry of construction followed, with a two-hundred-foot dock, a two-story administration building, boardinghouses, a laboratory, and a smelter. But all this was premature. One hundred pounds of ore was refined into nine pounds of silver, the full extent of the mother lode. On the north side of McKellar Island, I came across the black openings in the rock, slightly above water level, of an adit and crosscut, remnants of a mine started by three sons of prospector Duncan McKellar. The silver was too scant to be profitable, though barite, an ingredient for paint, was shipped to Cincinnati.

I stopped for lunch at the Thompson Island sauna. It was deluxe, with a paneled changing room. For hundreds of feet all around, the woods had been cruised for firewood, browsed by boaters wielding saws and axes. Trails laced the island around the cove. Someone had even built an outhouse. The island testified to the presence of builders. I walked over to a group of motorboaters on the wharf. They were standoffish, as though they recognized in me an alien philosophy. The sauna was cold, and I left, anxious to move on.

I skipped from island to island. Isle Royale occupied the horizon to my

left. Multicolored lichens covered the cliffs of Spark Island, where a waterfall trickled into the lake and deep gentle voices issued from the undercut
rock. With the sun nearing the trees, I crossed from Victoria Island to
McKellar Point. As I reached the mainland, a sudden wind rose, catching
me off guard. I took it as a warning against complacency. I pulled into the
shelter of Pine Point, where I could look across Pigeon Bay to the United
States. The bay stretched far toward the sunset (where the Pigeon River
emptied into Superior), with islands, dark hills, and rugged shores. Camping on a sweeping gravel beach, listening to gulls squawking on a nearby
cliff even as darkness descended, I felt the melancholy not only of traveling
alone, but also of knowing that tomorrow morning, weather willing, I would
leave Canada behind.

The protected cove of Thompson Island is a favorite with sailors, who have built a
sauna on the shore.

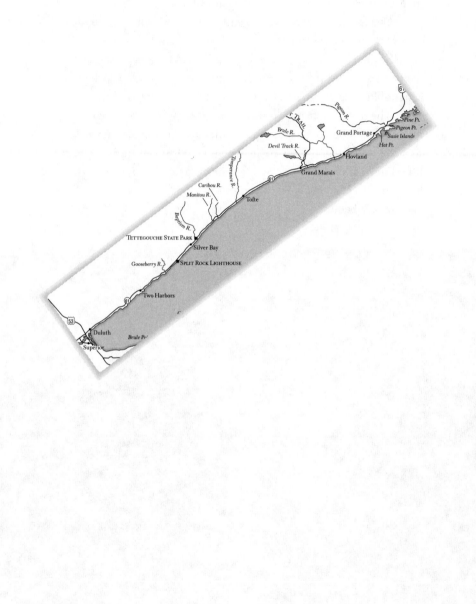

CHAPTER 6

Minnesota: Pigeon River to Duluth

THAT NIGHT I CRAWLED into my sleeping bag and saw water rising around me. *Oh God, don't let me dream about drowning.* But the next time I opened my eyes, I heard the voice of a white-throated sparrow.

I pushed off early and soon crossed over into U.S. waters and cleared Pigeon Point. I glided among the Susie Islands, the last islands of significant size or number that I would encounter along the North Shore. The Susies were the end of one shore and the beginning of another: the archipelago of the Canadian shore gave way to the straight, singular shore that stretched to Duluth.

The Susies are without development. All but one are owned by the Grand Portage Band of Ojibwa, which prohibits visitors, except band members, who set fishing nets in the channels. The largest island, Susie Island, is owned by The Nature Conservancy, a nonprofit conservation organization, to protect the community of oddball plants that exists along Superior's exposed shores and islands. Known as *disjuncts,* they include species characteristic of the arctic and subarctic, such as Norwegian witlow grass, purple crowberry, northern eyebright, pearlwort, and Arctic lupine. Probably quite common as the glacial ice retreated, they disappeared as the climate warmed, except on the cold, damp shoreline of Superior, especially on islands such as the Susies. The Conservancy calls the communities "unique," but they may be unique only in Minnesota. The Canadian islands I just passed probably support similar disjunct communities. When I suggested as much to a biologist with the Conservancy, he became a bit prickly, as though I were demeaning their mission. He acknowledged, however, that the Conservancy was comparing notes with Canadian biologists to learn if the disjunct populations were similar.

Conservation organizations and governments are sometimes misleading in proclaiming certain species rare or endangered, when in fact they are rare only within a particular jurisdiction, which may lie at the very edge of a species' range. The woodland caribou is a prime example, and the gray wolf is another. Proclaimed endangered (and later "threatened") in Minnesota, Wisconsin, and Michigan, the wolf remained plentiful across the border in Canada. In other words, some rare species are rarer than others. The opportunities for management differ, as do the chances of recovery and the implications to the biotic community if recovery should prove impossible. Extirpation from an area is a warning; extinction is an irretrievable loss. These distinctions are often lost in the politics and fund-raising of conservation.

All of this, however, was academic this morning, for I was no botanist and could not distinguish bistort from beef steak. As I paddled the shore of Susie Island and watched the clouds of midges hover above the rocks, I contemplated (and resisted) picking some samples of shoreline plants to bring into The Nature Conservancy office: *Say, are these the rare ones?*

I was finishing off the route the voyageurs had used over the northern part of the lake, down the long finger of Pigeon Point on the right, the Susie Islands on the left, then past Hat Point and into the shelter of Grand Portage Bay, site of the North West Company headquarters on Lake Superior during the late 1700s. I approached Hat Point expectantly. On its shore, quite apart from other trees, grew the Witch Tree. It was renowned as a sacred place, inhabited by a being that once appeared to humans as a gigantic eagle. Ojibwa and voyageurs would leave offerings of tobacco for the spirit. In recent years, the tree has become one of the most photographed sites along Minnesota's North Shore. To believe many nature writers, it holds deep spiritual significance for Grand Portage Ojibwa and is more properly called Little Spirit Cedar, the translation of its Indian name. For all the pictures I had seen of the tree, I had never seen the tree itself. I was eager to do so now, and especially to approach it silently from the lake, as the old Ojibwa and voyageurs did, in a way that the tree might produce its full drama.

I angled halfway down the point, aiming for a commercial fisherman's cabin, to make sure I wouldn't miss the tree. I reached land and turned slowly toward the tip of the point, examining every tree along the shore. This shouldn't be difficult; I had seen dozens of photos of the tree. But as hard as I looked, I saw nothing that resembled the Witch Tree. I paddled around the point, well into Grand Portage Bay. Nothing. So I backtracked all the way to

Southwest of the Susie Islands, the once-complex shore of islands and bays turns straight and singular.

the fisherman's place and even beyond and tried again, studying the shore every inch of the way back into Grand Portage Bay. Still, I could not find it.

I put to shore at Voyageur Marina and hunted up the owner, who was building a chain-link fence near his house.

Where was the Witch Tree? I asked. How embarrassing.

"You just about went by it. Did you go through the bay?" He meant Wauswaugoning Bay.

"No, I hit the point right near that fisherman's shack."

"Well, you missed it by about a block and a half. Are you the one who was up at Hole in the Rock a couple of days ago?"

"No, I camped across from there last night. I came from Thunder Bay yesterday morning."

Netting of lake trout continues near the Grand Portage Indian Reservation.

"Oh, if you've come that far, you've gone by thousands of witch's trees."

"Is there any way I can walk to it?"

He gave me directions, and straightaway, I walked up the road until I found a large sign: "Friends of the Witch Tree. From 1987 to 1990, the Friends of the Witch Tree raised over $97,000 to purchase this land for the Grand Portage Reservation. Over 2,000 donations were received from people in 40 states, Canada, Mexico, England, Holland and the Soviet Union. This is a spiritual area of the Ojibway Indian people. Hiking within twenty feet of the Witch Tree is not permitted. Reservation conservation laws are in effect." I hiked down a new boardwalk and lumber stairway. It ended about one hundred feet from the tree, which was situated down a steep rocky hillside, apparently to keep tourists from casually walking up to the tree. The owner of the marina was wrong: I had not seen a tree quite like it, so gnarled, so gray, so forlorn, so bare, so unnourished by anything other than rock. And I saw in its twisted crown a face—a woman's face, looking upward.

I paddled across the bay, just as the voyageurs would have, absent chansons and the final sprint to the landing, to the reconstructed North West Company post at Grand Portage National Monument.

From the late 1700s to 1805, Grand Portage was the crossroads of a lively trade extending from Europe to the front range of the Rockies and the northernmost reaches of the boreal forest in Canada. Each summer, Grand Portage was the meeting place of agents of the North West Company from Montreal, of voyageurs bringing trade goods such as cloth and kettles across the Great Lakes, of "winterers" carrying furs from the far reaches of Canada, of independent traders, of Ojibwa Indians who had settled around western Lake Superior in the previous decades, and even of African-Americans who were involved in the fur trade as slaves or voyageurs. The post was busiest during the summer "rendezvous," when Great Lake voyageurs met winterers to exchange goods and fur. "There are sometimes assembled to the number of twelve hundred men indulging themselves in the free use of liquor and quarreling with each other," wrote Alexander Mackenzie.

The operation of the North West post represented a terrific crisscross not only of goods, but also of cultures, especially European and Ojibwa. Through the fur trade, for better or worse, Indians throughout much of North America gained widespread access to manufactured goods, such as woven cloth, metal cookware and tools, flint and steel, firearms, and alcohol. In turn, they supplied English and Scottish businessmen with furs. They also taught the skill of building birch-bark canoes and revealed their well-worn trade routes. They even gave food so that traders might survive the hard winters.

The hustle-bustle of the North West Company is long gone, but Grand Portage enables modern-day travelers to become acquainted with the fur trade and the intertwining of European and Ojibwa history and culture. The reconstructed North West Company post stands on the lakeshore, on the exact site of the original fort. Actually, it is the second reincarnation of the fort; the first was struck by lightning and burned to the ground in 1969.

Grand Portage National Monument consists of a palisade of weathered pickets, the handsome hewn-log Great Hall, and an adjoining kitchen with a fireplace and hearth so large you could set a tent inside. In centuries past, a Scottish brogue would have filled the Great Hall as partners and clerks of the North West Company talked business over dinner, with place settings segregated by rank and the quality and quantity of dishes reflecting the hierarchy of the company. When I visited, the place settings were laid for partners who never showed. Samples of furs were laid out on the tables. Women baked fresh bread in the outdoor oven behind the kitchen. Role actors in the "Ojibwa village" outside the palisade lashed together the framework of a wigwam that would later be covered with birch bark.

Of course, there was much this scene did *not* say about the fur trade. John Askin, who cleared the land for Grand Portage in 1768 and later became commissary of troops in Mackinac, added this personal request to an order to build a barracks: "I need two pretty Slave girls from 9 to 16 years old. Have the goodness to ask the Gentlemen to procure two for me." What Wayland Drew wrote of recreated Fort William applies equally to Grand Portage:

> The visitors will not be threatened by dysentery, or cholera, or smallpox, or syphilis. Nor will they be visited by lice and fleas. Their sensibilities will be spared the stink of unwashed bodies in warm rooms, and the odours from stock yards, abattoirs, and privies. They will not be accosted by men demented by loneliness in the winter posts, and above the charming period costumes they will see few faces twisted by disease or hatred, by drink or despair. They will not encounter women whose bodies are chattel goods to be passed from one man to the next. If they stroll beyond the palisade, they will not discover the huts and hovels of worn-out voyageurs, nor the wigwams of indentured Indians. They will hear no blind cursing, no drunken laughter inside the *cantine salope,* no groans of beaten Indians, no keening for dead children and wasted lives. They will not be treated to such commonplace fur trade horrors as incest, murder, mutilation, rape, infanticide, and bungled self-destruction.

In the corner of the Great Hall I noticed a sign hung on a door: "Indian Craft Room. No cameras beyond this point." That seemed like an invitation, so I walked in. An Indian woman, in her early fifties, perhaps, was constructing a birch-bark basket, called a *makuk* by the Ojibwa. Another basket sat finished on the table in front of her.

"Do you mind if I take a look?" I asked.

"No, no. Go ahead."

I picked it up. It was surprisingly light and rigid, cylindrical, with the dark side of the bark facing out. It seemed naturally burnished, subtle, warm and sturdy.

"Is it a traditional design?"

"I just started making these. The other woman is teaching me how to do it." The other woman was not there at the moment.

"Oh darn," she muttered.

"What happened?"

"Oh, I broke the stitching."

The stitching was a light, thin fiber. I thought it might be watap, spruce root split lengthwise, the same material traditionally used to sew and lash the birch bark on canoes. "What is the stitching made of?" I asked.

"Raffia," she said matter-of-factly.

I told her how I had arrived, expecting to see the Little Spirit Cedar and how chagrined I was that I had missed it.

"How do people here refer to the tree?" I asked. I suspected the Anglicized "Witch Tree" had become politically incorrect. I figured they would call it *Manitou Geebigaynce* or the Little Spirit Cedar.

"Oh, just the Witch Tree," the woman said. "That's all I've ever heard around here. To tell you the truth, when I was growing up, no one ever talked about it. You know why everyone knows about it? Because an artist named Dewey Albinson from Minneapolis came up and made pictures of it. I never saw it until a couple of years ago."

By now the other woman had returned to the Indian Craft Room. She, too, appeared Indian. She was much older. Tiny with white hair, she had the fragile presence of a songbird.

"All I've ever heard it called is Witch Tree," the younger woman said.

"Yeah, yeah," the older woman said. "I've seen it only once."

I left, paddling west toward Grand Marais. A smattering of houses and mobile homes lined the shore. A near-mansion overlooked the lake from the bluff across the road. On some lots, the forest had been cleared for a lawn, where saplings were planted with geometric precision. Of course, that's what you do to a craggy, beautiful place: you make it over into a suburb.

Traffic roared by on U.S. 61, which ran within a couple hundred feet of the lake. The traffic was more annoying than the Canadian Pacific because it was nearly constant. The presence of traffic took much of the apprehension out of travel. What could happen? I would swim to shore and walk to the road to hitchhike. I began to conceive of the unlikely story of a man who kayaks through the wilderness of Canada, only to drown as traffic speeds by a hundred yards away.

I felt I was simply logging miles.

Late in the afternoon, I rounded a point and recognized the bay where I had spent so many autumn weekends as a child and a teenager. I landed and looked about. Yes, this was it, the same cobble beach, the same cabins perched on the shore. The view I remembered snapped quickly into focus. I knocked on the door of the tiny house that was once the office and home of the old fisherman and his wife. No answer. I walked a short way through the woods to a larger house and knocked on the door. Seconds later, a man I did not recognize answered the door. He was speaking on a portable phone.

"You'll have to come around back," he said through the screen door. "I've got an air lock for the mosquitoes."

I didn't know what to make of that. "Is the place next door still the Ongstads'?" I asked. "I used to come up here as a kid."

"Yes."

I told him no one was home. He called over on his phone. No answer. I offered to use my credit card to call Ray Ongstad, the son of the old fisherman, in the Cities: I wanted to ask if I could camp in his yard.

"Don't be silly. You don't need a card. Come on around to the back."

So we went around to the back and stepped into the mudroom. I shut the door behind me and we swatted mosquitoes for several minutes before he would open the door to the house. His name was Pat Smyth. He seemed trim and fit, in his forties, perhaps. He explained that he had bought the lot and the house from Ray Ongstad with the intention of remodeling it. He couldn't make the house conform to his plans, however, so he tore it down and built another. It was large, with light natural wood throughout, including silky birch floors, new kilim and dhurrie rugs, wallpaper with borders, a loft, and a large window overlooking Superior. Laid out on various coffee and end tables were lush books of Lake Superior photography. Wildlife and landscape art prints hung on the walls, including several by North Shore artist Howard Sivertson, which I thought ironic considering how cantankerous Sivertson could be about tourists and newcomers.

"It's for sale," he said, "for $275,000."

What did he do? I asked. "Semiretired," he said, acknowledging that he was "an evil land developer."

I called Ray. He remembered me immediately. Ray had grown up on the land. His father bought the lot in 1912 and built the house in the 1920s. He netted herring in the fall and ran the resort during the summer. Later on— for most of the years that I had stayed there—Ray and his wife, Lois, spent summers on the shore to run the resort. They got out of the business several years ago and now let their kids use the cabins. I asked Ray if I could camp on his land. "Well of course, by all means," he said. But even as he spoke, Pat offered the spare bedroom and asked if I wanted dinner.

Pat Smyth was certainly hospitable, though he seemed a bit lonely. He called himself the "hermit of Hovland" because he lived alone in this cabin and wasn't involved in the community, except through his business. He said the son of one of his old friends had left earlier in the day and he was feeling blue. "And then you come paddling around the corner."

Smyth, I gathered, wasn't much of an outdoorsman. We talked about hiking the Sibley Peninsula. "I'm strictly a day-hiker," he said. We talked about fishing. "When I go out fishing I like to run the boat," he explained. "People think I'm a guide, but I just like to run the boat. I don't know anything about fishing."

His family, he said, had been in the gas and oil business. They just sold a furniture business in Chicago. He came north because he loved the beauty of the area, but also to make money. Land, even this far north of Duluth, was in incredible demand. Lake Superior shoreline was selling for six to seven hundred dollars per front foot, he said. I imagined those prices would have been unfathomable to Ray Ongstad's father. Presently Smyth was building homes on eleven lots in Grand Marais.

He served up spaghetti. It was good to eat at a table again; better yet that I still had a view of the lake.

Starting out early the next morning, I paddled by more cabins than I believed existed along Superior. The view from the highway is misleading, because many properties are screened by trees. The vantage from the lake is different: I might as well have been paddling along a shoreline in a Twin Cities suburb. There were seasonal cabins and a few remnant homes of commercial fishing days. But there were also grand structures that dwarfed

Pat Smyth's home. Some were three stories high, with the woods cleared out in front for all to see. One was an enormous concrete building, unfinished, without windows or doors, modern, monolithic, and utterly out of place.

I landed near the mouth of the Brule and walked up to Naniboujou Motor Lodge for breakfast. Built in the waning days of the Roaring Twenties, the Naniboujou was intended to be an exclusive club. Its charter members included Babe Ruth, Jack Dempsey, and Ring Lardner. That's the story, at any rate. But the economy went in the toilet and the investors fled. Plans for the riding stables, tennis courts, cottages, and hunting lodge on MacFarlane Lake also vanished. The main lodge survived, however, an architectural curiosity with a cedar exterior and bright red and yellow shutters. At one end of the dining room stood a huge fireplace, said to weigh two hundred tons, constructed of lake stones arranged in geometric patterns. The walls and ceiling were a riot of painted designs, the color of tropical fruit: red, orange-red, orange-yellow, lime green, royal blue, dark blue. They were said to be Cree, but could as easily have been Pacific Northwest Indian, Aztec, or Javanese. The overall effect was pleasing, psychedelic art deco.

I asked the young waiter about the concrete monolith up the shore. He said the owner set out to build a modernistic mansion but died during construction. His heirs didn't want to finish it; so it sat without windows or an interior. The local kids skateboard down the halls, he said, and paint graffiti on the walls.

The rest of the day, I paddled down a shore that became less and less interesting. More homes. More highway traffic. The shore followed a constant bearing of 240 degrees. Two forty, two forty, two forty, an interminable grind. I was losing interest. What makes travel interesting is crossing gradients, whether gradients of topography, culture, or weather. I was plodding along a single contour, all the while thinking that the really interesting things were *up there*, on shore, while I was *out here*, as though closed off by a wall. Somehow, I had to make this shore more interesting.

So when I reached Grand Marais, I called Susan for a ride and went home.

Highway 61 had done its job. Built during the 1920s, it transformed the quiet home of a few hundred Ojibwa Indians and Norwegian fishermen into a tourist destination. In the process, the road and the development that followed have diminished the very qualities that attracted people to the shore. Who was hurt? Some fishermen, some woodsmen, and a few snobs who can travel the wilder shores of the lake by boat. Who benefited? Millions of tourists who enjoy an undeniably pretty drive. Viewed in those terms, preservation is hopelessly elitist.

The die may have been cast with the construction of the road, but the crush of tourism and development is more recent. I remember a distinctly wilder place, even thirty years ago as I searched the hills for trout streams. I recall driving into Tofte one day to ask directions at a gas station. For all I could tell, the gas station *was* town, and its entire population a grease-covered kid who laconically pointed me up the Sawbill Trail as flies buzzed around the station. A comparison with Appalachia was not out of line. What is Tofte like today? Holiday Stationstore, Holiday Inn Express (for people in a hurry), banks, shops, restaurants, Bluefin Bay resort, townhouses, condos. And Tofte is not the only community spawning this kind of development. It is happening from Duluth to Hovland. Meanwhile, up to 70 percent of the septic systems along the shore are failing.

And the highway? It has been widened and straightened. Multimillion-dollar tunnels have replaced the precarious cliff-side curves. The improvements have worked so well that now highway engineers use computer models to determine how to make drivers go *slower*.

I wanted to find traces of the North Shore I had known years ago. I owed it to myself and to the shore. Of the three transcendent moments I have experienced in my life, one occurred here, in the canyon of the Kadunce River. While fishing, I had wandered up the small stream until I climbed over a waterfall and found myself in a narrow canyon. Mosses and ferns spilled down from the rocks, and light drifted in like light snow. At that moment, it seemed that nothing at all existed but the rock, the looming shadow, and the strangely important rush of water.

I decided to start my exploration in Duluth. Were San Francisco not many times larger and already in possession of the name, Duluth might be known as the City by the Bay. Tucked snugly into the hillside at the west end of the lake, it was one of my favorite cities. I had lived there for two years when I worked on the city newspaper. The job put me in touch with the gritty, industrial side of town, a nexus of transportation. Grain trucks farted down the long hills to the lakeshore. Ore trains rumbled along the hillside to loading docks in the West End. The deep foghorns of freighters and ore boats cleared a path from the harbor to the open lake.

All things met at the harbor. Twenty years ago, Canal Park was a grungy agglomeration of factories, warehouses, and workingmen's bars. Today, the warehouses have been refurbished with shops, apartments, and studios. The streets are covered with pavers and the sidewalks are landscaped with young trees.

I was meeting environmentalist Janet Green in a sandwich shop in the basement of the DeWitt-Seitz Marketplace. We had never met in person and she surprised me with her cherubic appearance. She had a soft, round face, bifocals, white hair, and pale blue eyes. She had just come from the demolition of the old Flame Restaurant, future site of the Lake Superior Center, a museum of ecology and natural history.

Green and her husband, John, attended graduate school at Harvard. Forty years ago, he took a job as professor of geology at the University of Minnesota–Duluth. Compared to the Maine coast, where Green had sailed with her family, the North Shore was a disappointment. On Penobscot Bay there were islands to explore; here, just the unrelenting shoreline. "That's why I've become a real landlubber," she said. "There's a lot more to explore on the shore."

Bird-watching became her means for exploring the North Shore. Over time, she wrote several books on birds in Minnesota. She served as chapter president of the local Audubon chapter and sat on many conservation committees and task forces, including, most recently, the Minnesota Forest Resources Council, a board set up through state government to mediate forest issues on public land. "It's a form of arm wrestling," she said. "I felt that if you were interested in nature, you should be interested in conserving nature."

Recently, Green's greatest concern has been forest biodiversity along the North Shore, as logging for pulpwood has increased dramatically. Most of this wood—primarily aspen, with some softwoods, such as spruce and fir—is harvested by clear-cutting, which, carried to extremes, keeps the forest in a perpetual state of immaturity. A young forest benefits popular game species such as ruffed grouse and white-tailed deer, which feed on young aspen. Predators such as gray wolves respond to the abundance of prey. But so-called forest-interior species, especially many species of songbirds, suffer for lack of old-growth trees and unbroken mature forest.

"What we need is better long-term strategic management of our forests with a better idea of what we want them to be," Green said. The U.S. Forest Service, she said, has done far better than the state Department of Natural Resources in formulating a coherent plan for managing the forests for competing uses, including pulpwood cutting, logging for big timber, tourism, and conservation. In comparison, state land managers are "hermetically sealed within themselves." Despite talk in recent years of holistic forest management, relying on approaches and information from many disciplines, she said, state foresters have "no tradition of bringing a whole host of new information to management. Forestry thinks in terms of red pine and aspen."

Development along the shore fragments the forest with roads, buildings, and clearings. The greater danger, she said, is the transformation of communities in ways that, taken as a whole, no one wants. Money appears, land prices soar. Locals can't afford to live in their own communities. "It's a struggle for a community such as Grand Marais to maintain its identity," she said, especially when the habit of independence-minded locals is to let things go as they might and allow everyone as much freedom as possible. The result is the same kind of strip development you might see in any American suburb.

The North Shore highway, she said, "is no longer your scenic highway; it's just a place to go fast to get to where you want to go. It brings a type of person who doesn't care."

Driving the so-called scenic highway from Duluth to Two Harbors, I passed new houses, gift shops, and wide lawns. There were a few touches of the old North Shore, such as the cluster of fish shops at Knife River, with smoked whitefish and lake trout. I spent the night at Tettegouche, the largest state park along the Minnesota shore. Early the next morning, I launched my kayak in the estuary of the Baptism River. I dawdled in the rugged gorge and then powered over the shallow gravel bar at the river mouth and paddled into the lake.

During the last several years, kayakers have worked with the Department of Natural Resources to develop a "water trail" along the North Shore, a series of closely spaced sites allowing paddlers to travel and camp without trespassing. To date, the trail runs about forty miles from Two Harbors to the Caribou River. Some of that stretch suffers the same shortcomings I had experienced in paddling down from Grand Portage: a straight shoreline, the constant whir of traffic, and the unrelenting parade of homes. But some sites

along the trail are stunning, such as the long winding estuary of the Goose-
berry River and the lighthouse atop the cliffs at Split Rock, easily the most
imposing and beautiful lighthouse on the lake. I hoped to see another interesting stretch today.

The shore had a hint of Canada, with rugged rocks and cliffs. Paddling
southwest, I saw a young boy playing among the boulders along shore.
Dressed in a T-shirt and jeans, he might have been me more than thirty
years ago. I quickly reached the Palisades, which rise abruptly from the
lake some two hundred feet. I paddled through a little sea arch. Swallows
swooshed through the opening and scattered to the sky. Unfortunately,
about three miles to the southwest sat the Northshore Mining Company
taconite plant. Untold tons of taconite tailings formed an unnatural delta

The Palisades rise two hundred feet above the lake, the most dramatic cliffs along
the Minnesota shore. In the far distance lies the delta formed by tailings from a
taconite plant.

that reached far into the lake. The company's predecessor, Reserve Mining, was forced long ago to switch to on-land disposal of its mining waste, but its legacy will endure for centuries. I doubled back toward the Baptism River and noticed that a rocking horse, television, and other trash had been tossed from the rest area atop the Palisades and rested now in the talus next to the lake.

I continued past the mouth of the Baptism and followed massive Shovel Point far into the lake. Looking up shore, I saw a steady procession of headlands, long fingers that fell in gradations from green to gray and faded into the distance. As I paddled, I passed points and cliffs riddled with small caves and arches, including one opening that had the organic shape of a ventricle. I could hear the buzz of traffic. But unlike the stretch near Grand Marais, with its gradual shore open to the highway, the cliffs here were visible only from the lake. At the very least, by being out here, I was seeing something I otherwise could not.

I passed a couple of log ramps built by commercial fishermen to pull their boats up on shore. Long unused, they looked like organized driftwood.

The mouth of Kennedy Brook tumbled twenty feet from a cliff, splattered on the beach, and seeped through the gravel several yards to the lake. As I rested, I spotted a peregrine falcon as it flew from a cliffside nest, its location marked by white streaks of excrement on the rock. It landed in a nearby tree as a second peregrine soared overhead. Peregrines vanished from the North Shore—indeed, from the entire Midwest—during the 1960s and 1970s, victims of DDT contamination. Since the pesticide was banned and peregrines were reintroduced, they have returned to nest in the lofty crags along the lake. The peregrine in the tree scolded me with the sound of a coarse file over hard steel.

Finally I heard the roar of a waterfall and cleared a point to see the Manitou River spill thirty feet over a cliff, as though it poured directly from the rock. The falls were a stunning sight, but as if to gild the lily, the current flowed into Superior in the embrace of a sea arch. I paddled to within casting distance of the arch and pulled out my fly rod. It was a flawless scene. The falls, the arch, deep water the color of emerald. A silver, blue, and white streamer hit the water. Wouldn't it be perfect, I thought, if a big fish hit right here. In that instant I saw a dark shape and a flash of silver. It hit the fly and ran deep. For fifteen minutes I battled a fish I could not see. A light offshore wind rose and began to carry me into the lake. I paddled with one

Kennedy Brook spills over a cliff, just short of the lake. Peregrine falcons, once
endangered, nest nearby.

hand and held the rod with the other until I was able to land on a patch of
gravel among the cliffs. In another ten minutes I was able to bring the fish
close and scoop it onto the gravel. Twenty-six inches by the measure of
my outstretched fingers, the fish was silver and spotted, bullish across the
shoulders. Anadromous trout are hard to distinguish. One by one I eliminated species: not a Pacific salmon, not a steelhead, probably not an Atlantic salmon. I finally settled on brown trout. I had no way to eat the fish or to
keep it, so I unhooked it and cradled it in the water at my feet until it swam
into the deep shadows.

I wish I could say I packed up my rod and paddled back to the car in a
state of complete contentment. But I didn't. William Blake may as well have
been talking about fishing when he wrote: "You never know what is enough

The Manitou River, named appropriately with the Ojibwa word for "mystery" or "spirit," plunges into Lake Superior.

unless you know what is more than enough." I beat the water for another half hour until I paddled up the last few feet of river, then spun and paddled through the arch on my way back to the Baptism.

I drove back up to Grand Portage, this time stopping at Grand Portage State Park, one of Minnesota's newest parks, located within the borders of the Grand Portage Indian Reservation. I wanted to talk to Curt Gagnon, who was both a member of the Grand Portage Band of Ojibwa and a state park manager.

A small park, only three hundred acres, Grand Portage stretches three miles along the Pigeon River, the boisterous, rushing stream that divides Minnesota from Ontario. The rapids and falls of the lower Pigeon River are the very reason the Indians and voyageurs of the region used the "Grand Portage," a footpath nearly nine miles long that bypassed the unnavigable water and linked the placid upper Pigeon and Lake Superior.

I found Gagnon at the park office. Built solidly, he spoke softly and weighed his words. Gagnon explained that the Grand Portage is unique among state parks in that the land is owned by the band and run by the state Department of Natural Resources. "It's kind of a milestone in state and tribal relations because we're working as a team, in a partnership, and it's going well," he said.

Inside his office, Gagnon unrolled a topographic map. "The band has been looking at what has been happening up and down the shore," Gagnon said. "All the development, the huge encroachment, people building fabulous homes and large cabins and demanding recreation areas. The band wanted something for the generations to come, for people to enjoy and see what it's like, what we enjoy today."

In Grand Portage, as on most reservations, land once held in common by the tribe was "allotted" to individual Indians, ostensibly to give members a homestead and set them on the path to becoming farmers and landowners. In fact, allotment was an efficient way to pry land from tribal ownership and eventually get it into the hands of non-Indian buyers through tax-forfeiture and direct purchase. As a result, many reservations became "checkerboarded" with non-Indian land. Poring over the map, Gagnon tapped his finger on tracts the band had bought back, primarily with profits from Grand Portage Lodge and Casino.

Gagnon dragged his finger down the shoreline to Red Rock, a privately owned bay within reservation boundaries. Several years ago, a Twin Cities businessman bought the property and began to build a grand vacation home. "It was such an eyesore, it was such a huge building, it went above the treetops. The band got pretty upset because he was pretty arrogant in his way of dealing with the band. He didn't want anything to do with the band. 'They can't tell me what to do!'" Unfortunately for the landowner, his driveway encroached slightly on reservation land, a pressure point band members exploited to block shipments of building materials. "Then he said, 'I want an easement through your property so I can use my property.' I don't think so." Having stopped construction, the band bought the property and tore down what had been built.

"Everything south of Highway 61 is zoned a preservation area so that area can't be developed," Gagnon said. "Trails can't even be put in without going to the band. Nothing can be done in that area. So that area is going to be undeveloped and nearly pristine for, hopefully, generations to come." The zone includes Hat Point and Wauswaugoning Bay.

I asked Gagnon what *Wauswaugoning* means.

"*Waswaugon*" is 'spearing fish.' *Ing* means 'place,'" he said. "This is a real sandy bay. There used to be a lot of sturgeon in this area. They'd go there with their birch-bark torches and their canoes and spear sturgeon and white-fish. So it's a place where you spear fish. Wauswaugoning Bay."

During the sleepy middle of the day, Gagnon and I drove around the community of Grand Portage. We toured the harbor, where the band had bull-dozed an area near its sewage treatment plant. "We've had to expand the holding areas. It's real ugly but they couldn't get away from doing it," Gagnon explained. The reservation has grown—not all of the newcomers are tribal members. "It's probably up to five hundred individuals, not counting gam-blers," he said.

Casino gambling had meant not just money, Gagnon said, but also finan-cial independence. Casino profits were fulfilling wishes made years ago, when the only resources were federal grants. Now, the band had control. The casi-no had bought resource management, sewage treatment, and a community center housing a small library with new computers, a gym, pool, weight room, elementary school rooms, youth center, and senior center with a lunch room.

Along the waterfront, Gagnon pointed out Grand Portage Island. The island was also known as Pete's Island for Pete Gagnon, Curtis Gagnon's grandfather, who ran a store and fishing operation there in the early 1900s. His customers traveled by boat, including the well-known Lake Superior steamship, the *America*.

Curtis Gagnon was born in an Indian hospital in Cloquet, Minnesota, and came home to Grand Portage a few days later. During the 1950s, a fed-eral relocation program encouraged Indians to move to jobs and adopt a more American way of life. In this respect, federal bureaucrats resembled the missionaries and federal Indian agents who tried to make Indians into farmers. And with as much success. "So we moved to Gary, Indiana," Gagnon said. "Dad worked in a steel mill. After three and one half years we moved back." Back home, his father logged and then worked for the National Park Service at Grand Portage National Monument.

The family lived in a shack without plumbing or electricity. Gagnon's parents were Catholic and made him go to Holy Rosary Catholic Church. Then he told me an ironic story. "In the 1920s, an artist, Dewey Albinson, came up to Grand Portage and did some painting and mingling with people. Anyway, Dewey Albinson came up, he heard about this tree that some individuals would go down to and leave offerings. He wanted to see it. He went down and checked it out. He called it the Witch Tree. It wasn't known as the Witch Tree before. I don't know if it really had any sacred meaning, but when Dewey Albinson got a hold of it, it became popular and famous. People put more significance to it." Still, the lore of the tree had not taken root in the community. Growing up, Gagnon knew nothing of the Witch Tree, or the Little Spirit Cedar for that matter, until the nuns took him and other Indian children to the tree and told them it was important.

After four years in the Air Force, Curtis Gagnon came home. He served on the tribal council and lost a bid to become tribal chairman. Involved in the rough-and-tumble world of tribal politics, he was keenly aware of the legal fight by Ojibwa bands in northern Wisconsin to assert their treaty rights to manage their own hunting and fishing, free of state regulation. These treaty rights, Gagnon suspected, existed in Minnesota as well, and when he set out to put moose meat in his freezer in 1984, he left the house with a rifle in his hand and a chip on his shoulder.

Gagnon shot the moose near the border of the reservation. Maybe it was on Indian land, maybe not; he wasn't sure. But it jumped to its feet and ran off on a path that took it far off tribal land, where state regulations, not tribal rules, applied. And as far as the state was concerned, moose season was closed. Nonetheless, Gagnon tracked the animal until dark. He went home, considered the ramifications of what he was about to do, and then told the band game warden and tribal council that he intended to track the moose the next day.

"I told them I'm going after him tomorrow," he said. "Let the DNR game warden know. I can't leave it out there." The announcement was an invitation for his arrest. When he came home the next day, though he never found the moose, a state conservation officer wrote him a citation and took away his rifle.

Gagnon's case led to a long confrontation between the band and the state over Ojibwa hunting and fishing rights on non-reservation land. His case never went to trial, but the band sued the state in federal court, asserting that the treaty that had conveyed much of northeastern Minnesota to the federal government guaranteed that band members could continue to hunt and fish without state interference. The state and three Ojibwa bands, including Grand Portage, eventually reached an agreement—which Gagnon opposed in legislative hearings and meetings on reservations—to pay bands to keep their conservation codes consistent with state regulations.

Years later, after Grand Portage State Park was established, an opening was posted for a naturalist. Gagnon applied. It was a lark, really, and he was astonished to be hired. When the park manager position opened, he applied, again without any expectations. He got the promotion and again was keenly aware of the irony.

During the mid-1800s, when Robert Barnwell Roosevelt wrote *Superior Fishing*, brook trout were found throughout the lake's bays and estuaries. Spawned in riffly tributaries, they migrated to the lake by their second year and grew fat on small fish before returning to their home streams to spawn. These hefty anadromous brook trout, known locally as "coasters," were the fish Roosevelt caught in such abundance.

Yet even in Roosevelt's day, anglers had begun to notice a decline in fishing. In 1862, Roosevelt wrote that near Marquette, Michigan, "the waters are somewhat fished out." The decline continued as the sluice of logs downstream eroded spawning habitat, as sawdust from mills choked streams, and as commercial fishermen took brook trout as well as the more numerous lake trout.

Coasters probably grew even scarcer as the highway around the lake was completed and nearly the whole shore became accessible to tourists. "Brook trout are not the brightest bulbs on the tree," said John Johnson, the tribal biologist at Grand Portage. "They're very easy to catch in the springtime. They're opportunistic feeders, and they're going to snap at anything that goes by their noses."

These factors caused the coaster brook trout to disappear from most Lake Superior shorelines and estuaries, including the Grand Portage Indian Reservation, by 1950. Game and fish departments around the lake tried stocking fingerling brook trout in the streams tributary to Superior, but the effort was expensive and the results disappointing. Fish managers, especially those in the United States, where fishing pressure was greatest, simply gave up, concluding that the brook trout was too gullible, too finicky, and too frail to flourish. They turned their attention and resources instead to stocking more glamorous species, such as West Coast steelhead, Pacific salmon, European brown trout, and Atlantic salmon.

Nonetheless, the brookie continued to have its admirers. It was beautiful, with olive vermiculations along its back and flaming orange flanks. It had romantic appeal as a symbol of wilderness and a long-gone era. And, unlike the fish that replaced it, the brook trout *belonged* in Lake Superior.

Gagnon and I had stopped by to talk about the band's efforts to restore the coaster to reservation streams. Johnson and Lee E. Newman, from the U.S. Fish and Wildlife Service, were convinced that coasters had a future in the lake. The tribal government, already intent on reclaiming much of its past heritage, agreed.

Rather than to stock fingerlings, Johnson and Newman decided to stock fertilized eggs and newly hatched "fry." This approach promised to be cheaper. Moreover, the biologists hoped the fish, forced to survive most of their life in the wild, would be hardier than hatchery fish, better acclimated to the wild environment, and more strongly imprinted on their natal streams.

But what do you stock when the native coasters from the Grand Portage area are all but extinct? Grand Portage chose brood stock from the Nipigon drainage, available from the Ontario Ministry of Natural Resources. The Nipigon River lay less than one hundred miles up the shore, where conditions were probably similar. Attractive from a fisherman's standpoint was the great size of the Nipigon fish, one of which established the world record. "Everybody likes that big fish," Johnson said. "That's why we stuck with them."

Johnson and Newman began stocking several small streams with suitable gravel substrate for spawning. All probably supported coasters in the past. The biologists "improved" potential spawning sites, called redds, by diverting spring water into the gravel through flexible plastic tubing to ensure that the eggs were bathed in cold, oxygenated water. A man with a shovel could build a redd in a couple of hours; the only material cost was six dollars for the PVC pipe.

Success came quickly. Most, and in some cases nearly all, of the eggs appeared to hatch in the artificial redds. Newly hatched fry swarmed above the gravel. Juvenile brook trout soon roamed the stream. In 1994 two bright males, each a foot long, returned to spawn. The next year, silvery lake-run fish up to four pounds appeared in Grand Portage streams.

In 1995 band biologists installed tiny radio transmitters in twenty coasters and recruited reservation kids to "adopt" individual fish. Using radio telemetry receivers, the youngsters tracked the fish. They gave them such names as Brook, Hollow Rock Harry, Peety, Beach Baby, and Bay Boy. Bay Boy was tracked to Judge C. R. Magney State Park, twenty miles away, before being caught by the uncle of the girl tracking him. The children wrote up their results for a science project, which took top honors at a county science fair. Trout Unlimited awarded the kids and the band the Silver Trout Award.

"They're surviving," Johnson said. "I don't know if I'd go so far as to say that they're flourishing right now. We are getting natural reproduction in a couple of streams, which we didn't have five years ago. We fully expect to see a state record anytime. It's become a real neat fishery for the band. The band members have been just super about not overfishing."

At Grand Marais, while eating along the waterfront at the Angry Trout, I ran into Bob Pye. I had met Pye several years ago during a flap over a state plan to spend millions building harbors of refuge along the North Shore. A retired St. Paul firefighter who built a log cabin within a long cast of the lake, Pye, and many others, were opposed on two counts: $40 million was a lot of public money to spend for the benefit of a few pleasure boaters and recreational anglers; and harbor development, in Pye's view, threatened to bring ancillary development to coves and small boat accesses that were now undeveloped. Opposition eventually caused the "safe harbors" to disappear, for the time being.

Pye had nothing against boating. He moored his twenty-six-foot sloop at the marina in front of the Angry Trout. The lake was calm, so we took the boat out of the harbor under power.

As if the safe harbors dustup weren't enough, Pye ran for the county planning and zoning commission. He served five years but resigned because, in his view, the county granted variances and conditional-use permits too freely and allowed excessive development along the lakeshore. "I got tired of being the only one to say no," he said. "I was accused of saying no to everything." He described an "uproar" when Subway came to town, with plans to erect its standard yellow and black sign. "But it's in a commercial area," he said, so there wasn't much opponents could do. The Subway now stands next to the highway, at the edge of downtown.

As Pye talked, we struck a buoy.

"I should be watching where I'm going," he said.

A perennial issue was the snowmobiles on city streets. "I don't think they should even allow snowmobiles in town," Pye said. But they have, he explained, because the bars and restaurants insist on the business. Each year the town changed routes to placate the people who didn't like the noise.

We motored several hundred yards into the lake. The Sawtooth Mountains to the west slipped one behind the other, retreating into the distance in successive shades of grayness. A large flock of Canada geese had settled into the bay. The town looked lovely from this perspective, with the tiny knot of lights in its commercial district, the festive Angry Trout, and the boats nestled in their slips inside the breakwater. In the last minutes of daylight, cars rolled into town loaded with canoes, kayaks, and mountain bikes. It seemed to me that despite the best efforts of people like Bob Pye, Grand Marais was losing its fight to keep its character. The pressure of strip development was simply too great and threatened to overwhelm the little town.

Standing at the bridge over the Devil Track River, just off the Gunflint Trail, I watched the amber water dance amid the boulders and shadows as it raced downstream. The rushing water generated feelings of dread and anxiety, recollections of kayaks flying over impossible falls, surging currents flushing through narrow canyons, an unrunnable waterfall waiting at the narrow waist of the gorge. It was the first time, so far as I knew, that anyone had paddled so deep into the canyon. It was certainly the most frightening river I had ever paddled, and I never paddled it again.

Today I was equipped not with a kayak, but with a fly rod, a much better choice if you're alone, forty-something, and out of practice. The water was low. I enjoyed the pools of water and light, shadows and brightness, the lively green of trees and the sparkling light. I stumbled among the slick rocks, looking for pockets of calm in the river's swift descent. To a fish, depth is relative; in this case, a pool with two feet of water was more than enough. Brookies flashed at the drifting fly. In such a small stream, a ten-inch trout seemed large. There is no fight to such a little fish, just the wild vibration of fright. The thrill is coaxing them from their hiding places, the surprise of seeing such a tiny stream, with such transparence, offering up something live.

I decided to drive down to George Crosby–Manitou State Park. It was a backpacking park; no cars, no roads beyond the parking lot. I grabbed the rod, fishing vest, some water and, well into the afternoon, set out on Middle Trail, through a grove of mature birch and maple, toward the Manitou River.

Like the Devil Track, the Manitou was named for spirits. Unlike the Devil Track—a name transmogrified from *Manido Bimadagakowini Zibi,* "Spirits' Walking Place on the Ice River"—the Manitou retained the simple brilliance of the wonderfully elastic Ojibwa word for an array of qualities: spirit, mystery, the unseen nature of existence. Indeed, the Manitou had always seemed to me a magical place, of white water and black rock, the colors of basalt and rapids, of birch bark and the night sky.

The water was low, and I jumped from rock to rock, pool to pool, picking pockets for brook trout. The fish were few, and they were small. As I reached the entrance to a deep gorge, I decided that while this might not be the best trout fishing in the world, it might well be the most picturesque. For that reason alone it may be the best.

Looking at the streambed in low water, choked with boulders the size of cars, I tried to remember how we had paddled this stretch in high water many years ago. It must have been ferocious. I remembered a place where had I nearly broken my leg on a portage. And just downstream, a spot where I had spun out of control, sliding backward over six-foot falls. Today, by comparison, it was peaceful—the black basalt and sparkle of light in the birches and the cedars.

The gorge became more constricted and the canyon walls grew steeper. Soon I gave up fishing and began scaling a bluff to find easier walking. Picking my way across talus and the raw soil of a recent rock slide, I realized I was a good hundred feet above the river on a loose slope. What was I doing scrambling around like a mountain goat? Then I thought of spending the night with a broken leg. I have a morbid fear of struggling out of a place at night. This hike suddenly seemed far riskier than what I had been doing out on the lake in a sea kayak. When I finally eased myself back down toward the river and reached the trail, I recognized that one measure of wilderness is its effect on the heart. At least this much wildness remained along the North Shore: the single moment of panic in the breast. It is still a place where, if you look, you can be lost and alone.

CHAPTER 7

Isle Royale

IN THE MID-1700s, two large islands occupied the western end of Lake
Superior. At least they did on the maps of Jacques Nicolas Bellin, a promi-
nent French cartographer of the time. Bellin labeled the one island Isle
Royale. It was long and narrow and canted southwest to northeast.

Bellin called the second island Isle Philippeaux. He also used the Ojibwa
name, Isle Minong—"place of blueberries" or "a nice place to be." Isle Philippeaux was similar in size and alignment to the other island, but where Royale
had a lumpish, approximated shape, Philippeaux showed the very details
seen on present-day maps of Isle Royale, including Washington and Grace
Islands and Siskiwit Bay.

Literally, only one of these islands existed. But in a sense, they both did:
they were the Isle Royale of reality and the Isle Royale of imagination.

The two islands became one by the early 1800s as cartographers realized their error. How did such a mistake occur? It's possible that Bellin combined the sightings of several earlier explorers, some who viewed the island
from the north shore and others from the south. Perhaps unaware of the
distance involved, Bellin portrayed these stereoscopic views as two places—
cartographic double vision. Maybe the tricks of fog and mirages further confused explorers, as this early description of Lake Superior suggests: "There
lay a tall, bluish island, with which the mirage played in an infinity of ways
during our voyage. At times the island rose in the air to a spectral height
then sank again and faded away, while at another moment we saw the islands
hovering over one another into the air."

That early account came to mind as we departed Grand Portage aboard
the *Voyageur II* and proceeded briskly toward the island. Isle Royale is actually many islands: a main island a bit more than forty miles long surrounded

The ferry *Voyageur II* is the most reliable way to reach Isle Royale by kayak. The man handling the stern is Mark Rude, who fished with his father on the island. (Photograph by Katherine Breining-Hill.)

by more than two hundred small islands and skerries. But from my perspective, they were all a blue mass, twenty miles distant, floating on the silver mirage of the lake.

With me was my daughter, Kate, who was fourteen. Also on board were Susan and her two teenage daughters, Addie and Olivia. The *Voyageur II* was bound for Windigo Ranger Station at the southwestern end of the island. From there, we would motor around the northern shore of the island. Kate and I, with our kayaks, would debark at McCargoe Cove and paddle around the eastern end of the island. Susan and her girls would continue on to Malone Bay. From there they would hike the spine of the island, the most popular way of seeing Isle Royale. Four days from now, we would catch different ferries and rendezvous back in Grand Portage.

The thrumming engine grew tedious and I searched the cabin for something to read. On the walls were clippings and descriptions of the various shipwrecks around the island. The freighter *Emperor* struck the Canoe Rocks off the north coast of the island, killing twelve; now it is an attraction for scuba divers, who swim through its staterooms. The *George M. Cox* was the third ship to strike the "reef of the three Cs"—the first two were the *Cumberland* and the *Henry Chisholm*. The *Cox's* passengers were evacuated to the Rock of Ages Lighthouse, but the *Cox* remained stranded, bow in the air, for most of the summer as local fishermen relieved the newly refurbished passenger steamer of furniture, doors, dishes, and clothing.

I found a copy of the National Park Service management plan for Isle Royale National Park. Combined with the numbing movement of the boat, the plan's government prose would have put me to sleep, except for the endless supply of coffee available below deck. The plan described the long history of human activity on the island. For thousands of years, Indians paddled out to the island to hunt, fish, and, most interestingly, to mine veins of pure copper for tools, weapons, and ornaments. More than a thousand prehistoric pits and excavations have been discovered. The copper, of course, attracted the attention of early explorers and prospectors. In the mid-1800s, copper mines and stamp mills opened at Siskiwit Bay and McCargoe Cove. A single "nugget" of pure copper weighing nearly three tons created quite a stir, but the good deposits petered out, and both mines closed by the 1880s.

Commercial fishermen settled communities on the island's shores. Tourism became popular, relatively speaking, at the turn of the century. By the 1920s, a half dozen resorts operated at the water's edge. Belle Isle had a small golf course.

Efforts to make Isle Royale a national park began in the 1920s and the park was established in 1940. Albert Stoll Jr., the *Detroit News* conservation columnist and an early advocate of the park, wrote: "Isle Royale is part of an entirely different world than the one in which we live daily. It knows nothing and cares less of triumphs of modern civilization."

Since then, nearly all of Isle Royale has been designated wilderness, with the principal exceptions of the boat landings and ranger stations at either end of the island. Visitation is low compared with other national parks, but the island ranks highest in the number of overnight stays per acre of back-country. Many campgrounds are filled beyond capacity in July and August. Visitors complain of noise from boats, airplanes, and even other backpackers. Even now, as we were visiting, the park was reevaluating its management plan and considering the following options:

- Change nothing.
- Expand facilities at the ends of the island and create a more primitive experience in the center.
- Scale back all development for a more primitive park.
- Reduce the number of visitors.

Soon the *Voyageur II* passed the Rock of Ages Lighthouse, a weathered post standing on a skerry barely broad enough to support it. We motored on to Washington Island, where a fishing community thrived during the first half of the 1900s. The Island House, complete with bowling alley, operated for tourists. It was torn down long ago, though John's Hotel, in business only in the closing years of the 1800s, still stands on nearby Barnum Island. One family, the Sivertsons, still fishes commercially, and we dropped a couple of passengers at their dock, where several old boats moldered on shore.

We followed the long channel of Washington Harbor to the Windigo Ranger Station, where we had to register campsites. That was easy enough for the backpackers; Susan and her girls had known for days where they would stay. But for Kate and me, it all depended on the weather. I tried. I wrote down my guesses: Belle Isle, Caribou, Daisy Farm, Malone Bay. The exercise irritated me.

Leaving the harbor, we hovered several moments over the wreck of the *America*. The steamer, one of the most fondly remembered ships on the lake, shuttled goods, mail, and passengers along the North Shore. On 7 June 1928, as the *America* slipped from the dock at Washington Harbor, the captain turned over command to the first mate, who was unfamiliar with the water around the island and ran the ship onto a reef. The passengers debarked safely, but in the excitement, two brothers momentarily forgot that their dog, a water spaniel, was chained to the stern. When they returned for it, the boat began to sink; the brothers escaped, but Spike went down with the ship. The stern settled in nearly eighty feet of water, but the bow steadied only a few feet below the surface. It was clearly visible, quavering in the chop, as we looked down from the *Voyageur II*.

We turned down the northern shore of the isle toward McCargoe Cove. The shore was hard, often cliffy, and for that reason I chose not to paddle it with Kate. The passengers nodded off to the thrum of the engines. Addie played solitaire while Olivia and Kate read. I tried to read, but couldn't with the smell of diesel oil and the desultory roll of the boat in three-foot waves. Susan and I held hands and looked out the window. To the north, across the channel about fifteen miles away, the Canadian shore and islands rose in the humps, ridges, and mesas I had passed just a month ago. I tried to pick out the Sleeping Giant, but from this perspective I couldn't recognize it. Finally, the boat turned into McCargoe Cove. At the dock, Kate and I unloaded our kayaks and gear. The boat pulled out. We waved to Susan and the girls.

The cove was named for Captain Robert McCargoe, a British officer who hid his warship *Recovery* from American eyes in this narrow bay during the War of 1812. Once loaded and on the water, Kate and I soon reached the harbor entrance, where waves from the lake crashed into reefs. No harm. It was already late afternoon. We landed on Birch Island, where a screened camping shelter stood empty. No one else came by. We were alone, except for the moose a couple hundred feet back in the woods. Judging by the state of her bones and hide, I figured she wouldn't be bothering us.

The morning was calm, and we glided easily up Amygdaloid Channel. Up ahead, the loons were having a party. I counted nine. One occasionally ran across the surface of the water, sending up a sunlit roostertail. They disappeared and reappeared, singing their tremolo. A couple of young, almost the size of adults, were among them. Loons typically nest in protected bays and lakes, on small hummocks of mud and vegetation only a few inches above water level. Lake Superior, unprotected and wavy as it is, makes for poor nesting. Most loons spotted on Superior nest on inland lakes. On Superior itself, some of the few places where loons nest successfully are the protected coves of Isle Royale.

Loons, I discovered, are not the benign checkerboarded creatures you see in picture books. The previous day, after Kate and I had unloaded, an adult merganser and about a dozen ducklings had paddled busily about the bay near the landing. Hearing a commotion, we had looked up to see a loon sitting on the water and the mergansers fleeing toward shore. The loon must have attacked, surfacing in the midst of the ducks. (It seemed unlikely

that the loon could have swooped in from the air without our hearing it.)
For several seconds, the loon seemed to stalk the brood, then it dove and
disappeared. The mergansers hugged shore, the mother looking anxiously
toward deeper water.

"When a pair of loons stakes out their territorial claim to a lake or part
of it, they pronounce themselves lord and master of all they can see," writes
wildlife biologist Paul Strong in *Call of the Loon*. "Not only do they fend off
the advances of rival loons who would have the place for their own, but
they often make life miserable for other animals living there. . . . Numerous
accounts of loons submerging at a distance and swimming to a brood of
ducklings have been reported in the scientific and popular literature." The
loons' motives may not be clear, but their intent certainly is. "Typically, the
ducklings disappear as they are pulled below the surface and are killed, but
are not eaten," writes Strong. "Larger ducklings and adults are killed by a
powerful thrust of the loon's sharp bill into the abdomen." Loons will occasionally follow and bother large swimming animals, says Strong, even bears.
One group of loons distracted and harassed a swimming coyote until it finally drowned. Strong himself was skinny-dipping one evening after a day
of fieldwork when he was approached and then surrounded by about a
dozen loons. They closed to within about ten feet. He was astonished by
their size. As he tread water, they repeatedly dove and resurfaced, as though
to gauge how much of this creature was underwater. "All I could think of,"
writes Strong, "was that I didn't have on a bathing suit."

While loons on small bodies of water are highly territorial, loons on
large lakes must often mix with other loons, and they usually lose much of
their territorial aggression. Loons without territories and mates often gather
in groups as large as sixty, and trespass freely in other loons' territories. These
birds are called "floaters." Occasionally, Strong writes, a breeding loon seems
to try to join the group to lead the floaters out of its territory. "Rogue loons"
among the floaters sometimes seek out nesting pairs to kill unattended
chicks.

The loons weren't the only wildlife we spotted. Paddling through an
area of long craggy points and skerries known as Five Finger Bay, we spotted several cormorants and two eagles, including an immature bird hounded
by a swarm of tiny songbirds. At one point, as we paddled side by side
about thirty feet apart, a female merganser surfaced between us. It seemed
agitated, calling its harsh *cronck, cronck,* as if gnashing its teeth. (If any bird

could gnash its teeth, it would be the merganser, which has teeth-like ridges for holding fish.) Suddenly, little mergansers began popping to the surface between us, swimming frantically and rowing with their wings, until their mother finally herded them from between our boats.

Throughout the morning, though I didn't want to, I urged Kate along. The wind was light, but that could change, and I didn't want to be stuck on the exposed, northern side of Blake Point and miss our ferry. We paddled in the shadows of the Palisades, where a buoy marked the resting place of the wooden-hulled steamer *Monarch*. We looked beneath our boats, but with a light chop, we couldn't see any of the wreckage. We heard the horn from the Passage Island Lighthouse, three miles to the east and watched a large freighter pass through the channel en route to Thunder Bay. Before rounding Blake Point, I glanced back toward Canada and was surprised to finally recognize the Paps and the Sleeping Giant. Then we turned the corner into the slivers of channels, points, and islands that characterize the eastern extreme of Isle Royale.

The pressure was off. Having cleared Blake Point, we suddenly had no compelling goal. For the next two days, we were free to meander in the protection of Merritt Lane, Rock Harbor, and Moskey Basin, where only a near-hurricane from the south would put us to shore. So we ate a long lunch, looked at the map, and imagined where Susan and the girls might be at this moment. Almost surely they were climbing the Ishpeming Trail, a route that rose more than 250 feet a mile. At the moment, they were either struggling under the weight of their packs or resting in the cool shade of the forest. There was something magical about laying out the map and thinking, yes, they are right *there*.

I read a travel essay by the playwright David Mamet, who at long last had forced himself to take a family vacation—and surprised himself by enjoying it. Removing the pressures of the workaday world, he found he had no need for a new idea. An old one sufficed: the restorative power of Nature. "I thought of Hippocrates and his hospital on the island of Cos, where the sick were treated to a peaceful view, and warm winds, and the regenerative rhythm of the surf—to a place where man could be healed because the natural order was allowed to reassert itself." As we sunned on the rocks, the natural order may well have been asserting itself, but without an immediate purpose, with no immediate goal in sight, I felt indolent. *Doing something* was the thing that gave a trip drama, narrative force. It was the difference between a description and a story.

At Rock Harbor, small runabouts, sailboats, big fishing boats, kayaks, and even canoes crisscrossed the opening to the marina and the park visitor center. Seaplanes took off from Tobin Harbor and roared overhead. Kate and I landed to look for a campsite. Backpacks, clothes, and gear were spread out on the shelter porches, on tables, on clotheslines. We could tell if a party was beginning its trip or ending by the amount and condition of laundry. All the sites within a half mile of the landing were taken. The only sites available were far back in the woods, too far away to carry our kayaks and gear.

We stopped a Park Service employee. He looked across the channel to Tookers Island. Don't see any boats, he said. Maybe we'd find something there.

We hurried, because it was already late in the afternoon. As we paddled, a boat with two men appeared to pull out from Tookers and motored toward us. I waved.

"Is there room?"

"It's full."

We paddled on. What choice did we have? Approaching the dock, we saw a man filtering water on shore.

"The two shelters are taken, but you'll probably find room for a tent," he said. He had long curly hair and a ponytail. "I hear Threemile is filling up. A boatload of kids got off this morning and they were all headed down there."

Kate and I hiked up the path. A family with several kids occupied one shelter. Unattended gear claimed another. I asked the family if they would mind terribly if we camped nearby.

"Suit yourself," the father said, "but thanks for asking."

I felt sorry for him; he probably thought he was coming to a national park in the middle of Lake Superior to get away from it all.

By the time we arose at seven, the man with the ponytail and his tent were gone. The unattended shelter was occupied—by fishermen who clattered around and spoke in hard voices. We talked to them down by the dock. One pulled a handful of green gemlike pebbles from his pocket. He called them greenstones and said he had collected them on the beach by the lighthouse. (They were actually chlorastrolite, not to be confused with

the metamorphosed basalt also known as greenstone.) Then he talked en-
thusiastically about a couple of brothers he met recently. They were paddling kayaks around Superior. "A couple of nice young men," he said. The
fisherman was about my age, but already seemed to imagine that a vast divide separated him from young men who would attempt something so
physical and time-consuming as paddling around Lake Superior. "That's
quite a dream they have," he said.

Kate and I paddled back to Rock Harbor. Families were poking about
the gift shop. Campers walked the trails between campsites. The crowd was
a mix of casual tourists and grubby, seasoned backpackers. This is what a
national park will get you. It was by far the greatest human traffic I had seen
in my travels, except in towns. If solitude lies at the core of your definition
of wilderness, then Isle Royale was as little like wilderness as most places I
had seen on Superior.

I was beginning to understand the two Isle Royales: the island I saw
and the island a recent issue of *Newsweek* had included among its "unspoiled
hideaways."

That islands are fortresses, isolated from the effects of the mainland, is partly true, but mostly untrue. In effect, the channel separating an island from
the mainland is like a semipermeable membrane—allowing some things, living and nonliving, to pass and preventing others. That is what makes islands
so interesting as natural history.

Ten thousand years ago, as the last glacial ice retreated, the bedrock rebounded, and proto–Lake Superior found lower levels, Isle Royale emerged
as an island, wiped clean by glaciation and inundation, a biological tabula
rasa. Immediately, spores and seeds from the tundra vegetation along the
margins of the glaciers blew across the channel from the mainland. Initially,
their chances of success were slim, since the island was composed largely of
bare rock. But eventually these pioneers found sand, accumulations of dust,
the beginnings of soil, and took root—first lichens and mosses, then spruces,
willows, birch, cedar, pines, and various hardwoods.

Most birds had no problem crossing, but poor fliers such as ruffed grouse
and spruce grouse, common on the mainland, apparently never made it to
the island, or if they did, they died out. Only the sharp-tailed grouse, less
common than the others in the northern forests but a stronger flier, eventually reached Isle Royale and survived. Bears, which hibernate in winter, are

not present. But animals, such as snowshoe hares and red fox, which are active during the coldest winters, when ice bridges the gap between mainland and Isle Royale, have made the crossing. Others, such as beavers and otters, undoubtedly swam. We can only speculate about the arrival of some species, such as the deer mouse, which almost certainly did not swim, but may have arrived as a stowaway aboard a boat or even flotsam, such as a drifting log. (Interestingly, deer mice exist only on the main island and on small islands within a couple hundred yards of the main island.)

Some of the species that arrived on Isle Royale no longer live here. Passenger pigeons, once seen all along Superior's shores, became extinct. The sharp-tailed grouse, which requires brushland and openings, vanished as the island was logged and the burned forest matured. Woodland caribou, long the only ungulate on the island, disappeared as white settlers hunted and cleared forest during the late 1800s.

Of the nearly fifty animal species on the nearby mainland, only fifteen have reached Isle Royale and survive today. This simplified ecosystem, with fewer interactions and where very little migrates in or out, has provided an ideal laboratory for one of the longest running and most important ecological studies of wolves and moose.

Moose arrived on Isle Royale in the early 1900s. They might have walked across the ice, though it was certainly within their capability to swim. By all evidence, this was the first time they had appeared on the island: archeologists have found stone flakes and pottery with fish and bones of caribou, but no bones of ancient moose. With no predators and little competition for food, the moose had found heaven on earth. The population exploded. By 1930, biologist Adolph Murie estimated their numbers at more than one thousand, perhaps as many as three thousand. The forest was heavily overbrowsed; young balsam fir were hardly to be found. Murie predicted a train wreck, and that is what happened. With severe winters during the mid-1930s, moose died by the hundreds. In 1935 state biologist Paul Hickie estimated the population at four hundred to five hundred. Another buildup followed, and so did another die-off, in the late 1940s. Boom and bust seemed inevitable.

Then in 1948, after a cold winter that froze the lake between Isle Royale and the mainland, the track of a large canine was discovered on the island. Coyotes were present, but this appeared larger than any coyote. In 1951 ranger Bob Hakala made a plaster cast of a footprint, which laid all doubt to rest. The track was gigantic. Clearly wolves were on the island.

As wolves increased, coyotes waned. No love is lost between wolves and their smaller competitor. Coyotes, which had appeared on Isle Royale in about 1900, were last seen in 1958. But as the coyote disappeared, *its* close competitor, the red fox, became more common. The wolf and the red fox were different enough in size and habitat requirements to coexist.

And so the laboratory had been set up. In stepped Durward Allen, a wildlife biologist from the U.S. Fish and Wildlife Service and Purdue University. Allen began to study the interactions between moose and wolves with the help of a young researcher named L. David Mech. Hanging from the window of a two-seater plane, Mech captured on film for the first time the scene of wolves hunting moose. Some of these wolves may have been the founders that arrived from the mainland; the rest were the first and second generation born on Isle Royale.

During the next twenty years, the moose and wolf populations seemed to fluctuate in tandem. As the moose population rose, the number of wolves rose proportionally about a decade later. The moose population topped out at about 1,400 and then slowly fell, but not lower than about 750. It appeared the two populations had achieved a dynamic equilibrium, replacing the wild fluctuations of the past. I remember, as a young forestry student at the University of Minnesota, studying the moose-wolf relationship on Isle Royale as a classic example of the balance of nature, how wolves had stabilized the moose population within the limits of their habitat.

During this period, in 1969, a young college student, Rolf O. Peterson, applied to work on Allen's wolf research. The next year, Allen sent Peterson to Isle Royale to continue examining the dominant predator-prey relationship on the island.

Flying over the island in winter, when the deciduous trees were bare, Peterson fought off air sickness and watched in fascination as wolves and moose faced off. He and his pilot tried to be absolutely predictable in their overflights to acquire the trust of their subjects. Peterson suspected that after a time, the wolves viewed them much as they would ravens, which often accompany wolves at kills. "Our occasional low passes are similar to the teasing of low-flying ravens, and I suspect that the wolves would like to catch us," Peterson writes in *The Wolves of Isle Royale*.

Peterson watched in fascination as moose successfully stood their ground or ran away; or, conversely, as wolves successfully brought down their prey. During more than twenty seasons, Peterson witnessed about two hundred confrontations between predators and prey. In only ten did the wolves succeed. That statistic is in line with other studies: predators usually fail. They test their prey and then abandon the chase as too dangerous or difficult. On one occasion, Peterson discovered a moose that had been wounded and remained standing as wolves waited nearby for the animal to die. Peterson kept tabs on the animal, which stood for seven days, with the wolves in constant attendance, until it dropped.

Once, when they briefly put down on the ice, Peterson and his pilot found a pack of wolves near a moose they discovered was blind with cataracts. They checked throughout day, but the wolves and the moose never made contact. The next day, however, they again spotted the moose standing on open ice on Lake Superior. This time, however, it was surrounded by wolf tracks. They saw no blood, no obvious wounds. The sound of the plane triggered stomping and kicking—that apparently was how the moose had confronted its attackers. On day three, they again spotted the moose, still standing, farther out on the ice, surrounded by new tracks. The next day, the moose—and the ice on which he had been standing—were gone, apparently carried out into the lake by the wind. Superior, not the wolves, finally claimed the old fighter.

Over the years, Peterson watched the wolf packs ebb and flow across the island. Dominant packs split into new packs; packs subsumed other packs. Like nations, packs rose and packs fell. In 1967, several black wolves appeared, evidence that new blood had wandered over from the mainland. But within five years, they vanished, suggesting a bloodline had come to an end. Following an increase in moose numbers, wolves multiplied to fifty animals in 1980, the greatest number observed on the island and the highest density of wolves found anywhere in the wild.

But then something surprising happened. For the wolves, it was catastrophic. Between 1980 and 1982, at least fifty-two wolves died. Some wolf pups were born to offset the losses, but the population plummeted to just fourteen. Two years later, they numbered only a dozen, the lowest observed in thirty years. They weren't dying for lack of food: in the absence of serious predation, the moose population had soared to twenty-four hundred.

Predictably, they starved during the next stretch of severe winter weather, numbering only five hundred in 1997.

What had happened to the dynamic equilibrium?

Peterson suspected canine parvovirus had killed the wolves, whose blood showed the presence of antibodies to the virus. The disease probably came to the island by way of campers' dogs. The antibodies disappeared within a few years, indicating the virus no longer infected the population, but the wolves failed to multiply, despite an abundance of food.

Meanwhile, genetic evidence confirmed that Isle Royale wolves, which had descended from a single maternal ancestor, were seriously inbred. Only the alpha animals in each pack reproduce. In a population as small as Isle Royale's, the "effective population" of breeders is, in Peterson's words, "almost laughably small—usually four to six wolves." Were the Isle Royale wolves becoming too inbred to succeed as a population? "In the late 1990s alpha positions in wolf packs will be filled by a new generation of young wolves, disease-free and well-fed through their lives," Peterson writes. "Their reproductive success should shed light on the important issue of genetic variability in small, isolated populations."

The travails of the wolf population suggested troubling philosophical questions. "Creeping in through my mind's back door in the 1980s, as shock followed shock, was the possibility that any single equilibrium, even a dynamic equilibrium, might be a myth," Peterson writes. Indeed, the Isle Royale ecosystem seemed more of a "disequilibrium system." Ecological relationships were buffeted by disease, weather, and other confounding events until they seemed to spin beyond the ability of the ecosystem to correct itself. Any illusions that scientists could predict the events of even such a simplified ecosystem were severely tested. "This is not a sign of growing incompetence or scientific senility," writes Peterson. "It actually illustrates a classical paradox in science, wherein the longer one studies a particular living system, the less once can say with certainty about its behavior."

The burgeoning moose population led Peterson to wonder if the Park Service's management of large mammals such as moose was based on a fallacy. Since the late 1960s, the Park Service had managed herds of ungulates under the policy of *natural regulation,* in the belief that mortality in large herds was sufficiently "density-dependent" that the herds' numbers would stabilize, even without predators. In this view, predators had little effect on the size of a herd; wolves would simply kill animals that would otherwise die of other causes.

But as the Isle Royale wolves struggled with first parvovirus and then their own failure to reproduce, the boom and bust of the moose population suggested to Peterson there was no natural regulation to speak of. The supposed density-dependent suppression of reproduction never materialized. Moose bred like, well, rabbits, until they starved by the hundreds.

The Park Service's hands-off attitude toward wildlife management had troubling implications —troubling at least to Peterson if his beloved Isle Royale wolves were to die out. What then?

Park Service policy was rather ambiguous. The policy states that "the primary objective . . . will be the protection of natural resources and value . . . with a concern for fundamental ecological processes." The service "will seek to perpetuate the native animal life . . . defined as all animal species that as a result of natural processes occur or occurred on lands now designated as a park. Any species that moved onto park lands directly or indirectly as the result of human activities are not considered native."

What is the fundamental process that must be protected? Extinction through inbreeding? Or the eternal relationship between predator and prey? On the face of it, the policy would seem to forbid any intervention, such as transplanting wolves, but Peterson disagreed.

"Rote adherence to a simple tradition of hands-off management will not suffice in a world with pervasive human influence," he argues in an article in *Ecological Applications.* "Of course, this raises the difficult question, 'What is natural?'"

Clearly, wolves are natural. They are also native. They reached the island under their own power under the natural conditions of a hard winter. Would their dying out be natural? The initial cause of their decline, parvovirus, most likely spread to the island through domestic dogs. If wolves had disappeared under the "natural" conditions of two centuries ago, they might quickly have been replaced by wolves from the mainland. But today, the human population and highways around Thunder Bay hinder the movement of wolves that might colonize Isle Royale. On a larger scale, if global warming is taking place because of fossil-fuel emissions, the ice to Isle Royale is less likely to freeze than in the past. Is the Park Service obligated to compensate for this "unnatural" barrier by reintroducing wolves should the present occupants disappear?

For that matter, how "natural" and "native" are the moose themselves? Caribou inhabited the island until humans killed them off. Moose wandered in only after logging and fire opened up the forests along the North Shore and on Isle Royale itself. If the Park Service wants to perpetuate natives, perhaps it should hunt moose to the last one and reintroduce woodland caribou.

Such is the illusory nature of *wilderness*—a state of nature free of human influence—and the conundrums that arise when humans are considered "alien" to a natural ecosystem. The deeply roooted notion that humans stand separate from nature, writes ecologist Daniel Botkin in *Discordant Harmonies*, is "one of the main impediments to progress on environmental issues." We already play a role and have a responsibility and a capacity to intervene gently on behalf of life, Botkin argues. In fact, the smaller the natural island, the greater the need.

"The more one is drawn into this question, the more convoluted the answers become," Peterson remarks in his book, cautioning that "leaving humanity out of nature is simply naive." To break through the tangle of logic, Peterson clearly sides with the wolves that have been the subject of his study for so long, even if it means giving them a helping hand: "It seems only prudent to maintain wolf predation on Isle Royale as long as moose continue to inhabit the place. No one can say how long that might be; over the span of centuries, few things in nature are permanent."

As Kate and I paddled deeper into Rock Harbor to Mott Island and the Park Service administrative headquarters, we saw two things of note. The first was a moose, swimming across the channel a quarter mile ahead. By the time we approached close enough to see clearly, it had reached shore and disappeared into the woods. The second was the *Ranger III*, which appeared suddenly from behind Mott Island. Sky blue and 165 feet long, it seemed to fill the channel. It wasn't about to disappear anywhere. The largest piece of movable equipment in the Park Service inventory, it hauls passengers and equipment from park headquarters in Houghton, Michigan. We watched in amazement as it turned in front of us—still a couple of hundred yards away—and sidled up to the wharf. The landing was suddenly abuzz—passengers debarking, park service employees materializing and hovering like bees, freight swinging through the air on the *Ranger III's* crane. Kate and I landed to watch the activity. Amid the hubbub, Rolf

Peterson, the wolf researcher, was organizing a party of Earthwatch volunteers to search the backcountry for wolf and moose remains. Then, as suddenly as it all began, the *Ranger III* pulled out, Peterson and his volunteers departed, various small boats dispersed, and the dock was quiet.

We continued to Caribou Island Campground. Several spots I wanted to see—Historic Edisen Fishery, Rock Harbor Lighthouse, and the tantalizingly named Cemetery Island—were clustered nearby, so even though it was only midafternoon, we decided to camp. One plywood shelter was taken by two young men. One was pale and flabby. He wore a T-shirt with a picture of a stripper: *Foxy Lady, the memory lives on. Friction dancing, Providence, Rhode Island.* The other, with sandy hair and a goatee, had a harder face. His T-shirt had a figure with a blazing machine gun and the words *I'd rather be killing terrorists.* Their canoe sat on shore. The flaccid blonde whined about bucking a headwind and two-foot waves, though I couldn't remember seeing any weather like that today. The terrorist killer offered to move their gear to one side so that Kate and I might share their shelter.

"Thanks. I don't think so."

We set up our tent some distance away. Both men seemed eager to talk and hovered about, waiting for a conversation to draw them in. Kate and I made a getaway to our kayaks.

Cemetery Island was overgrown with scrubby woods and thimbleberries. We followed a trail to a wooden fence on the crown of the island. The wood was weathered gray and covered by old-man's beard. Rings of stones marked—what?—graves, perhaps. There was a wooden cross as well. Nearby was another enclosure with a weathered wooden marker: "William Hanks of Coventry, who departed this life on Sept. 11, 1851, age 24." Another: "In memory of infant daughter of Maurice and Johanna Mickey, died Oct. 20, 1854." And another: "Erected in memory of Jeremiah Colbert of Bonmahon County, Waterford, Ireland, died Oct. 18, 1853, age 25 years."

"Sad," Kate said.

I am always astounded to see a grave in the middle of nowhere, because to see where people have died is to see where they have lived. The remotest areas are well traveled, crisscrossed by people's lives. As I learned elsewhere, these were graves of copper miners and their families. The wood was in good shape, the nails galvanized. The markers and fences had been replaced recently. But by whom? Relatives? Or just those who wished to maintain

The graves at Cemetery Island are reminders of the many people who once lived on this island "wilderness."

such things? Is this the work of the builders? I couldn't imagine sea kayakers doing this. I couldn't imagine that I would do it.

We arrived at Rock Harbor Lighthouse, which faced the bay, protected from the lake by a small skerry. The lighthouse was brick, covered with white plaster. It was pretty in a clean, simple way. Built in 1855, it guided ships to mine docks, according to a sign. But mining ended virtually as soon as the light was built. After only four years, the keeper extinguished the light and departed. The lighthouse reopened briefly, but closed for good in 1879. Several island families had lived here, but the building was abandoned in 1939 and decayed rapidly. Photos from the 1950s show a sorry structure with broken windows and dilapidated siding. The Park Service stabilized the foundation and started to refurbish the building in the 1960s.

Inside, light gleamed off varnished pine floors. Our footsteps echoed. A display told of the wreck of the *Algoma* in 1885. The ship "struck the rocks and broke apart. Approximately forty-five persons perished, the greatest loss of life in a Lake Superior wreck." John McLean, the ship's waiter, testified, "It was dark and freezing cold, with a terrible sea. There were two ladies and three little girls that I noticed. They were swept away with the cabins. We could hear the ladies and the girls calling piteously, but no one could help them. After awhile their voices ceased, and we all knew they were out in the Lake."

Another exhibit recalled the mystery of the *Kamloops*, which disappeared with a crew of twenty-two on 6 December 1927 on the north shore of the island in subzero weather, with snow, fog, ice, and gale winds. The next year a trapper in Canada found a note in a bottle, signed by Alice Bettridge, an assistant steward: "I am the last one alive, freezing and starving on Isle Royale. I just want mom and dad to know my fate." Her body was found in June, near the wreck. A piano from the ship was found onshore, fifteen feet above lake level.

Many photos showed the fishing families and children that grew up on the island during the early 1900s: Andersons, Mattsons, Gustafsons, Carlsons, Eckels, and Sivertsons. Kate and I climbed the old wooden stairway up to the beacon. "Dad, look, oh cool." We saw paired photos from the late 1800s and a century later in 1979, showing nearly identical views from the lighthouse. Remarkably little had changed, except for the tree line. Boorish people had carved their names in the woodwork. It was very hot, but the

The Rock Harbor Lighthouse nearly fell into shambles before it was restored by the National Park Service.

view was cool, up Rock Harbor in one direction and across the limitless lake in the other.

Walking across the point to the Historic Edisen Fishery, we encountered another wooden marker: "Arthur Lee Scott, born Aug. 17, 1845, Nineveh,

The author at the Rock Harbor Lighthouse. (Photograph by Katherine Breining-Hill.)

NY; died March 5, 1878, Isle Royale." The Edisen fishery was itself a kind of marker, marking the lives of the Edisens, who married early and worked here nearly sixty years. The camp looked much as the Edisens had left it in the 1970s: herring skiff with engine amidships, net reels, cabins built of tongue-in-groove boards, tar-papered fish house at the end of the dock. This was typical of the forty or so seasonal fishermen's homes on Isle Royale. There was a boathouse with old outboards, a stash of old oars, flags to mark nets, piles of gill nets, machinery, grinders, drills, winches, and an old saw. The people who lived this life had a genius for manipulating, fixing, building. All that was missing was the smell of fish.

By the time we reached our Caribou Island camp, the dock was crowded with four runabouts, two sailboats, and a canoe. As Kate and I cooked din-

The Historic Edisen Fishery is an artifact of a lifestyle once common on Isle Royale.

ner near the dock, a family of otters appeared. The little ones galumphed around, grunting *runk, runk, runk*. Then they dove into the water, where they suddenly became as lithe as trout. They frolicked beneath the dock as people walked from one side to the other, trying to see them. At one point, everyone in camp, sixteen people in all, were watching the otters, which ran from the water and made a move on Kate's dinner. We jumped up and I took a step toward the single adult, which backed off reluctantly and made a threatening *huff*. Nowhere except in this national park, this managed wilderness, had we seen such bold animals.

Early the next morning, while the guys with the T-shirts slept, we paddled out of the gap and passed down the long exposed southern shoreline of the island. Near the opening of Conglomerate Bay, a little boat bobbed on the small gray waves. As we drew closer, we saw that an old woman was drawing a net over the gunwale hand over hand; a man of similar age was pulling large fish from the mesh. In the clear water, we could see the net beneath us and the nearly luminescent bellies of the netted fish.

"How deep was your net set?"

"Right to the bottom," the man said. About forty feet at the shallow end, eighty feet at the deep end.

They were Leslie and Donna Mattson. His family had fished for years out of Munising, Michigan. She was talkative, with curly hair and a bright face. He had fewer words. He wore a yellow slicker and a cigarette dangled from his lips as he worked.

"Is that a linen net?" I asked.

"It is and it's rotten," Donna said. "If the Park Service saw what we do, they wouldn't let us do it. This boat is too small for us." Their boat was about sixteen feet, aluminum, with a fifteen-horse Evinrude.

"We catch trout for the lodge," Donna said. During the summer they lived at the Edisen fishery. "It's kind of a show-and-tell fishery," she said.

As we talked, they hoisted eight large trout and two large whitefish aboard. The cigarette never came out of Leslie's mouth. I remarked on one large trout with a dark green back and silvery flanks with several circular wounds.

"What do you figure he would go?"

"Oh, about maybe fifteen pounds. A lot of lamprey scars."

The victims of sea lamprey attacks often survive their wounds, but enough die that the lake trout fishery collapsed as the lamprey advanced through the Great Lakes. Native to the Atlantic Ocean, the lamprey sneaked into the upper lakes with the deepening of the Welland Canal in 1919, reaching Lake Erie in 1921, Michigan in 1936, Huron in 1937, and Superior in 1946. It targeted large fish. Lake trout were especially vulnerable. Ten years after it appeared in Lakes Michigan and Huron, the lake trout there were essentially extirpated.

Quite possibly lampreys wrought such havoc because Lake Superior was a simple, immature ecosystem. In the mere ten thousand years since it was formed after the Ice Age, its species have adapted only modestly to their environment. Compare, for example, Superior with fewer than three dozen native species, none of which are endemic, to the ancient great lakes of eastern Africa. In Lake Malawi alone there are more than two hundred species of the single family of fish known as cichlids; all but four are endemic.

Recent research at the University of Minnesota demonstrated that a diverse grassland remained productive during times of stress, in this case drought, because as certain species faltered, others were able to take advantage and prosper. Less diverse grasslands suffered greater losses in productivity. It's not unreasonable to suppose that aquatic ecosystems perform in similar fashion. As lake trout and burbot disappeared, no other species were poised to compensate.

Meanwhile, there was evidence that Lake Superior was already in decline by the time sea lamprey arrived. Early fisherman mistook great *concentrations* of fish for abundance. In reality, Superior was—and is—cold, infertile, and not very productive, a near vacuum of fish life. Fisheries biologists now estimate the sustainable catch from Superior may be as low as a single pound per acre. The lamprey may simply have hastened the end of a fishery already destabilized by more than a century of effective, but poorly regulated, commercial fishing.

Lake trout have made a remarkable recovery in recent years through intense stocking and costly (and continual) poisoning of lamprey in their spawning streams. Sport angling for lake trout is allowed, but commercial fishing is limited to Indian tribes and a small "assessment" harvest. To that extent, the entire commercial enterprise has become, in Donna Mattson's words, a kind of "show-and-tell" fishery.

Mark Rude grew up on Isle Royale, the son of a commercial fisherman in the waning days of that era. Living through the transformation of Isle Royale from commercial fishery to park, he saw both Isle Royales—the island wilderness and the island rich with human life, the illusion and the reality. I met him aboard the *Voyageur II*, where he occasionally filled in as captain. Age fifty-nine, he had a buzz cut, a wiry build, and gnarly forearms. He smoked heavily. His family fished out of Fisherman's Home Cove on the south shore of Isle Royale, at the end of Houghton Point. His grandfather, from Norway, had been fishing there since 1919.

"My family lived in Duluth, Minnesota, and went out to the island during the summer," he said. "I guess I was first out there when I was about two months old. My dad normally would go out some time in April, beginning of May, depending on the season. They'd usually get me out of school a little bit early."

Fisherman's Home Cove was remote in comparison to other Isle Royale fishing communities. "Down in our area, the nearest neighbors were in Hay Bay, and that was three miles away," he recalled. "Our next nearest neighbor was the Holte family. They were eight miles away. But when you got down to Washington Harbor, there were some twenty different commercial fishermen—my gosh, that was just like a little city there.

"The area that my father fished, my grandfather fished, and my grandfather fished, I'm sure, was the same area that Seglem [the previous fisherman at Fisherman's Home Cove] did before him. When another fisherman would get into your territory a little argument would ensue. One of the fishermen set a net across the top of one of my dad's nets. When we got down to the end of our net, an anchor rock came up. His net came up with it. It had just kind of slid along as we pulled our net up. But the anchor rock got caught in it. Well that was good exercise for my dad, 'cause he just pulls from both ends and just puts it in a huge big ball. That's all there was—a huge messed-up ball with the webbing in it and two anchor rocks and a long anchor line and he threw it overboard, and that net went down in one huge ball with holes. It was just a ripped-up net, you know. And never again did that guy ever come close to us."

The Rudes fished for lake trout, whitefish, and herring. In the mid-1950s, trout brought fifty cents a pound, whitefish only slightly less. Herring and menomenee earned only five to ten cents a pound. Fishing from wooden skiffs, Isle Royale fishermen used mostly gill nets. After the war they began suspending the nets above the bottom and they began to catch more fish. They also fished "hook lines," lines up to a mile long with dropper lines and hooks, baited with cut herring, set at twenty-foot intervals. Bringing in a hook line was excruciating work. One man pulled the boat along the "hook line" hand over hand while the other pulled off each "down line," perhaps with a wiggling trout or eelpout, and tied on a new down line, already baited. That could take all day.

The effect of sea lampreys was immediate, Rude said. "Nineteen fifty-four was a wonderful fishing year and then in '55 it just fell off; '56 was worse, and it really went downhill fast. It got to the point where probably 80 to 90 percent of the fish we caught had either fresh or healed lamprey

scars on them. By 1960 a lot of fishermen just started pulling away from
Isle Royale. It was obvious that there was not going to be any money to be
made as a commercial fisherman." Rude himself left, and without much soul-
searching. "It was just to go out and find a real job and get on with the business of raising a family." He married and lived in Rockford, Illinois, for more
than twenty years. He worked in the service department of a manufacturing
company. Later he started a small manufacturing company in Illinois. He divorced and, during the 1980s, returned to fishing, netting under his mother's
assessment permit. These days he pilots a charter boat for divers and fills in
on *Voyageur II* to make enough "to keep the wolf away from the door."

"When the park was formed," he said, "there was this segment of fishermen, like the Washington Harbor bunch, that resented the park coming in
and taking their land and taking their houses and so forth. I guess old Sam
Sivertson was probably the ringleader of the Washington Harbor group. He
was a crusty old guy, and he didn't like being told what to do. . . . Because
Sam Sivertson didn't like what the park was coming and doing, neither did
almost all the fishermen in Washington Harbor. But as far as Fisherman's
Home was concerned it really didn't make any difference to us. My grandfather wasn't interested in the land. If they came along and said, 'We're
going to pay you for these buildings, and we're going to let you use them
and stay there for life,' well, this was not a bad deal. That's what they did
with all the fishermen.

"So when the Park Service started coming around, my family never had
any real gripes with them. They weren't too authoritative. They showed up
once in a while in a boat and came in and sat down and had dinner or coffee
and chatted. We continued to catch fish. Then we heard a lot of stories from
Washington Harbor and other areas where they got to be pretty confronta-
tional. You couldn't bring a gun out to the island anymore. You couldn't go
shoot a moose because you wanted a little moose meat. There were a lot of
rules and regulations that came into being that people didn't like, especially
in Washington Harbor. Well, heck, we didn't very often get a moose anyway.

"The management plan for Isle Royale National Park had always been
the philosophy of whoever happened to be the superintendent at the time,"
Rude said. "About three years ago the Park Service decided that there should
a long-term management plan. It seemed like a good idea to everybody that
the park should have some guidance." Rude soon discovered, however, that

he disagreed with the Park Service over the fundamental nature of the island. "In a statement of purpose, the park said Isle Royale is a 'primeval wilderness, isolated from the rest of the world by the size and fury of Lake Superior.' I looked at that and I thought, 'You wonder why you're having problems with people who come up and camp on the island and complain that their wilderness experience has been compromised by boat noise and by too many other hikers and campers.' *Isle Royale is a primeval wilderness, isolated from the rest of the world by the size and power of Lake Superior.* First of all, there is no primeval wilderness left on Isle Royale. Maybe a little chunk on the Siskiwit Swamp. Other than that, there is no primeval wilderness. . . .

"Isle Royale has been trampled over by man both historically and in modern times. Therefore it's no longer primeval wilderness. It's not isolated from the rest of the world. . . . They had cruise boats that regularly went to Isle Royale. From the turn of the century, everybody who wanted to go to Isle Royale, all they had to do was get on a boat and go. So this is not isolated. It never has been isolated. It's a strip of land forty-five miles long, nine miles wide at its widest, probably average width about five or six miles, and there's probably one spot on the trail where you can get three miles from Lake Superior, right up at the wide part of the island, right up on the Greenstone Ridge. The rest of the time, you're going to be one or two miles or even less from Lake Superior. So you have people that come out there and they can't get more than a mile or two from Lake Superior and all of a sudden it's a foggy day and the boats are going by and they're required by the Coast Guard to sound a four-second-long blast of their whistle once every two minutes. They hear boat whistles. On a nice calm day you can hear boat engines. They come in there in August with their group of four people and they go up to Hatchet Lake and they expect that they're going to be all alone in their shelter. Well, whoops, now there's a group of Boy Scouts next to them. 'Well, shit, let's go to Desor.' So they go up to Desor and here comes a group coming from the other direction. And they write a little thing that says, 'Our Isle Royale experience was much compromised because there are too doggone many people out here.' What those people are really saying is that there's too many people out there other than *my* group. But collectively they are the problem.

"The one thing you can pretty much bet on is that when some government agency designates something as wilderness, it will become less of a wilderness than it ever was before. Sometime it would really be nice to see some person in a position of authority like a superintendent out on Isle Royale stand up and assess Isle Royale for what it is—it's a maritime park. Some of the people say we should do away with all motorboats out there. How in the world are they going to get out there? Are they going to swim? Well, fine, do away with Park Service boats and do away with all motorboats. You want to come out there? You kayak or swim. . . . The Park Service can run the park with about six employees."

You would think, listening to him, that Mark Rude does not like the Park Service, or the park, or the idea of a park. But that is not true. Recently he was out on the lake with a fisherman who had been dressed down by a park ranger because he had not monitored channel sixteen, the emergency marine channel.

"That damn Park Service," the man said. "I wish they'd have never been here."

Rude disagreed: "I said, 'Oliver, look around at Siskiwit Bay. Had this not been a national park, Siskiwit Bay would be filled with condos and you'd be asshole deep in boats out here. You wouldn't be able to move because of boats.'

"Somewhere along the line, my dad, my grandfather, could have said, 'We're going to claim this land and make money here.' Well, I wouldn't trade. If it was a million-dollar-a-year exclusive fishing resort, I wouldn't trade that for what it is. Isle Royale is a wonderful place and it is because it became a national park."

We had the whole day to make the boat landing at Malone Bay, a distance of only fourteen miles. As we paddled, the wind began to rise. Our kayaks pitched and bobbed in two-foot whitecaps. Kate seemed to enjoy wandering far out into the waves.

"Get over here!" I yelled above the whipping wind. "How are you doing?"

"Fine," she said, so nonchalantly that I took her to be telling the truth.

Finally, I heard her let out a cry of delight and looked over in time to see her kayak teeter on the crest of a three-foot wave. I began to look for a break in the cliffs where we might land until the wind died.

"Oh, Dad."

We dodged into Blueberry Cove, where we read and snacked for the rest of the afternoon. A moose and a calf swam across the bay in front of us. We ate dinner in preparation for an evening of paddling. Finally, the waves seemed to drop.

"It looks like it's quieting down."

"Oh, poop."

"Why? You want to stay here?"

"No, I want to paddle on rough water."

The lake turned to mercury as we paddled into the evening. Kate stroked hard, mile after mile, but as the sun touched the horizon, we realized we would not make Malone Bay before dark. As we drew near Schooner Island, Kate pointed out a horseshoe bay.

"There's a big beach."

I had hoped to make the campsite at Malone Bay. But why? Because of

Kate prepares our final camp on Isle Royale.

a rule? Because we had told the ranger we would? So we could stumble in the dark looking for a campsite that might not be available? So we landed. The beach rose quickly to a gravel plateau where we set our tent. We had a snack and made hot tea. We saw no one else that evening. It was the best site of all.

CHAPTER 8

Apostle Islands: Brule Point to La Pointe

I DECIDED TO SKIP Duluth and Superior. Sea kayaks aren't much good for touring cities. Except for the rusted hulls of ships in the harbor, what could I see that I couldn't see more easily by car? Instead, I decided to pick up my trip somewhere to the east of Superior, safely outside the shipping lanes, along the red clay banks and sand beaches that stretched past the Brule River to the beginning of the Apostle Islands. It was a landscape I wanted to see, but quickly. Except for three small towns, I didn't anticipate much of interest. So one day when Jim Weseloh suggested we take his sixteen-foot catamaran on Superior, I said, "Let's sail from Superior to the Apostles."

We rendezvoused on the hill overlooking Duluth and drove across the bay to the lowlands of Superior toward the South Shore. Superior is Hoboken to Duluth's Manhattan, Cicero to Duluth's Chicago. Its downtown is gray and faded as an old photo. We drove past docks for loading iron ore, past blue-collar houses pressed against the highway, past weedy chain-link fences, past slack rivers and ponds, red with mud.

At the mouth of the Brule River we untrailered the Hoby Cat, assembled the mast, lashed our gear on board in waterproof bags, hoisted the sail, and waited for the wind.

And waited.

We bobbed listlessly on the dead calm lake until a brisk wind raced across the water, whipping it into four-foot whitecaps, which concerned the living hell out of me, and drove us back to the Brule River, where we flopped ashore gracelessly in the surf. We dragged the boat onto the beach and waited the rest of the day for the wind to drop, but it never did.

The second day strong winds and four-foot waves blew us into Port Wing, where we sailed straight up on the beach and hung out at the quiet, weedy marina for the rest of the day, waiting for the wind to drop. It never did.

The third day, there was no wind at all. We sat on the pontoons and paddled fifteen miles to Cornucopia, where a gust near sundown spared us the embarrassment of paddling into the marina. That night, we camped at a malarial site by the lagoon in the terminally quaint village of Cornucopia— Corny as it is known among the boaters. The marina, small though it was, had the whiff not only of diesel oil, but also money and far-off travel. Its slips were filled with sailboats, including the *Mouja*, a lovely ketch with brass-trimmed portholes and natural-wood spars. After dark, colored lanterns hung from the awnings of the camper trailers tucked cheek to jowl along the marina. Voices drifted through the shadows. The night reminded me of a village in Indonesia as I saw glimpses of human forms in the dimly lit windows.

Finally, on the fourth day, we had a wind strong enough to sail but not so strong as to tear the mast off the boat. We wafted into Squaw Bay, past the sandstone cliffs, riddled with small caves and arches, past the prickly nests of cormorants in the dead trees on Eagle Island, until, with sails full of a freshening wind, we sped on the light chop into Little Sand Bay and the red-rock beauty of the Apostle Islands.

Like many now-wild places with a long history of human occupation, the Apostles provide much to wonder about. Do the dark shadows of the sea caves really hold the sacred birch-bark scrolls of Ojibwa *Medaewaewin*? What thoughts pass through the mind of a sailor in the moment before he drowns?

And what of the name *Apostles*? The islands number twenty-two; the original apostles numbered ten fewer. There are stories of a short-lived band of pirates who called themselves the Twelve Apostles and hid their boat on Oak Island, the highest and most rugged of the islands. But by most accounts, the islands were named by French missionaries. Were they so determined to honor the original disciples that they neglected to count? Maybe it was the meaning of the word itself—*apostolos*, "person sent forth," as though the islands ventured from Wisconsin's shore northward into the unredeemed wilderness of Superior's icy waters. Maybe the name derives from those who have made the pilgrimage *to* the Apostles, washing up on the islands in waves of exploration and settlement. Perhaps the notion of refuge was uppermost in the mind of the early missionaries. Just as their parishioners should cling to the bosom of Christ, early Jesuit travelers should seek the protection of the Apostles. "You have a boatload of people with a religious background passing through a vague area," local writer and guide-boat operator Dave Strzok once explained. "You can almost hear them saying, 'Cling to the south. Don't veer north. Cling to the Apostles.'"

I first saw the Apostles in college, visiting a friend from school whose parents owned a summer home on Madeline Island. It was one of the first times I had brushed up against money—not great wealth, but more money than I had known. At the same time, there was a kind of tumble-down casualness about the place, where island hardscrabble met the well-off. My friend and I sailed his parents' boat in the channels between islands. The sails tightened and the boat heeled until water lapped the rail, yet I felt secure, as though I knew the islands would protect us from Superior's infinite horizon.

Many years later, I visited the islands on a magazine assignment with my friend Layne Kennedy, a freelance photographer. We joined a commercial kayak tour of the islands. The eight members of our group launched at Little Sand Bay. In the distance, the low wooded Apostles sat like thin wafers on the calm gray lake. As we bobbed like baby ducks, our guide led her brood across the three-mile channel to Sand Island.

After setting camp, our fleet of kayaks set out to explore the Sand Island caves, gouged from the soft island by nor'easters barreling down more than two hundred miles of open lake. The caves were small and tortuous. We glided through the kaleidoscope of spaces and listened to the lake speak its deep voice as waves slapped the back of the chambers.

As evening settled in, the sun hovered blood red in a foggy pall, the un-worldly effect of widespread forest fires in Canada. We continued down the shore to Sand Island Lighthouse. Built in 1881 of native sandstone, the lighthouse burned these days with a solar-powered beacon. Looking north-west toward the setting sun, I imagined the sight in 1905 when the freighter *Sevona*, running before a gale in the open lake, sought refuge in the Apostles. Blinded by the storm, the captain crashed into Sand Island Shoal. From his lookout in the turret, lighthouse keeper Emmanuel Luick watched helpless-ly as the *Sevona* broke apart barely more than a mile away and seven sailors drowned in the surf that was pounding the rock at his feet.

The next morning we awoke to foghorns, the deep dialog between ships. As other campers washed up and fixed breakfast, I hiked down the beach. There, in front of a lakeside cabin, I found Howard Palm. He was a retired railroad worker who had summered on Sand Island since he was three. As a

181

child he had accompanied his uncle, a commercial fisherman. He recalled watching the nets surface through fathoms of clear water, and the white flash of whitefish and trout caught in the mesh. His grandfather had been a fisherman, too. His boat had vanished in an April storm, when ice still floated on the water.

Refuge takes many forms. While sailors and fishermen looked to the Apostles for shelter from inclement weather, Palm's family took refuge from the Depression, living on the island for nearly a year. "My father was a salesman," Palm said, "and who could afford to buy insurance during the Depression?" Palm, his parents, and three siblings wintered in a log cabin, drawing water through a hole chopped in the ice. "We all missed a year of school, which was all right with me. It was one of the most memorable and enjoyable years that our family spent together."

At one time, up to one hundred people lived on the island, Palm said, though by the time he moved there, the population had dwindled to four families. The men were commercial fishermen. One kept dairy cows. A telephone cable ran out from the mainland, though a storm eventually put an end to phone service and it has never been restored. The island had a post office and, through 1928, a school. Every Saturday night during the summer, island residents danced at the West Bay Club. A road ran along one shore of Sand. Not far from Palm's house, two old cars rusted in the forest.

"All the people are gone now," Palm said. He seemed vigorous, even youthful, in his baggy khakis and bright yellow Hawaiian shirt. Yet I thought of him somehow as porcelain, frail beneath translucent skin. "I guess you could compare it to going to a movie with a packed house. Everybody left and you're the only one left," he said. "That's how it feels. It feels lonely."

When the Apostle Islands National Lakeshore was established in 1970, only Madeline, the most populous of the islands, was excluded. The government negotiated with residents of other islands to sell their land. About two dozen clung to their properties through long-term leases, mainly on Sand and Rocky Islands. Palm's own lease was set to expire at the turn of the century. "I've always been in favor of national parks," he said. "Anytime they take a beautiful area like this and preserve it for future generations, I'm in favor of it." Still, he regretted he couldn't pass the place on to his son. "Our roots run pretty deep. It's going to be tough to leave."

After an overnight rain, our group glided silently by the wet red rock and dark woods of Oak Island, sticking close to shore, for nothing is more invisible and vulnerable in the fog than a kayak. Suddenly the quiet was shattered by the thunder of jet boats, roaring out of the Bayfield marina. They disappeared around a point of the mainland, but for fifteen minutes I felt their power as an inaudible throb deep in my belly. Watchful for other boats, we crossed to the mainland.

We suddenly confronted the ribs of an ancient ship near shore. It was the *H. D. Coffinberry*, scuttled in shallow water in 1913 after she outlived her usefulness. The ribs curved upward, like two rows of gnarled, black fingers reaching to the sky. We paddled between them as waves slapped the wood and tree swallows played tag above us.

A few yards from shore, our guide gathered us over the sunken remains of the *Ottawa*. When she was launched in 1881, the *Ottawa*, at 151 feet, was the biggest tug on the lake. In 1909 she hauled the *James H. Hoyt* off a shoal near Outer Island and towed the big freighter to the shelter of Red Cliff Bay. As the two boats rested at anchor that night, the *Ottawa* suddenly burst into flames. The crew fled to the disabled *Hoyt* as the *Ottawa* burned and sank. Looking into my own shadow, I saw its ribs and timbers beneath me. Jabbing deep with my paddle, I felt the dead thump of waterlogged wood.

Down the shore we came upon another surprise—several gulls sitting on the ribs of the *Fedora*. Rusted bolts stuck barely above the surface, poised to puncture the hull of the careless sea kayaker. On a stormy September night in 1901, the *Fedora* had steamed southward through the Apostles toward Ashland when a kerosene lantern exploded in the engine room. In minutes, flames filled the ship, which continued to run full speed. The captain turned the ship toward shore and ran her aground. The crew escaped in lifeboats, but the *Fedora* burned to the waterline.

The hull formed a three-hundred-foot diagonal, a bridge between two worlds. The bow lay buried in drifted sand, gradually achieving the permanence of a fossil. The stern provided a perch for birds. We glided back and forth over the submerged timbers, clearly visible just a few feet below. In a kayak I felt as light and lively as sunlight on the water, and just a bit arrogant, as though I mocked the wreck. These shipwrecks reminded me that refuge is neither safe, nor secure. The best of plans and the most perfect lives can be upended in a moment by bad luck, carelessness, arrogance, or simple change.

At dusk, Layne and I borrowed a small rowboat from a family that lived just up the shore from Bayfield. Rowing to the *Fedora*, we set a camera and tripod in the shallow water and opened the shutter for a time exposure of the twisted black stern. As we waited several minutes for each shot, we smoked cigars and contemplated, among other things, the changing fortunes of these islands and the links of the past to the present. As we sat, two paddlers in bright plastic kayaks paddled along shore and weaved among the wreckage in the low light.

Later, as I looked at Layne's photographs, I saw fleeting ghosts of pink and green amid the solid black architecture of the *Fedora*. I was struck by the transitory nature of the present amid the firm landscape of the past. Yet I was keenly aware of this paradox: it is that moment, no matter how fleeting, that makes the past. Will my own life seem as ephemeral as the image of the kayaks? That evening in the Apostles reminded me of my relationship to those who have come before, and confirmed the humble thought that we too shall pass.

On Devils Island, in the Apostles' outer ring, Layne and I rode a small boat into the sea caves, which bellowed even in this mild chop. On shore we clambered over slabs of sandstone that had been undercut by waves to the point of collapse and, in the lake's wilder tantrums, tossed high onto the brutalized shore. Examining a ledge, I found a colony of delicate violet brook lobelias. Only three inches tall, they had held out against the elements in a rocky crevice.

On South Twin Island, in an old resort converted to a Park Service cabin, we visited Jim dale Vickery, writer and summertime park ranger. On the wall of his cabin hung a nautical map. Notations recorded his seven summers in the islands: *Rescue 2 lost boys. Boat wreck. Boater rescue. Gulls nesting. Butterworts. Challenge rescue.* "There's a force the lake has," Vickery said. "Sometimes it's concealed. But sometimes it's released. Sometimes it's destructive. Sometimes it's beautiful. You're at the mercy of the lake."

Like the delicate lobelia, Vickery and others on the islands had found in the Apostles a crevice of shelter where they could live, work, and play amid Superior's cold, tempestuous environment. This refuge defined their relationship. Each night during the summer, sailboats gathered in his picture window, which looked to the cove. "Different villages of people congeal around you every night," Vickery remarked. "You're sort of floating through it like a salmon. In the morning, everyone goes their separate ways. There's an ebb and a flow."

Over time, the ebb and flow has been greatest on Madeline Island. Iroquois, Fox, Huron, and Dakota had passed this way. Sometime before the arrival of European explorers and traders, Ojibwa had made the island their home.

For the Ojibwa, Madeline was the latest of many homelands. Several hundred years ago, according to William W. Warren, his ancestors lived "on the great salt water toward the rising sun," near the mouth of the St. Law-rence River. By all accounts, they were having a tough time of it. They bat-tled frequently with the Iroquois and other powerful eastern tribes, and seemed to suffer a sort of spiritual malaise. They looked for deliverance in a vision—a great seashell that alternately rose and set like the sun, leading the Ojibwa westward from the Atlantic, along the St. Lawrence. Each time the shell sank from sight behind the curtain of yet another of the Great Lakes, Warren wrote, "death daily visited the wigwams of our forefathers." The tribe settled for a long time at the Sault before once again moving westward, splitting into two groups. One group moved along the northern shore of the lake; the second, larger group followed the southern shore, battling the Fox and the Dakota. Finally, the shell led the latter group to Moningwunakauning—literally, home of the golden-breasted woodpecker— "where it has ever since reflected back the rays of the sun, and blessed our ancestors with life, light, and wisdom," wrote Warren. On Moningwunakaun-ing—Madeline Island—the Ojibwa finally found refuge from their enemies and woes. Ojibwa religion and society reached full flower, Warren reported, and the people of Moningwunakauning led full and secure lives.

The French called the Ojibwa community La Pointe, a name that remains to this day. During the summer, on the half hour, the ferry from Bayfield brings workers and tourists to La Pointe's docks. The white-shingled post office stands there, in a building built in the 1830s as the Protestant mission house. Casual restaurants and bars spread along the waterfront.

Just up the road from the docks sits the original one-room schoolhouse. Built more than a century ago, it has been moved and converted to a public library. One day several years ago, I found the librarian, Constance Ross, hidden by stacks of books and camouflaged by mottled shadow and sun-light. She grew up in St. Paul, she told me, and summered on Madeline before moving there permanently. "I'm getting to like the winters more and more," she said, "because in summer the tourists are starting to take over."

Nearby I found the Madeline Island Historical Museum. The back room is filled with old-fashioned museum stuff—lots of *things*, from musket balls to Bibles, with only a thin veneer of context. The majority of the collection was donated on the condition that it not be changed. "Basically, it's a museum of a museum," a curator told me. Stone tools, beaded buckskins, and a birch-bark canoe recalled the days when the Ojibwa played lacrosse and stick games on *Moningwunakauning* and paddled to the mainland to hunt and gather wild rice. Beaver pelts, brass kettles, ceramic beads, and clay pipes told of the fur trade, when first French, then English, and finally Americans established posts on Madeline to buy furs from the Indians. Fishing nets, a logging sled, oxen yoke, and old school bell portray the settlements of the late nineteenth century, when the fur trade vanished, shipping switched to mainline ports, and Madeline's population dwindled.

Tourism revived the island's fortunes, though the permanent population remains less than two hundred. In 1898 Colonel Frederick and Eliza Woods led the first wave of wealthy summer residents. They bought property along the shore and invited their Nebraska relatives to join them. They did, building houses up and down the road still known as Nebraska Row. At the end of the road sits Woods Manor Bed and Breakfast, covered with raw wood shingles and blue and yellow trim. Built by the colonel's son, it was later owned by Frank Woods Petersen, who spent the summers of his childhood in the 1950s and 1960s absorbing the laid-back island life. "When I grew up here I knew about 90 percent of the people on the island," he told me. "I probably know 10 percent of the people out here now."

Still, there are few enough that if you spend any time on Madeline, you're bound to see the same people over and over. Chances are good you'll spot them some hot summer night down near the dock at Tom's Burned Down Café, seeking refuge from the quiet sameness of island life. Part big top, part bar, the cafe was born in 1992, when Leona's, a popular night spot, burned to the ground. "Thirty-six hours after the fire we were tapping beer on the front lawn," said owner Tom Nelson. Recognizing a good thing, Nelson propped up the surviving floor and deck with two old Cadillacs, stretched a tarp overhead, and backed a semitrailer up to the makeshift bar to hold the beer and snacks. Signs greeting patrons convey the informality of the place: "Build it first; design second." And: "No shirt, no shoes, no problem."

"How's business in the semi-outdoors?" I asked.

"Great," said Nelson. "Higher ceilings, lower overhead."

An inveterate collector, Nelson had gathered tons of metal scrap and other odds and ends on the site. "One broken shovel is junk," he said. "When you've got eighty-five, then you have something." Nelson wrangled a Wisconsin Arts Board grant to sponsor a "live art workshop." Regionally recognized sculptors have transformed Nelson's junk pile, which had rankled local residents, into the Phoenix Art Gallery.

Among Nelson's collections were clay pipes, delicate artifacts from the fur-trade days with the subtle patina of alabaster. As he showed them off, he mentioned that they were combed from the beach just south of town, so I drove down there. Known as Grants Point, the area was the site of a seventeenth-century French fort and later British and American trading posts. Old Fort Road led past tennis courts to a sandy beach.

I searched the beach, determined to find a clay pipe. I pocketed wave-polished quartz, beach glass, and a chalky white stone the shape of Lake Superior. I picked up a piece of birch bark. Who knows? Perhaps a fragment of a voyageur canoe or a piece of sacred Ojibwa scroll long hidden in a sea cave. I found what appeared to be a fragment of curved pottery. But no matter how hard I willed it, not a single clay pipe, not a single fragment of pipe, materialized.

On the isthmus between the marina and the lake, just down the hill from the golf course designed by Robert Trent Jones, I found a cemetery behind a rusting iron fence. Called the La Pointe Indian Cemetery, it was established in 1836 by Frederic Baraga. At the height of his mission, the dynamic Austrian priest conducted five services each Sunday, two in French, two in Ojibwa, and one in English. Many of the graves were still covered by low wooden houses, built long ago by Christianized Ojibwa to protect both the dead and the food left to sustain the spirit in its four-day journey to the hereafter. Some of the houses had collapsed; raspberries grew through the planks.

A marble stone marked the grave of Michel Cadotte, manager of a fur-trade post (and maternal grandfather of historian Warren, who wrote of wandering island trails past Indian gardens of corn and pumpkins). Cadotte died in 1837. Nearby, in an unmarked grave, lies his wife, Madeline, daughter of chief White Crane. It was for her the island was named.

Another stone marked the grave of Chief Buffalo. A year before he died in 1855, he signed the treaty by which the Ojibwa gave up claim to Madeline and agreed to move to mainland Wisconsin. When I visited, goods were spread out in front of the headstone: a deer antler lashed to a wooden staff, a feather trimmed with turquoise and red wool, pennies, blackberries and raspberries, a pouch of Half & Half tobacco, fresh flowers, and an Atlanta Braves baseball card. A hundred fifty years ago, Dakota scalps might have hung here as well.

Something had happened here in the days before the arrival of the white men, Warren wrote. Something evil. The old men he queried were reluctant to speak of it. But he detected the undercurrents of something horrid. Over time, Warren came to understand that the Ojibwa of *Moningwunakauning* had fallen under the sway of evil medicine men who practiced cannibalism. They were expert in the use of poison and would take revenge on other members of their tribe and serve the flesh of victims to their unknowing families. What circumstances caused these powerful people to turn to such evil? Warren asked. He never learned the answer. The wailing souls of the victims drove the Ojibwa from *Moningwunakauning* in terror, as if in shame over their own wickedness. The island was essentially abandoned until the appearance of the first French traders.

I sat on a wooden bench under a spreading oak and remembered my first visit to the island. Not far from this spot, I had sipped wine at a tony reception with some of the island's richest families. What a difference between the country club and this poor cemetery, where sumac and blue aster pressed in around the graves, as if waiting for any opportunity to rush in and claim the site. Odd, I thought, that the very people who colonized the islands and first found refuge here had, in effect, been exiled. It seemed their absence had opened a gulf as deep and wide as Superior itself. Across the road, a halyard blew against a steel mast. I listened to the steady clang. It seemed to be tolling for the dead, calling them home, home to the Apostles.

Over the years, I have revisited the islands. One day, on Sand Island, a flag hung at half-mast in front of Howard Palm's old cabin. His brother and sister-in-law, who worked as Park Service volunteers, said the man with the porcelain vulnerability had died.

Most recently, Susan and I had pulled into Bayfield, on the mainland, across the channel from La Pointe. Bayfield had done a better job than most

On one of several trips to the Apostles, Kate and I toured the Raspberry Island
Lighthouse.

towns around the lake cashing in on tourism while avoiding the most egre-
gious development. On Friday night, downtown was crawling with tourists.
Cars carried kayaks, canoes, and dirt bikes. Despite the crush of customers
and the ching-ching of cash registers, downtown made for a pleasant walk.
Old store facades fronted the streets. Victorian houses overlooked the lake.
Even the roads into town were blessedly free of franchises and cancerous
strip development. We had appetizers and beer at a restaurant before camping at Red Cliff, the local Ojibwa reservation.

The next morning, we rendezvoused with other kayakers on Stockton
Island. Smaller only than Madeline, Stockton supports one of the densest
populations of black bears in existence. The Stockton bears, like the caribou of the Slate Islands, are the runts of their species. Cubs average half the
size of mainland cubs, and females breed for the first time at a later age.

Kayakers explore the wave-hollowed excavations along the shore of Basswood
Island. Sandstone was mined from a quarry on the island during the late 1800s.

Stockton is also one of the most beautiful of the islands. A long sandy tombolo joins the island to what, five thousand years ago, was a second island and is now Presque Isle Point. Along the sandy shore, widely spaced red pines grow gnarled and stunted from the wind's constant abuse. In early August, blueberries grew, exuberant and dewy, the most prodigious I'd ever seen. With an open view among scattered trees and grassy dunes, Stockton presents the picture of verdant savanna, perhaps our species' original habitat. Was this Eden—an endless sand beach and unlimited blueberries?

That evening we gorged on potluck, including barbecued chicken and Susan's jumbo Cajun shrimp, carried frozen to the island. After dark, paddlers set out on Quarry Bay under the full moon. Sunday we paddled back down channels filled with bright, taut sails. I paddled with Susan, dreading the parting. And when it was finally time, we kissed and she paddled with

Paddlers approach Honeymoon Rock, at the north end of Basswood Island.

the others back to Red Cliff, while I headed south, alone again. I would see
her next week in Houghton, Michigan, 130 miles to the east.

The wind rose; the day turned humid and hazy. As the makings of a
thunderstorm appeared over the Bayfield peninsula, I pulled onto the public
beach at Madeline Island. I made the rounds—first to Tom's Burned Down
Café ("Tommy's playing softball") and then down to Joni's Beach (No Overnight Camping Permitted). I walked on to the marina, where cabin cruisers
and sailboats up to fifty feet filled the slips. I walked by the Indian cemetery,
but the iron fence was tied shut and a sign posted by the Bad River Indian
Reservation said the cemetery was closed. I sipped coffee at the Beach Club,
taking refuge from the threatening storm as I watched cars queue up for the
end-of-the-weekend ferry trip back to Bayfield. Ragtag and breezy with a
whiff of money—that was Madeline Island, and I liked it a lot.

By evening, the bad weather had passed. I paddled down the shore, past
the site of the old forts, and crossed the channel to Long Island, a delicate
curving finger of white sand, a barrier spit that all but seals off the opening
to Chequamegon Bay. As I paddled, I heard a roar—like that of the Canadian Pacific but louder. There were no trains in the area that I knew of. Ah,
but there, far off toward Washburn, was the rooster tail of a jet-boat, sharing decibels with people three miles in every direction. Its thunder echoed
off the hills. What kind of self-centered person runs one of those?

I passed down the beach past the Long Island light and a broken-down
dock. My map suggested the first several miles of Long Island belonged
to the National Park Service and the remainder to the Bad River Indian
Reservation. As far as I knew, I wasn't permitted by either to camp. So I paddled till sunset and then dragged my kayak across the sand beach. With no
one in sight, I set up my tent.

The beach was deliciously empty, just a sandbar with a scrubby topping
of hardwoods, jack pine, and tamarack. My tent was surrounded by nothing
at all except sand, odd pieces of driftwood, and tracks of gulls and small
mammals. In the gloaming, with the red sun on the hazy horizon, it was
one of the most desolate scenes I could imagine.

The rolling dunes of Long Island—perhaps this very place—had been
the site where Ojibwa warriors from La Pointe had ambushed a Dakota
raiding party that had trapped and killed two Ojibwa boys. "Over the
whole point of Shag-a-waum-ik-ong, are still strewn small particles of bone,
which are said to be the remains of the warriors who fell in this bloody

Forlorn Long Island is at times an island, at times a peninsula, depending on the deposition of sand.

fight," Warren wrote much later. In 1886, the three-masted schooner *Lucerne* cleared Long Island but soon disappeared in a winter storm. She was found washed up on this beach with three crewmen, who apparently climbed the masts to escape the icy waves, frozen stiff in the rigging.

Wasn't it ironic that the Apostles, a place of refuge, would provide me with so many stories of death? I supposed that the very notion of refuge suggests its opposite—that the world is a dangerous place. As the night grew darker, a galaxy of twinkling lights covered the hillside at Bayfield. My sand spit, with a clear view for miles, seemed lonelier than ever.

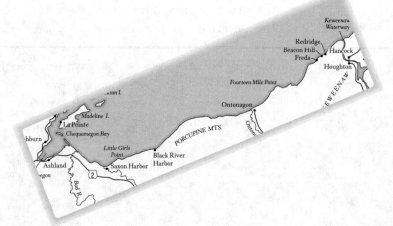

Keweenau
Waterway

Redridge
Beacon Hill   Hancock
Freda
Houghton

Fourteen Mile Point

Ontonagon

...ton I.

Madeline I.
La Pointe
Chequamegon Bay

hburn

PORCUPINE MTS.

Ontona...

KEWEENAW

Little Girls
Point   Black River
Ashland   Harbor
Saxon Harbor
...egon   2

Bad R.

CHAPTER 9

South Shore: Long Island to Houghton

I EMERGED FROM MY TENT to a kind of stunning solitude, surprised to awaken on the same desolate beach where I had fallen asleep. The sun rose red and hazy, and the air was thick.

That morning, I wanted to fish in Chequamegon Bay for smallmouth bass. But how was I to get into the bay? I had already paddled several miles down Long Island—too far to want to double back to the shipping channel. So after breakfast, I continued east down the long point, separated from the bay by only the thin strip of sand and a sorry fringe of trees and grass. My map showed a possible break in the spit, with the cryptic notation *Uncovers*. Apparently this was the area that, depending on the strength and direction of major storms, opened up to the lake or filled in with sand. Many times over the centuries Long Island had changed from island to peninsula to island again. But after a couple more miles of paddling, I failed to find a channel. At the moment, I guessed, the island was a peninsula. So when I saw a low swale, I landed and dragged my kayak across the sand to a broad marsh on the protected side of the barrier spit.

The wetland, formed in the soggy delta of the Kakagon and Bad Rivers, opened into the whole of Chequamegon Bay, which was warm and, compared with the clear empty water of Superior, as rich as a jungle. I waded out through loon shit and paddled through arrowhead and phragmites. Wild rice, though not yet ripe, dropped a few kernels as my kayak brushed by. Beaver sign was plentiful: severed limbs, stripped branches, chewed-off stumps. Frogs sang and red-winged blackbirds scolded as they clung to waving vegetation. As I followed a gentle current out into the bay, muck gave way to sand.

The warm, shallow confines of Chequamegon Bay support fish rarely found in the cold, open lake. Among these are smallmouth bass, including some real bruisers of five pounds. The log booms that supplied Ashland's sawmills leaked logs by the millions of board feet, many of which now lie on the bottom of the bay, providing attractive cover for the bass. I looked down at hundreds of them right now, crisscrossed on the bottom.

In recent years, enterprising divers began recovering these submerged logs for their value as timber. The logs were red oak, maple, birch, hemlock, cherry, and elm, slow growing, solid, and relatively free of knots. The logs were well preserved by Superior's icy waters, even though some of the trees began life more than five hundred years ago. Prized for furniture and musical instruments, with a quality no longer found in the cut-over forests of the Great Lakes, the logs fetched up to five hundred dollars apiece.

Not without complaints, however. Among those objecting was Roger LaPenter, a local fishing guide. I had fished with LaPenter before, cruising the bay in a wide boat built for fishing the flats in the Florida Keys. We would cast poppers and streamers to visible logs and fish. LaPenter worried that with fewer logs, there would be fewer bass.

I tried for those same fish today. I cast to logs sticking above the water and logs lying in piles on the bottom, but after an hour I had caught no bass. Well, that's the way bass are. So I began to look for a way back to the main lake.

Rather than backtrack up the marsh, I cut straight to the barrier spit and began dragging the fully loaded kayak three hundred yards over a double ridge of sand dunes, through what turned out to be some of the most profuse poison ivy I had ever seen. Which would come first: Keeling over from a heart attack in this heat? Or dying from a terminal itch in an unreachable spot inside my boat?

I continued eastward, down a shoreline I knew next to nothing about. There were few parks of consequence. It was not much discussed in travel guides. Hardly anyone I had talked to had paddled along it. Those who had, had told me nothing about it.

The peninsula joined seamlessly into the mainland, and a sand beach stretched ahead. As I approached Marble Point, red clay bluffs rose a hundred feet above the lake, a thin strand of sand at their base. Unlike Minnesota's North Shore, roads here visited the lake only briefly before they ducked back inland, and it was there I would see cabins or small groups of people along the beach. Many people were swimming—rare along the

Long beaches stretch eastward from the Apostles.

North Shore, but more common here in the sandy shallows, especially this year, when the water was far warmer than normal.

By late afternoon, the lake took on its look of liquid mercury. The shadow of the boat rippled like a dark flag along the sand bottom, and drops from my paddle made halos of shadow and light. It was that still.

About three dozen boats sat in Saxon Harbor, a quiet public marina. Nearly all were runabouts. Sailboats seemed to frequent the more fashionable—and frankly, more interesting—spots, such as the Apostles. I had a Coke at a bar up the road. The bar was decorated with fishing lures. I told the bartender I was kayaking. She was about my age, a bit heavy. I asked about the Montreal River. My charts didn't show it clearly.

"That's about three-quarters of a mile down the shore. You haven't missed it."

I mentioned that we used to run kayaks down the river when the water
was up. Rapids ran through a sheer conglomerate canyon with walls more
than a hundred feet high, one of the most dramatic in the Midwest, before
the river tumbled over a falls into Superior.

"Yeah, yeah, we took inner tubes down in the summer."

She surprised me; I didn't think she had it in her.

I wondered aloud whether I should move on or stay here.

"Well, you could make Little Girls Point. That's just a few miles up. They
have a nice city park right down by the water."

Perfect.

Between Saxon Harbor and Little Girls Point, the beach gave way suddenly to cliffs, which rose from the lake. Entranced by the color of the rock
in the late afternoon sunlight, I cruised within a paddle's length of the cliffs.
I studied the ripple marks of ancient beaches and the tiny plants attempting
to gain a foothold in the shaly crevices and indentations.

My heart jumped as I came upon a man and a woman sitting in a grotto
by the water. I could have touched them with my paddle.

"How did you get there?" I stammered.

They appeared as startled as I was. "We just walked along the edge."

It was only by luck we weren't thoroughly embarrassed, since they apparently believed they were as alone as I assumed I was.

As I rounded Little Girls Point, the cliffs gave way to another sand
beach. Though it was nearly dark, people continued to frolic in the water
and comb the beach at the local park. Two motorboats, one pulling a skier,
carved large wakes in the bay. I dragged my boat onto the beach and set
up my tent by some burned wood and beer cans. I hoped the party-goers
wouldn't return.

As I finished dinner, the stars appeared one by one, and the swimmers
vanished. I could barely see when two men and a boy strolled by. One of
the men explained that they camped here with their families to drive all-
terrain vehicles on the public forest land.

His companion and the young boy said little. The second man did not
seem to be curious about the kayak or my trip. When he spoke, he talked
only about ATVs.

But the first man seemed eager to talk. He asked about the kayak and
what I had seen. "It must really keep you in shape," he said, adding that he
would like to try it sometime. I sensed he had had his fill of off-roading.

Perhaps that was simple projection on my part, but he did say this: "My wife and I decided we're just going to sit on the beach, look at the lake and not do much of anything for four or five days." He said it as though he believed it would be a good thing to do.

Early the next morning I saw the man again, walking the beach alone. We said hi. I felt, both last night and this morning, that something weighed on him.

I walked across the road to investigate a sign that said "Indian Cemetery." A trail wound through a shadowed grove of old spruce, huge cedars, yellow birch, and—a sign I was gradually moving into an area of greater rainfall—hemlock. Ferns, wild ginger, and clintonia carpeted the ground. The trail led to a rickety fence of saplings, surrounding what appeared to be a grave, or several. Someone had laid white asters on the grave. A post, like a totem pole, stood nearby, with drawings of a fish, deer (or moose or caribou?), and perhaps a bear. All could be construed as totems of clans, images of which often marked Ojibwa graves, though I didn't know if that was the case here. The thought that life simply ends is too much for any culture to bear. At what early stage in our evolution did humans become blessed, or cursed, with this self-awareness? Graffiti had been carved into the pole. I was always quieted by these places and disheartened by the disrespect.

I had barely pushed off when a headwind began to rise. The shore became rockier, with fewer places to land. By midday a steady parade of whitecaps marched toward me from the northeast, so I decided to lay up at Black River Harbor. In the shelter of the twin breakwalls, I pulled up on a small beach, stripped down, washed and shaved, rinsed my clothes, and spread them out to dry.

I hiked to a large stone U.S. Forest Service shelter with picnic tables and a phone. I called Porcupine State Park, located a few miles down the shore. I was concerned about finding a campsite.

A woman said I could camp at the mouth of the Presque Isle River, Speaker Creek, Little Carp River, or Carp River. "You have to register in advance," she added.

"How do I do that?"

"Over the phone, with a credit card."

Once again, I was being asked for an itinerary. Not knowing how the wind might build or when it might die, I decided to skip the campsite.

Instead, I wandered past the marina to a long beach crowded with sun-bathers. Three-foot whitecaps crashed onto the sand. Kids played in the surf. One girl paddled a little blue recreational kayak. It bobbed in the waves as if to mock me.

I returned to my boat to find something for lunch. Suddenly a kayak appeared in the harbor. And what a kayak! It was a folding boat of some kind, low and lumpy in profile, like a U-boat. The paddler had a long beard and a striped long-john shirt. Wiry, with craggy features, he said his name was Norm Hopkins.

An impressive story unfolded. Last year he had paddled from Duluth up the Minnesota shore to Grand Marais. As he paddled, his wife walked the Superior Hiking Trail. Each evening, they would rendezvous at a site. Since Hopkins traveled the shorter distance each day, he set up camp and fixed dinner. Great deal for his wife, but Hopkins spent a lot of time waiting. No matter. He was hooked on the big lake and decided to finish it off this year. So nineteen days ago he set out from Grand Marais, heading north and east (paddling in the opposite direction I was). In that short time he had traversed the Canadian shore along the top of the lake, down the Pukaskwa, down the East Shore, across the narrows from Coppermine Point to White-fish Point (cutting off all of Whitefish Bay), and past the long beaches of Michigan to where we sat today. He had set a goal of forty miles a day and already was two days ahead of schedule. Today alone, setting out from the other side of Ontonagon, he had paddled more than forty miles, and it was still early afternoon. My best day was a paltry thirty-seven miles. Obviously he didn't let a few waves stand in his way. He figured he would make Duluth in four days.

He worked for a telecommunications firm in Rochester, Minnesota, and had two grown children. He had traveled extensively, including a long canoe trip down the Yukon, where he met several Germans paddling folding kayaks. He liked the portability of the boats. He bought one and set out on the Mississippi, starting at Lake Itasca (the headwaters) and paddling down through Minnesota deep into Iowa. He picked up the route again in Memphis and paddled all the way out the mouth of the river, poking around the little Cajun towns on the delta. "I'd ask them questions," he said. "I knew what they were going to say, but I just loved hearing them say it." Finally he paddled into Lake Pontchartrain to the New Orleans airport, where he disassembled the aluminum tubing that formed the skeleton of his kayak, packed the frame and rubber-and-fabric hull into a bag, and flew home.

On this trip, he had lived on a steady diet of dehydrated meals. I offered him pasta and red sauce with pepperoni.

"Do you like garlic?"

"Yeah, it would be pretty hard to name something I don't like."

"I had the feeling that anyone who's traveled a lot must like garlic."

At the Agawa pictographs, he said, he met a woman, also a kayaker, who suggested he take special note of a particular image, which was drawn by a shaman. She asked Hopkins if he had read *Deep Water Passage* by Ann Linnea. Subtitled *A Spiritual Journey at Midlife*, it is the autobiographical story of a wife and mother who gives the impression of being on the ragged edge, seeking a sea change in life. She sets out with a friend on a kayak trip around the lake. To many who have read it, it is not so much an exploration of the lake as it is a journey of self-absorption and mysticism. One night the spirit of a recently deceased friend appears in the author's tent. It seemed, said Hopkins, that the author had had trouble not only in circumnavigating the lake, but also in navigating life. The woman at the pictographs, he offered, "seemed to be in synch with Ann." She revered pictographs in a way that struck Hopkins as reflexive, adulatory, and, well, phony. "I'm sure she was wishing for some tobacco that she could sprinkle around the site," he said.

Talking to Hopkins, I began to question my own decision to take the lake in several trips instead of one. I said I wasn't sure I could stand being alone that long, that I would dash desperately toward home.

"That's what I'm doing," he said.

How did he make such mileage? He was on the lake every morning by six, he said, and he paddled until dark, camping wherever he happened to be.

After dinner, the wind began to die and the whitecaps disappeared. Hopkins asked about the shore to Little Girls Point.

Cliffy, I said. Not much for campsites.

Still, he said, he hated to let the last two hours of daylight go to waste. I gave him a half-dozen packets of coffee for the small thermos he kept in his cockpit. He packed up and disappeared around the breakwater.

Unlike Hopkins, I felt I had little to gain by setting out now. I wasn't sure if campsites were available farther along the shore. Besides, I was comfortable and, frankly, lazy. I found a ranger and asked if I could camp on the grass near the marina. He said camping wasn't allowed. So I waited until

dark, when everyone had left the beach. Then I set up my tent and went
to sleep.

Shamed by Hopkins's ambitious schedule and anxious to leave before someone spotted my camp, I rose early, struck the tent, fixed breakfast, and
pushed off. Six-forty. Hopkins had paddled three miles already.

Morning unfolded as a kind of dream, induced by two hours of steady
paddling before my first rest. After three minutes, I began paddling again.
Nudged along by a slight following breeze and mystery swells from the
west-northwest, I traveled well over four miles an hour. In my reverie, I
nearly ran over a large trout, cruising inexplicably at the surface.

Porcupine Mountains State Park, at sixty thousand acres one of the
largest protected areas along the southern shore, stretched twenty-one
miles, with soaring hills of hardwoods, hemlock, and pine. The shore consisted of a wonderful variety of rocks—at one point, gravel beach, at another, rounded sandstone cobbles, and at another, toothy slabs of sandstone
conglomerate. A pyramid island rose just off shore. On my map, it was
marked *rky*. Rocky? Or rookery? The rock was covered with cormorants,
gulls, and guano. Since the Apostle Islands, I had seen several bald eagles
along the shore. Just now two flushed from the trees. One headed for the
trees along shore, while the second sailed far out over the lake, where it descended to grab something from the water.

By early afternoon, I had traversed the entire park. Behind me, its hills
rose like Norman helmets. Now the highway ran along the shore, and
people appeared. Sunbathers and waders populated the beach at Union Bay.
At sleepy Silver City, where a Best Western sat along the highway, people
looked out at me and I at them, each without eyes for the other.

The sky was big and blue, the day languid, languorous, somnolent.
Creeks oozed from the boggy land, seeping through sandbars into the lake.
Kids swam, families lounged on the beach. Cottages bravely fronted the
open lake. As the day grew late, I spotted the smokestack at Ontonagon.
Soon I saw the breakwater, but, like a mirage, it seemed to loom forever in
the distance. It turned out to be nearly a half mile in length. I had been baffled by the scale of it. The small white objects floating near the opening,
which I took at first to be gulls, were in fact fishing boats. As I passed the
harbor entrance, I heard the steady groan of the paper mill. A group on the

beach pointed out the location of the public campground and, with the sun about to set, I landed.

Ontonagon was a lumber town and a natural harbor. The area is most notable for the Ontonagon Boulder, a nugget of almost pure copper weighing nearly two tons discovered in the bed of the Ontonagon River. Negotiated away from a local Ojibwa chief for cloth, tobacco, and earrings, it was hauled away on a temporary railroad track and displayed briefly in Detroit before the federal government claimed it and sent it to the Smithsonian.

At the moment, however, I was interested in none of that. I wanted a pasty. *Pasty*, of course, is not pronounced *pay*-sty. That would be found on the nipple of an exotic dancer. I was looking for a *past*-y, which is a meat and vegetable pie brought to the Upper Peninsula by Cornish miners.

I hiked over to the park office, set amid a knot of RVs, trucks, and tents. I explained to the teenager there that I had just paddled from Black River (I couldn't resist the opportunity to brag) and was exhausted. Did he have any sites near the lake?

"Nope. All taken."

Suddenly a boy about eight popped up in the back of a pickup.

"Did you come in that?" he asked, pointing to a nearby toy raft. I ignored him for the moment.

"Would it be possible to camp in the picnic area? I have my boat there. I'd like to stay near my boat."

"Yeah, you can camp in the picnic area," the boy said. "You can camp right on the beach."

"Yeah, I suppose you can," said the teenager.

"I hear there's a place in town that makes really good pasties."

"Syl's!" the little kid said.

"Yeah, Syl's," the teenager said.

"How do you know so much?" I asked the kid.

"My, uh—"

"Cousin," the teenager said.

"Cousin," the kid said. "My cousin used to work at Syl's."

So I trudged back to the kayak, pulled out gear, and fumbled with the poles and fabric until the tent stood at the edge of a grove of pines, looking out toward the red sun setting in a puddle of mercury. It was a beautiful site, even if it was on the edge of town. Then, taking a headlamp, I walked downtown to find Syl's and a couple of pasties. By my reckoning of my charts, I had paddled forty-six miles, and by the time I would get back to bed, I would have walked four more.

Late in the morning, I landed in the shelter of Fourteen Mile Point, where a reef of red sandstone broke the surf and a brick lighthouse stood on the edge of the woods, fifty yards from shore, amid blueberries, birch, and fire-weed. The windows were missing, as was most of the roof. Bricks had fallen from crumbled mortar. Graffiti marked the walls, despite this handwritten note: "Please respect our Fourteen Mile Point Light Station. Your help in preventing further damage to these buildings is needed." If the lighthouse were to be preserved, it would have to happen in a hurry, or the owner would soon be in the used brick business.

All of Lake Superior's lighthouses, once manned by keepers and their families, have been deactivated or converted to automated operation. Some have been dismantled, some have been purchased by public agencies to be operated as historical displays, and others have been sold to be converted to bed and breakfasts. Fourteen Mile Point, decommissioned in 1934, is none of the above. According to Wes Oleszewski in *Great Lakes Lighthouses—American and Canadian*, "Of all the abandoned lights on Lake Superior, this one appears as the most hopeless. The site's location and the isolation of the wooded shore has not spared it from vandals. The buildings are rapidly being ravaged, and there's little hope of their preservation. In July of 1984, some mindless vandals set the lighthouse afire. Now only a shell remains. This is a sad place." *A Traveler's Guide to the 116 Michigan Lighthouses* was more discouraging: "We do not recommend visiting this light."

I, on the other hand, rather liked it the way it was. The crumbling walls provided interesting nooks and crannies. The vertical reach of a lighthouse, like the steeple of a church or the vaulted ceiling of a cathedral, suggests a link to the spiritual. And this one seemed positively transcendent. I felt as though I were touring an ancient religious shrine, with the sight lines of an M. C. Escher drawing—empty windows visible through windows, visible through windows, a view within a view, and a clear view of the light tower by way of the missing lower roof. Unfortunately, this lighthouse didn't have much of a future, except as a vivid demonstration of entropy.

Around a point of red sandstone lay the long beach of Misery Bay. The name derives from the deprivations of traders who stayed there. I could

The Fourteen Mile Point Lighthouse: "This is a sad place."

have understood better if they had called it Poverty Bay, for the poverty of cold, the poverty of biting insects, the poverty of anything unpleasant. Hiking the old trails that ran through a clearing, I found assorted stone-filled depressions, suggesting the foundations of old buildings, and abundant trees with tart ripe apples. Someone had carved a memorial into a sandstone ledge along shore, accompanied by the petroglyph of a guitar: Buddy Lindgren, 6-4-38 to 6-3-86.

Through the day, I paddled away from the wind. Each point provided a little more shelter, so that I was carried along on gentle waves. But late in the afternoon as I approached Rockhouse Point, the shoreline swept northward in a butt of land that caught the eastward-marching waves nearly straight on. At the same time, the shore rose abruptly from the lake in a line of red cliffs—strikingly beautiful cliffs in the late afternoon sun. The waves reflected off the rock, intercepting incoming waves and producing dancing pyramids of water. Nearing Rockhouse Point, I looked up and saw dancing pyramids by the thousands.

As I paddled alone, I often lost perspective. Every lean became a tip, every tip became a brace with my paddle, every brace nearly a capsize and the need to roll, every roll potentially failing. The short version of this: every tip was life-threatening. My fear was irrational, but real. And as I turned away from the cliffs, moving gradually farther into the lake, I tried hard to keep from unraveling. Stay centered. Stay calm. Don't look at all the waves at once. Paddling in these waves took little skill; it was almost entirely a mental game.

Finally I saw a break in the rocks and a long beach of dark sand and, beyond that, more cliffs as far as I could see. I could land on this beach, at what appeared to be the mouth of the Graveraet River. But as I neared shore, damn, I saw little cabins tucked into the woods beyond the beach. Then as I drew closer to shore, I saw an umbrella and a man back by the trees. I shouted and waved. He walked down to shore, a big man with a ponytail and a full beard. I found a biker hangout. No, a young girl walked with him.

As I bobbed in the waves just beyond the surf line, I shouted: "The waves are bad off the cliffs. It's getting late. I don't want to round any more cliffs." So far as I could tell from my map, the town of Freda lay near the end of the beach.

"Is there anyplace to camp in Freda?"

"No, no, there's not anyplace to land up there."

"Would it be possible to camp along this beach?"

"It's my wife's family's property. If it's all right with her, it's all right with me."

By now a blond woman had appeared on the shore. "Absolutely," she said. "Camp on the beach. We've got more than a thousand feet. Set up your tent anywhere you want to."

The beach was deep, stretching perhaps seventy-five yards back from the lake. Huge chunks of driftwood—bolts of pulpwood and entire trees stripped down to gray bones—had been tossed up onto the sand. I had just put up the tent and set my teapot on the stove when the man and his daughter came back down to the beach with a paper plate covered with aluminum foil. "Don't heat up too much water," he said. "We've got dinner for you. You came just in time."

Their names were Brad and Anna Liisa Schourek and this was their summer house. Brad said his wife, Kris, grew up nearby. Her father worked in the stamp mill in Freda, where copper ore from the Champion Mine was crushed and concentrated; the dark waste rock, the so-called stampings, spewed into the lake, covering the beaches with coarse, dark sand.

"When we got married fifteen years ago, it was black," Brad said.

"They call it black sand, but it's really kind of gray," Anna Liisa added.

"But it's getting lighter all the time as other sand gets mixed in."

Brad grew up near Chicago and came to the Upper Peninsula to attend Michigan Technological University in Houghton. "But like a lot of Techies, I never moved away," he said. "It's a little too nice a place to go to school." Unable to find a job in his field, geology, he became a carpenter instead. "I think it's more important to live in a place I like and take whatever work I can find," he said.

They left me to eat dinner. I peeled back the foil: a heaping plate of fresh cucumbers, coleslaw with purple and green cabbage, saffron rice, grilled chicken, and a roll. I wolfed it down. If only there had been more. As I sat by my tent eating, I looked out to the cliffs I had rounded off to the left, and the cliffs of Freda and the smokestack of the old mill off in the other direction. Surf crashed on the sand as the sun set over the lake.

After dark, the Schoureks built a bonfire up the beach and invited me to join. As Anna Liisa and her older sister, Sylvia, roasted marshmallows, I talked to Kris. She taught high-school biology in Houghton. She had done

much of her biology fieldwork on Isle Royale. She was also a painter and a
nature and wildlife photographer, using the name Kris Raisanen Schourek.
Some of her best-known photographs are of gray wolves, she said, mostly
of a captive pack that used to be located near Negaunee. Attitudes toward
wolves had changed from twenty years ago, she said, when "people were
shooting wolves just to shoot wolves. There aren't nearly as many dairy
farmers up here now." The wolf population in the Upper Peninsula had
grown substantially since the wolf became protected under the federal Endangered Species Act—to the point, in fact, where the wolf would soon be
taken off the list of endangered species. Still, Kris had detected relatively
little wolf hatred. With several colleges on the peninsula, she said, "we have
a fairly well-educated group of people."

Kris had an icy blond complexion and a broad face not inconsistent
with her heritage. Her grandparents all came from Finland, she said, as did
many settlers in the area. She lived a year in Finland, northeast of Helsinki
in the country's lake region. She spoke Finnish and had researched some of
the old Finnish homesteads in the area. "I can't believe the places they built,
the places they lived in," she said. "I can't believe the way they would eke
out a living." They typically kept a few cows and chickens and cut hay from
the low meadows. "I found little homesteads with fenceposts in cedar
swamps," she said. "You'd have to take a four-wheeler out there now."

Her father was born and raised in nearby Redridge. He rented a one-
hundred-foot-square lot along the beach from the mill and built his first
house on skids so it could be moved if he lost the lease. That house is now
the sauna. When the plant closed in 1967, the mill sold off land and he
bought the lake frontage. At the time the mill closed, Kris said, houses in
mining towns sold for one hundred dollars. The mining company would
pay fifty dollars if the owner would tear down the house and take the materials elsewhere. "We did that to build our place here," Kris said. Nearby
Beacon Hill became a popular retreat for hippies and other back-to-the-
landers who moved into the hundred-dollar houses, despite the lack of utili-
ties. Since then, the mining towns of Freda, Beacon Hill, and Redridge have
become bedroom communities for Houghton.

All the copper mines have closed. The White Pine Mine near Ontonagon, the last to operate, ended production in 1995. A recent proposal to re-
open the White Pine, using sulfuric acid pumped underground to extract
the remaining copper, caused an uproar, both from environmentalists and

the local Ojibwa. "The Native Americans were really the heroes in that fight," Kris said. "They said, 'No way are you going to take trains filled with sulfuric acid across our land.'"

After an hour of talk, I gathered up my thermos and headlamp and started back toward my tent. Kris offered the sauna, which was just now getting warm, but I didn't want to intrude any further and said it was getting late.

"We're glad you stopped by—that you picked our beach to land on," Kris said.

"That was my good luck."

"Do you know Tom Waters?" she asked out of nowhere. Waters, a fisheries professor from the Twin Cities, had written books about Lake Superior and Minnesota streams.

"I've fished with Tom Waters."

"Oh my gosh. He's married to my cousin. If you say you were on the Freda Beach, he would know exactly what you meant."

In my tent I listened to the surf and watched silent far-off flashes of lightning. A thousand stars glimmered outside my door. Not a single electric light shone along two miles of open beach. I could see a faint glow in the northeast toward Redridge.

I had asked Kris about the condition of the shoreline from Redridge to the entrance to the ship canal to Houghton. "It can't be more than a couple of miles," she said. In fact, it was much farther, unless my navigational maps were wrong by a factor of four. I have found that locals often have a wildly distorted sense of distance. What seems a short way—a few minutes to Houghton by car—would take me most of a day. Which shows, I suppose, both the value and the shortcomings of paddling a kayak around Superior.

The next morning the breakers crashed onto the beach, bigger than ever. I had a day and a half to make Houghton, so I decided to skip paddling and explore the old mill towns.

I walked up the beach road, a simple bulldozer swath through the maple and thimbleberries. I soon reached the magnificent stack of the old stamping mill. The concrete cylinder, more than two hundred feet tall, had begun to crack. At the base of the crumbling stack sat a trailer. I wondered if the owner had given any thought to moving, especially when the wind blew strong off the lake.

The road opened onto a wasteland of concrete where the mill once

The smokestack from the stamping mill at Freda recalls a time of industry, picnics in the park, and black sand beaches.

stood. The Champion Mill, as it was known, was built between 1901 and 1903 to process ore shipped from the Champion Mine in Painesdale, ten miles inland. Ore, delivered by train, was crushed (stamped), pulverized, and separated into waste and a slurry of 40 percent pure copper. The concentrated ore was shipped by train back inland to smelters near Houghton; the tailings were flushed into the lake. After the best ore played out, the Champion Mine closed. At the same time, the federal government threatened to put an end to the dumping of tailings. The day the Champion Mill closed, Ray Durocher, the master mechanic, turned on the mill's siren, according to local historian Clarence J. Monette. "Usually it was the morning call to work," said Monette, "but this time, residents came out on their porches and saluted and wept as the old mill ground to a halt, and an eerie silence crept over the town site."

The buildings, including the mill, were torn down and hauled away, leaving foundations and rubble. There was the burned-out hulk of a car and the sound of wind and beer cans blowing across the concrete.

The town of Freda was a weedy place, perched above the mill site on the sandstone cliffs, as unapproachable from the lake as a castle. Lake access wasn't important, I guess, only that the mill have a source of water and a place to dump its tailings. Front and center in town was the Superior View Restaurant, clad in weathered clapboard. In fact, it had once been the office of the stamping mill. A sign said it was for sale. Another said it was closed till noon.

Nearby was a "roll of honor" of war dead. With a few exceptions, I might have been reading this in Finland: Melvin Raisanen; Arvo Raisanen; Eino, Uno, Veikko, Wilho, and Wiljo Asiala. Eino Asiala, Oliver Asiala, Onnie Asiala, Veikko Asiala. Wilho Asiala, Veikko Asiala, Carlo Raisanen, Eion Raisanen. Many Rajalas. Honkanen, Hiltunen, Hakala, Hannula, Hautala, Heltunen, Puumala, Hyttinen, Karkkainen.

I walked down the highway a mile to Beacon Hill, another fallow place with willows, old apple trees, and chokecherries. Trails into the woods led to abandoned cars and even an abandoned milk truck. Beacon Hill seems to have reached an advanced entropy, ready to fall into complete disassociation. Houses were abandoned, and others seemed about to be abandoned. Others should have been abandoned. Woodpiles were scattered and weeds grew up everywhere, though I saw a path mowed to a sauna.

As I walked down the road toward Redridge, two miles away, an old maroon Chevy passed. Its brake lights lit up.

"Where you going?"

I climbed in, kicking the two Old Milwaukee empties to the side. The driver, small and fat, wore no shirt. He had scraggly whiskers and heavy black glasses. Immediately he began to talk about the weather. "Without this wind it would be muggy," he said.

Then he stopped.

"This is Redridge?"

"This is it. You're looking at it."

The old school had been converted to a house. The Finnish Evangelical Lutheran Church (which, according to a photograph, was in good repair as recently as 1983) stood vacant with an open door and broken windows. I

The Finnish Evangelical Lutheran Church stands in downtown Redridge.

found my way down to a second stack, the location of the stamp mill for the Baltic Mine. Five mills operated at various times along this short stretch of beach, each stamping hundreds of tons of rock a day and transforming the sand beaches into coarse black tailings. The life of the mills, and the mines they served, was short. Most folded by the 1920s. They operated a single generation, but left a scar on shore still obvious nearly eighty years later. I searched through the sand and concrete and found broken clay pigeons, shotgun shells, beer bottles, and the charred remains of old campfires. It seemed only right that there should be some law of proportionality: that the benefit should last as long as the damage. But that, I knew, was an impractical, romantic notion.

Walking the highway back to Freda, I heard a car behind me and stuck out my thumb. They were two old guys in a light blue Mercury, pulling a boat and trailer.

"Where're you going?"

"To Freda, to the restaurant there."

"Oh, we're going to Freda, too."

"You from around here?"

"I've got a place down in Portage," the driver said. His name was Wilbert Lund. His friend's name was Ernie. But at the moment, they were going to family property, where Lund had grown up, on the beach past Freda, at the mouth of the Graveraet River.

"You know we've got this boat on the back," Wilbert said. "It's fiberglass. It's kind of heavy. We wouldn't mind having a hand with it."

"Sure, no problem."

We drove down the hill at Freda onto the dirt road that ran along the beach. Lund said the Copper Range Railroad ran along the bluff. Before World War I, the railroad would carry passengers to Houghton for a dime apiece. People would pile off the train and walk down the bluff for picnics at Freda Park, which had a pavilion with a hardwood dance floor where an orchestra would play. I wouldn't have known. All obvious traces of the park were gone.

We pulled up to Lund's cabin at the river mouth. "It's a choice piece of property," Lund said. "It has both the river and the lake." The Graveraet River was named for a trader, shot to death by one of his voyageurs. Today it sustains runs of coho and steelhead. At streamside sat a vertical-log sauna that Lund and his father built from eight-foot bolts of pulpwood collected from the beach.

"Sixty years," Lund said, "still standing." His name, he said, was Finnish. Finns would write it *Lunde*. In this country, his family removed the *e*. "Now it's a Swedish name."

Lund wanted the boat stored upside down, next to the sauna. We slid the boat off the trailer, balancing it on a timber so that we could spin the bow toward the river. We turned it over and then tried to move it the final couple of feet into position. It was just a small runabout, but it must have weighed four hundred pounds. We strained and grunted. Lund was a little crippled in the legs, and I could not lift an end by myself. It was only when Ernie put his broad back into it that the boat moved.

"You wouldn't think it would weigh so much," Ernie said.

Right. I tried to imagine the conversation between Lund and Ernie as they slowed down to pick me up: *There's a young guy. Kind of skinny but looks pretty strong.*

With the boat off the trailer, I noticed Lund's license plates: Ex-POW.

"Did you serve in Europe or Asia?"

"In Europe. I flew B-17s. Mine was a sad story. When I was over there, twenty-five missions was considered your tour of duty. I had twenty-one in when they came to us and said, 'We've got fighter cover for you all the way. Now you have to fly thirty missions.' I don't know if that was official or not, but I got shot down on my twenty-sixth." He spent the rest of the war in a German prisoner-of-war camp. When he came home, they had logged the land across the river from his cabin.

Just before midnight, the wind rose and the crash of the surf grew louder. I awoke and saw the threatening whiteness of waves outside the tent door. I had guyed the tent to the kayak to hold it against the wind, and I imagined the kayak and the tent rolling in the surf together. I took a headlamp and walked around the beach to scout out new places for my tent. I put the pots and pans in the kayak. Now, if it became necessary, I could pull the kayak and the tent in two movements up to the next ridge. Meanwhile, until the water lapped at the tent door, I would try to sleep. Each breaking wave sounded like a train wreck.

By morning, the front had passed, bringing cold air. My feet felt like a bird's: bony, bloodless, cold as stone. But the waves had begun to subside and grow round. By midmorning I launched and paddled along the cliffs at Freda and Redridge, staying far out on the lake to avoid the reflection waves.

I soon covered the twelve miles to the entrance to the Keweenaw Waterway. The channel had been dredged from the natural waterways (including Portage Lake) that Indians and voyageurs followed to cut across the finger of the Keweenaw Peninsula at the middle joint. As I neared the entrance I saw a large ship, far off to the north. For a few minutes I thought I might enter the waterway well ahead of it. But as if to illustrate how difficult it is to estimate speeds and distances over open water, the ship closed the gap and entered the waterway at least a half mile ahead of me. It was the *Ranger III*, arriving from Isle Royale. Despite its size, it glided into the canal as quietly as a cloud.

Moments later, from nowhere, came a hammering buzz. A Jet Ski appeared over the horizon and followed the *Ranger III*. It seemed ironic that a boat designed to carry one person should make so much more noise than the largest vessel the National Park Service owns, designed to carry 125.

Once inside the canal, I sped past beachfront homes, trailers, and fishing boats. The Jet Skis were abundant—like mosquitoes—racing from one end of the canal to the other. I was the only human-powered craft on the water. When I reached Houghton, Susan was waiting for me in a park that was a knot of activity, with reunions, swarms of children, and Jet Ski gatherings. I tried not to let my crankiness show. In fact, one group of skiers helped me carry my fully loaded kayak up to the car.

"And they say people from Detroit aren't nice," said one woman. Moments later, a woman in the group, who had been doting over a baby, carried the child to a car and handed it to the driver, apparently her husband. Then she walked around, climbed in the other side, shut the door, and shouted, "Shut the fuck up, just shut the fuck up!"

My trip had been lonely and thoroughly satisfying, but the canal was a drag, and I was glad to be done with it.

CHAPTER 10

Keweenaw Peninsula:
Houghton to Marquette

HOUGHTON WAS ABUNDANTLY industrial. But that is the first impression of any city you first see from a working waterway. Minneapolis, Manhattan, Houghton—from the water, they all look like the backside of a factory.

Once we loaded the boats and drove around, I saw a town that was historic and picturesque, its downtown streets filled with tourists. Many of the old buildings along the waterfront had been reclaimed. On the hill above downtown stood the Houghton County Courthouse, built in 1887. It had a copper roof and sandstone trim, reflecting, according to a sign, "opulent high Victorian design." The stone was striped like revel ice cream. Sharing the hill was the Richardsonian Romanesque Grace United Methodist Church and St. Ignatius Loyola Church. The original St. Ignatius was dedicated in 1859 by Frederick Baraga, the so-called snowshoe priest of Lake Superior. The present church was completed in 1902. Its sandstone facades and stained glass windows were encased by an addition with the windows of a modern office building, as though the stained glass windows were butterflies under glass.

The hills were steep, steeper it seemed than those of Duluth. I couldn't imagine how you would begin to climb them in winter, especially a Keweenaw winter, when the warm, moist lake winds dump more than three hundred inches of snow on the town. The magnitude of that statistic had never impressed me until an acquaintance who had grown up in Houghton showed me snapshots: sidewalks and driveways were canyons of snow. A sign on a telephone pole marked the record snowfall. The sign was more than twenty feet off the ground.

Susan and I intended to paddle from the entrance to the Keweenaw

Waterway (where the *Ranger III* had cut in front of me) up the raw western shore of the peninsula as it curves into the middle of Superior, around the exposed tip (like a frostbitten nose in a bitter wind), down the concave eastern shore, and then over the hump of the Huron Mountains eastward to Marquette, the largest city in Michigan's Upper Peninsula. The route was deceptively long—about 180 miles. I didn't know what kind of shore we would find, but considering the exposure to waves, I suspected cliffs, rocks, and few places to take shelter.

But first things first. We needed to arrange a car shuttle. Through friends of friends, we had located two young women willing to drop us off and drive our car back to Marquette, where it would be waiting for us at the end of the trip. So that night we drove the so-called highways of the Upper Peninsula to get the girls.

Residents of the Upper Peninsula call themselves "Yoopers," as much in self-deprecating humor as in boastful independence. Talk of declaring the U.P. the fifty-first state shouldn't be taken too seriously, but it does suggest the alienation of a region that lies as far as four hundred miles from the capital in Lansing. Most Yoopers feel they have nothing in common with, say, residents of Detroit. "It's an edgy place," wrote John G. Mitchell in *Audubon* magazine. "I mean, in the sense that it still hangs on out there like a rawhide flap of the old frontier, outposted from the swirl of mainstream America."

The U.P. has escaped many of the amenities of the late twentieth century, including modern highways. John Voelker, a Yooper, former Michigan supreme court justice, and author of *Anatomy of a Murder*, wrote, "The best thing that could happen to the U.P. would be for someone to bomb the bridge." He meant the spectacular bridge crossing the Straits of Mackinac, joining downstate with the Upper Peninsula. With attitudes like that, you can hardly blame the feds for not building freeways. During the evening, we rolled down a narrow, curvy, and very dark two-lane highway, pushed to the shoulder by the onward rush of trucks overloaded with pulpwood. There were a few bright SuperAmericas and Hardees, but mostly we saw dimly lit, little, never-heard-of places, like the Beefaroo Restaurant and the Imperial Hotel on the outskirts of Marquette, where we stopped for the night, exhausted.

Our drivers had to be back home at some ridiculous hour to go to work. So, still exhausted, we picked them up before daybreak. Their names were Aria and Misty, aged sixteen and nineteen. I had trouble telling them apart, which I attributed to several factors: it was dark, they sat in the back, I was barely conscious, and both had similar multiple body piercings.

As we drove back toward Houghton, they talked about music. One said she liked Hanson, the teenybopper heartthrobs of the moment. Hanson was big with nine-year-olds, I thought, not with someone old enough to drive our car.

"They're so smart," she said. "They wrote a song that was, like, about Einstein and the relationship between, uh, you know, his theory of, uh, something being, uh, turned into something or related like, uh, you know, it's early in the morning."

We drove through Houghton and Hancock. To avoid having to paddle through the Keweenaw Waterway, we drove to a county park near the entrance to the canal. Aria and Misty were in a hurry, so we unloaded the boats and threw our gear into a pile. As the car disappeared up the road, I watched anxiously, hoping the huge pile of gear included everything we would need for the next week and that somehow it would all fit in our two small boats.

We dragged the boats and gear to the beach and loaded up. The boats seemed full—as though we had everything we needed. We launched with a brisk wind building at our backs. We made great time, pushed up the peninsula by two-foot swells. Soon they were three-foot waves. Then four-foot. The waves were big and sloshy, breaking occasionally and shoving the boats forward. Susan disappeared in the troughs. Every once in a while the entire horizon would vanish behind a wall of rapidly receding water. I began looking anxiously toward shore for a sheltered beach on which to land.

When landing in surf, you try to catch a large wave and surf it far onto the beach, beyond the reach of the waves that follow. That's the theory. My wave deflated, stranding me in the surf zone. Succeeding waves plowed into my boat, turned me sideways, and crashed over the deck. Attempting to get out of the boat, I threw my paddle up on the beach. That was unfortunate. The next wave floated me up and then sucked me back into the surf. Still sitting in the boat, I tried clawing up the gravel ridge with my bare fingers. I bailed out of the boat, tumbled into the surf, and dragged the boat up onto the beach. Susan, meanwhile, calmly drifted in. When she reached shore, I simply reached out and pulled her up on the gravel.

Eating salami and oranges, we waited for the wind to die. This was not good. With only a week to cover 180 miles, we couldn't afford many weather days. If we could make Sevenmile Point, just three or four miles away, we could turn south just enough to find shelter from the waves for the rest of the day. As I ruminated on our bad luck, Susan and I spotted the glint of paddles in the distance. Someone was following us up the shore. My god! It was a canoe. Just a plain old canoe with a woman in the bow and a man in the stern. We watched it creep by. I didn't wave; I figured they would be too preoccupied, or terrified, to wave back. They finally disappeared up the shore. A canoe! Suddenly, the waves didn't look so big. Both encouraged and shamed, we finished lunch and launched into the waves, staying just out from the surf zone, taking what shelter we could from the shore. The next point, small though it was, forced us into the larger waves again. We saw the canoe again, this time coming back.

"Are you OK?" I yelled as we passed.

"Yes," said the man in the back. "Are you?"

They carried no gear to speak of. They were simply out for a spin. The guy seemed to be enjoying himself; I wasn't so sure about the woman in the bow.

Rounding Sevenmile, we left the largest waves behind. At Fivemile Point, we stopped at a square lighthouse of yellow brick. It had been converted to a bed-and-breakfast, but no one was home, so we pushed on. Sand dunes along the shore turned to cliffs. The small town of Eagle River had a maritime look. I would have loved to stop, but the weather report said the wind would be shifting to the north tomorrow. I wanted, if possible, to round Keweenaw Point—the very tip of the peninsula—by then.

We stopped at a sandy bay, where the coastal highway ran along the shore. As we snacked, a truck stopped and, right behind it, a four-wheel-drive. Brad and Kris Schourek and the girls stepped out. They had been driving back from an art show in Copper Harbor, where Kris had exhibited her photography. What was the chance that four of the very few people I knew on the Upper Peninsula would drive by during the twenty minutes of the day that we spent near the highway? After the Schoureks left, Susan asked what I made of such coincidences. I confessed I didn't make anything of them; I was simply astounded.

The town of Eagle Harbor was arrayed around a natural harbor with a narrow opening, complicated by rocks and rock cribs. A marina and the former U.S. Lifesaving Station sat at the east end, the lighthouse and town at the other. When we arrived at the marina, no one was around. We planned

An old lifeboat sits outside the Sand Hills Light, now a bed-and-breakfast, on Fivemile Point.

to set our tent in a grassy clearing, but as we unpacked, we noticed a sign: "No camping except in designated sites." There were no designated sites that we could see. In fact, all we could see with any bearing on the matter was a second, smaller sign that said "No camping." So we decided to walk into town for dinner and come back to the marina after dark to set up camp. No adult, at least no one my age, should have to skulk around like this, but I found myself doing it all the time.

In town, the homes and few commercial buildings, mostly of white clapboard, projected a maritime feel, as though they faced the Atlantic. A block off the waterfront sat the Eagle Harbor Store, established in 1859, the oldest store in Copper Country, according to a sign. The store was closed. So was the only restaurant we saw.

"It's very hard coming the back way into a town," Susan said. She was right. Tourist businesses are built to greet you as you approach from the highway. Arriving by water, you simply show up, like an unexpected guest.

We asked around and found the Eagle Harbor Inn on a hill overlooking town. It was dark by the time we finished dinner and walked back to the boats. The beam from the harbor light swept through the trees along the waterfront. A terrific wind blew. Lightning flashed in the distance. Fumbling in the dark and wind, we set the tent at the edge of the clearing by the marina, near the No Camping sign. We spent the night hoping that the stakes would hold against the storm, that the tall white pines would not fall on the tent, and that no one with any authority would come and tell us to move.

In the morning, endless formations of wild white waves marched into the harbor, thrashed the rocks, and ricocheted about the shoals.

Susan found me by the shore.

"That's not even borderline for me."

Nor for me. For that reason, I felt no anxiety, no ambivalence. There was no decision to make: the lake was horrid.

I hoped the wind would give us squatter's rights in the no-camping zone. This was a harbor of refuge, after all.

We made breakfast, grabbed a few things, and walked again toward town. Straightaway we saw the North Winds Bookstore, a two-story stucco house with a big front porch tucked in the woods. The titles were tilted strongly toward nature, travel, Indians, history, and the Great Lakes. They had two recent photo books about kayaking around Superior, Craig Black-lock's *The Lake Superior Images,* and Gary and Joanie McGuffin's *Superior: Journeys on an Inland Sea.* They made an interesting contrast. The McGuffins' book, to its credit, showed people on the lake—though there was too much of Joanie in brand-new outdoor gear. Blacklock's photographs were lush and artful, but they showed no human signs at all, reinforcing the fallacy that Superior is an unpeopled wilderness. In fact, the lake had scarcely emerged from the glaciers before humans began to swarm along its shores.

The North Winds specialized in hard-to-find Great Lakes titles, said the owners, Patricia and John Van Pelt. "What's the point in carrying things that you could find at the mall?" John said. "People aren't going to come up here for them. Word-of-mouth is important. Readers do find us." The bookstore seemed to me a wonderful retreat against the long winters and the isolation that comes with twenty feet of snow on the shore of Superior. I imagined that in such a setting, I might be able to finish the reading stacked up at my bedside.

In town, we saw where Horace Greeley landed on 15 June 1847, break-ing through a skim of ice to reach shore. We found, tucked amid a grove of trees, Holy Redeemer Church, yet another parish established by the ubiqui-tous Father Baraga. We toured the lighthouse (home of the Keweenaw County Historical Society) and looked at exhibits in a nearby building about the U.S. Lifesaving Station, established in 1912. Rescue crews launched oar-powered surf boats and a thirty-six-foot lifeboat in pounding waves to snatch survivors from foundering wrecks. The boats were decked and sealed against the weather, as watertight as a barrel. In training, the crew stood on the rail of a surf boat, capsized it, and then rolled it upright, as if it were a kayak. Also on display was a seventeen-hundred-pound piece of "float cop-per," the native metal venerated by Indians and mined commercially in the mid-1800s. The irregular mass, the size of a tabletop, was so pure that when I rapped it with my knuckle, it rang nearly as clear and long as a bell.

During its heyday, Eagle Harbor had a population of a thousand, said the guide at the lighthouse. But these days, during the long winters, the number dwindles to twenty-six. Because of its vacant quaintness, Eagle Harbor was quickly becoming my favorite of the small, small towns I had encountered on Superior. The town struck me as a small version of Bayfield thirty years ago. The road winding along the shore up the peninsula—at least what little I had seen—showed none of the blight that had spread along Minnesota's North Shore and was creeping up the Bayfield Peninsula. How long would Eagle Harbor's charm last? Susan and I agreed we couldn't have picked a better place to be wind bound. Along the road, chokecherries and black cherries hung from the trees. The cherries were abundant, with thin skin, small pits, and the sweetest taste imaginable.

The next morning we beat laboriously against the wind. It howled in our faces. The boats seemed not to move. The paddles felt as though they were stuck in mud. What had happened to predominant westerlies? Out on the lake, a freighter passed. Unruffled by wind and waves, it seemed serenely rooted, more like an island than a ship, until it disappeared magically over the horizon. I fixed my sights on a house a mile down the shore and watched hopefully for signs it was getting closer. After perhaps two hours, we landed in a small conglomerate cove, where I worked on a knot in Susan's shoulders and she began to cry in frustration.

Through the afternoon, the wind continued. It screamed. It ripped. It thrashed. The tops of the waves churned and evaporated. The wind was a bully, pressing his face into yours. By some accounts, the voyageurs called the wind *La Vieille*—Old Woman Wind. If that is so, then Susan did them one better. "Fucking whore of a wind," she blurted out. Finally we saw the green light and white tower marking the entrance to Copper Harbor.

Like Eagle Harbor, Copper Harbor occupies a natural amygdaloid basin, nearly surrounded by rock, snug in almost any wind. It is far larger than the former, however, more than two miles long. And it made a much different first impression. Three big motels faced the water. Several other businesses sat along the waterfront. We landed near town and the municipal dock. We found a woman in a shop; out back was a stack of kayaks.

"Is there a place we can camp with the kayaks?" I asked the woman. She wore a bulky rag wool sweater, glasses, and (when I asked the question) a look of utter confusion

"Well, the campground is up there." She pointed vaguely. "Several blocks away."

"Is it a place accessible to the water?"

"What are you asking?"

"Is it a beach or a cliff?"

"Ummmm . . . "

Why was this so difficult? Sometimes conversations derail, and they might as well be trains for all the effort it takes to get them back on the tracks. I had assumed she had something to do with the mess of kayaks out back and would understand that we needed to camp near the water, but as I struggled to explain myself, I began to realize she had nothing at all to do with the kayaks and probably knew nothing about the needs of kayakers.

"We want to get our boats to the campground. We want to sleep next to our boats." I'm sure that sounded odd, if not actually perverse.

"Oh, it's away from the lake."

Finally she sent us down to the marina, at the far end of the harbor. There was a wharf where large boats could tie off, a boat ramp, a large parking lot, and a small store. But no campground. A woman staffed the store. Around dinnertime she locked up and drove off in, of all things, a silver Corvette. Then we promptly set up our tent between the store and the wharf, where it wasn't likely to be seen by a cop tooling through the parking lot.

I had become ever more amazed at the dinners Susan prepared. Last night, spicy sausage and red sauce on pasta that she had dehydrated at home before the trip. Tonight, a ground beef paprikash with fresh biscuits. What did I offer in return? Hiding our kayaks in the weeds and setting up our tent under cover of darkness. Stick with me, baby.

After dinner, we walked up the main road into town. A parade of cars, trucks, and motorcycles roared by, and dozens of cars were parked in a lot near the municipal dock. Much of this activity could be attributed to the traffic heading to Isle Royale National Park aboard the *Isle Royale Queen III*, which departed daily from the municipal dock, and also to U.S. Highway 41, which runs down the spine of the Keweenaw and ends at Copper Harbor. Copper Harbor reminded me of Minnesota's North Shore, with traffic, tourists, and trinkets. The Old Country Store with Gifts. The Gift Center with Moccasins. Minnetonka Motel. Shea's Gifts. Swede's Keweenaw Minerals.

"It's a good thing," Susan said, "we got wind bound in Eagle Harbor, instead of up here."

It was still early when we cleared the harbor, under the gaze of the brick lighthouse. We passed a shoreline of conglomerate cliffs, until, nearly at the end of the Keweenaw Peninsula, we paddled into an unusual cove, unlike anything I had seen on the lake. A break wall of conglomerate, barren except for a veneer of lichen, led us to a small gravel beach. Next we followed a "hallway" of conglomerate, barely wide enough to paddle through. Off to the right sat a snug little cove, perfectly sealed from winds from any direction.

"This is really beautiful."

"This is what I had hoped for," Susan said.

In the era of voyageurs, this tiny spot was known to canoemen throughout the lake. It was the perfect shelter for a canoe or rowboat rounding the exposed knob of the Keweenaw and encountering a headwind or sudden storm. "This is the finest harbor for small craft that I ever saw," wrote William Boutwell, who accompanied Henry Rowe Schoolcraft's 1832 expedition. "For safety, strength and beauty," he said, "nature has so far excelled all that art could have invented."

We paddled among stark islands of conglomerate, narrow channels,

This weather-tight cove at the tip of the Keweenaw Peninsula was well known to voyageurs and other long-ago Lake Superior travelers.

lines of outcrop, and gravel beaches. Tiny grottoes, topped by twisted red
pine, pocked the shore. The conglomerate was stark, nearly black but for
the dusting of orange lichens. We scared a merlin off a bare rock. It flew
into the sunlight. Then an adult bald eagle flew out of a red pine. It banked
and soared back toward Copper Harbor.

"Do you like hanging out with me?" I asked.

"Are you taking credit for this?"

"I suppose if I take credit for this, I have to take blame for the wind."

"I was about to say—"

Through the night the wind had dropped. It was rising again, according
to the weather radio, from the south-southeast. Through the morning we
had paddled in the protection of the Keweenaw Peninsula. But as we crept
around the fingertip of land, the wind was there to greet us, blowing harder
with each slight turn to the south. According to the marine radio, waves on
the open lake would be building to seven feet. Canadian radio predicted
even larger. Were we actually to clear Keweenaw Point, we would paddle
along a shore fully exposed to the southerly wind. Unfamiliar with the
shore, I didn't know if we could find shelter or if we would be forced to paddle for miles with seven-foot waves striking us broadside. Being prudent and
somewhat cowardly, I suggested we lay up to wait for the wind to shift or die.

We landed in a gravelly cove on the bitter end of the Keweenaw. Across
a narrow channel lay Manitou Island. A lighthouse on a skerry at the tip of
the island (known as the Gull Island Light) resembled a grain elevator it was
so square. It seemed to float in the distance. Manitou, of course, is Ojibwa
for "spirit." The Ojibwa called the island Beaver Island. Even this seemingly
prosaic name referred to a spirit: beaver were plentiful because of the manitou that protected the animal at the tip of the Keweenaw. Indeed, fearing
the spirits, the Indians rarely traveled here. I could understand. Thrust in
the middle of the lake, as if nudged in the back by a finger of rock, I, too,
felt in awe. I was reluctant to so much as curse the wind. Under these circumstances, I could believe that Nature was willful and filled with spirits.

Of course, the Ojibwa had a more practical reason to avoid the end of
the peninsula: it was out of their way. *Keweenaw*, according to a John Johnston translation in 1808, means "the way made straight by means of a
portage." Indians traveling the southern shore took the shortcut through
Portage Lake, now the Keweenaw Waterway.

In the shelter of a small outcrop, we napped on the beach, gathered rocks, washed clothes, and bathed, even though the wind and currents of the lake had moved a mass of icy water onto shore. By late afternoon, the whitecaps had moved offshore, suggesting the wind was dying or shifting toward the west.

"You want to go?" Susan asked.

We clambered over the outcrop to look and were smitten by the wind. We ducked back down behind the outcrop, where we set up our tent.

It rained during the night. The rocks glistened like coal and oiled leather. Fog hung over the water. The wind had died and we wasted no time in clearing the tip of the peninsula, sneaking quietly so as not to wake the wind.

On a beach we spotted four canoes and a kayak. Several campers appeared to be in the standing-around stage before dropping their tents and breaking camp. They had been stuck there three days, waiting for the wind to die, one man said.

The eastern shore of the Keweenaw was more dramatic than I had imagined. We followed a line of cliffs, with soaring forested hills, fading by gradations into the distance: green to dark green to dark gray to light gray into clouds. Bete Grise Bay, according to Schoolcraft, was so named because someone had seen a gray beast in the area. More probably, the expression derived from the gray cliffs and hills that served as landmarks to the voyageurs.

It was not a momentous day, but we were able to paddle twenty-six miles before camping on a beach a couple miles above Gay. It was a lovely camp, if you discount blackflies and mosquitoes. The beach was made of "singing sand"—or more descriptively, squawking sand. The grains were angular and with each step we heard the coarse song of a raven. That evening we discussed whether we could make Marquette on time. It was a stretch: nearly one hundred miles to go in four days, if Susan were to return to work on time. It would be possible, I said, to make Big Bay and pull out there. Then I could hitchhike to the car in Marquette.

"If we make Big Bay, we're going all the way to Marquette. To pull out there would be silly."

Well, there you have it. Barring horrendous weather, we were going to Marquette.

The next day we began paddling by six-thirty. To be on the water that early felt pure and good. It seemed possible to reach Marquette in four days. Early in the morning, anything seemed possible.

As we paddled southward toward the town of Gay, a long gray finger seemed to emerge from shore. Another gray beast? We paddled on and on, but the gray mass seemed to get no closer, suggesting that whatever it was, it was huge. Gradually, it transformed into a vast gray delta of tailings. In the first decades of the century, Gay was the site of the Mohawk and Wolverine stamp mills. Now, nearly seventy years later, we paddled by mile after mile of barren, crushed rock.

"I don't want to be near it," Susan said.

Bones of driftwood lay on the dead beach. A few widely scattered beach peas sprouted from the tailings. A merlin appeared to attack a sandpiper. Otherwise, we saw no life. According to my map, something called the Scenic Shoreline Drive set out from here.

Tailings from stamp mills cover the beach at Gay, the beginning of, if you care to believe it, the Scenic Shoreline Drive.

Miles of layered cliffs run along the shore south of Gay.

Beyond the poisonous landscape of Gay, the shoreline alternated between bays and headlands. As the day wore on, the rock predominated. Rising directly from the lake, the cliffs were composed of banded layers suggesting the recollection of time, like rings on a tree. Each was distinct, like a fingerprint. One was composed of creamy rounded rectangles that suggested Tlingit art to me. Another was perforated with small arches and caves, which the waves lapped suggestively.

The cliffs ran on for miles. The wind, quartering from the rear, began to build. The swells from behind merged with the reflection waves from the cliffs, creating a troubled sea that, mile after mile, grew tiresome and increasingly unnerving. The cliffs, which earlier in the day had been objects of beauty and admiration, became objects of dread. Finally, at the old lighthouse at Jacobsville, the rock gave way to the sandy mouth of the Portage

River and the lower entrance to the Keweenaw Waterway. We landed to relax. We had paddled thirty miles, yet there was plenty of daylight. Should we go on? Ahead, across the entrance to the waterway, the land seemed to rise steeply.

"If I see more cliffs," Susan said, "I'll go crazy. I'll just lose it. I'll flip out."

From the entrance to the Keweenaw Waterway, where we camped and ate breakfast, the shoreline continued many miles southward to the towns of Baraga and L'Anse, deep in the narrow bight of Keweenaw Bay. I would have liked to see them from the water. But to venture the full length of the bay and travel back up the opposite shore would have added nearly thirty miles to our trip, an entire day. To reach Marquette, we would have to take advantage of every opportunity, and one presented itself now in the form of a glassy lake emerging from patches of fog, and the forecast of a calm morning. So a bit before seven, we set a straight course across Keweenaw Bay—nine miles of open water at that point—marking the bearing on a compass should the fog close in again.

We paddled steadily for the first hour. We took a brief rest and took up the paddles again. Two things are true of crossings such as this. First, the apprehension of paddling away from the safety of shore is palpable. Second, the first half of the crossing seems to go quickly; the last half is interminable. The reason is a matter of perspective: by the time you are a third of the way across, you perceive you are halfway across. By the time you get halfway across, you believe you are nearly done. In the last mile or two, it seems as if someone were actually drawing the shore away from you. Finally we reached land, a bit more than two hours after we began.

We made good speed up the Abbaye Peninsula. The lake was flat calm. The gray water reflected gray sky and the horizon melted away. We seemed to fly through some new medium. A dozen loons floated with us between water and sky. Was such a moment the beginning of George Morrison's abstract art, the paintings without the unifying horizon? In *Turning the Feather Around*, he writes, "I . . . sometimes let go of space entirely."

At Point Abbaye, we turned into a terrific headwind that had been lurking on the backside of the peninsula. Peaked waves and whitecaps marched in from the east. We landed and ate lunch. From time to time we checked the lake, but the wind continued to build. Defeated, we huddled beneath our tarp, cooking soup and gnawing on beef jerky.

231

By morning, the wind had switched again, this time to the southwest. We paddled quickly across Huron Bay, through the swells left over from yesterday's blow. If only the beast would remain still for a few hours, we would be able to find protection as the shore curved gently toward the south.

As we paddled, Susan said she thought it best to travel without expectations, to paddle when the weather was good, to stop when it was not. Expectations led to disappointment.

"If the wind holds like this, we can easily make Big Bay today," I said.

We paddled on, past the Huron Islands, a national wildlife refuge for colonial nesting birds. The slight wind propelled us down the shore toward the Huron Mountains.

"Ten more miles to Big Bay and then only twenty-seven to Marquette," I chirped, turned suddenly optimistic by the favorable winds.

We tucked in behind Huron River Point for lunch. Old cedars and hemlocks formed a cool glade. All was green and shadows. I thought it was lovely, but Susan was annoyed.

"It feels like the pressure is on," she said. "I thought we would come out here and it would be fun. We would be like vagabonds. And that's the way we explained it to people, but this is something different. We've got schedules and deadlines. It's the furthest thing from being vagabonds."

She was right. The schedule was getting the best of me. She was the one who had to get back to work. If she didn't worry, why should I? I hadn't been steadily employed for years. We launched and paddled on. Soon, in a sandy bay at the mouth of the Pine River, framed by two red cliffs, we saw a line of two dozen weathered houses. Two things were striking: first, that the houses were uniformly gray, and second, that they were all grand two-story affairs. At center stage rose a tall pole topped by the U.S. flag. My map showed no indication of a village of any kind.

What better time to start vagabonding? We turned toward shore. Following swells surfed us onto the beach in front of a central lodge of some kind, where five young men talked on the porch.

"What is this place?"

"Huron Mountain Club."

So this was the legendary Huron Mountain Club. Its existence was hardly a secret, but I never knew quite where it was located. Fiercely private, the club hadn't exactly advertised its location.

"I notice none of these places are painted."

"If someone did, they'd probably be ostracized," one of the men said.

We asked if there was a phone. Susan wanted to call her daughter.

"No phones."

I asked about cars. I didn't see any.

"Can't drive anything newer than 1970," said another man. I was sure he was putting me on.

Two of the young men walked down to the beach. Peter Lawrence was tall, handsome, and clean-cut with glasses. His younger brother, Josh, had tousled hair and a thin beard. They asked us about the kayaks, while we tried to learn more about the Huron Mountain Club.

The club was established in 1889 by a group of wealthy men from Marquette. John Longyear, the club's first president recognized that the "serenity of woods and lakes and fish-filled streams" was in short supply. Get a piece of God's country while it lasts, he urged, seven thousand acres in the heart of the Huron Mountains, sold in shares, with annual dues. Longyear also recognized that he owned a steamship, the only means of public transportation to the area.

Conservation and private ownership were not incompatible: as the serenity of the woods grew scarce elsewhere, the club added to its holdings, eventually growing to twenty-three thousand acres, including large tracts of virgin pine and more than five thousand acres of undisturbed maple-hemlock forest—some of the largest preserves of old-growth timber left in the Upper Peninsula. Aldo Leopold, the grandfather of ecology, wrote about the club's holdings in 1938. Ecological studies of the club's holdings have described everything from ferns to mayflies to wolves.

While the club began as a local endeavor, ownership passed on to wealthy families from the Midwest (such as Detroit and Chicago) and the East. Members built their tasteful cabins in one rank along the shore and a second rank of conforming houses along the indolent lower reaches of the Pine River. The number of cabins was limited to about fifty, each passing down within each family. Josh said his family flew into Marquette from New York City, where they lived near Central Park on the West Side. He spent his childhood summers here with his cousins.

"It's pretty incestuous here," he said.

We stood at the edge of the beach, barely out of the water. I expected that soon someone would order us back onto the lake. At the same time, rain clouds seemed to be gathering. I said I was a bit concerned about the weather.

"Gee, I don't think anyone would mind if they were on the beach here," Peter said to Josh, somewhat anxiously I thought.

"By all means, don't think you can't sit up here on the deck," Josh said. "No one would make you go back out on the lake if it were storming. If anyone says anything, tell them it would be unchristian to send you out in a storm."

I noticed that as Josh and Peter had come down to the lake, the other young men had disappeared down the boardwalk. Then, as Josh invited us back to his family's cabin, Peter suddenly excused himself. "I'm going to take a walk, OK? See you in a while." And he disappeared.

We walked down the boardwalk and across a weathered wooden footbridge spanning the Pine River. The riverbank was developed in a way that only the rich can develop something. The cabins that fronted the river, like those along the lake, were tasteful and restrained, but not timid about being on the water; the decks of several overhung the river. All the cars were tucked away in a single parking lot, screened by woods.

At the cabin, Josh pointed to a faucet by the steps. "You can wash your feet off there," he said. Then he invited us to step inside.

Susan and I looked at each other. We were sweaty from a day of paddling. Our neoprene and paddling jackets were probably the only thing that stood between a noxious odor and the world at large. But Josh insisted.

"C'mon in, c'mon in. Please, c'mon in."

Once inside, I watched my wetsuit drip on the sisal rug.

"Please, sit down," Josh said.

A man sitting at the piano played "Moonlight Sonata" artlessly but intently, never looking up until Josh introduced us. I think Josh said the man was his father. The man grasped my hand and looked directly into my eyes, as though this were an extremely sincere moment. Then he returned immediately to the piano and resumed his pounding.

Josh disappeared into the kitchen for tea. The cabin was simple and rustic, with a large map of the Huron Mountains and the boundaries of the club. Josh returned with a man and a woman. I didn't catch the relationship, but Josh explained that we were kayakers. The woman said "oh," as if kayaking were quaint or pitiable. Then they disappeared.

Sipping our tea, Susan and I described our trip. Josh explained that he had just graduated with a history degree from Kenyon College. He said he wanted to write for newspapers and was moving to Portland, Oregon, perhaps simply as a stop on the way to Alaska. He was drawn to Alaska, he said, just as he was drawn to the book *Into the Wild*, by Jon Krakauer, which tells the story of a young man from a well-to-do family who gave away his savings and car, burned his wallet, and headed into the Alaskan bush. Inexperienced and unprepared, he died within the year. The story appealed to him, Josh said, not because of the result, but because someone had given up everything to live simply.

As the conversation and "Moonlight Sonata" continued, I began to wonder if Josh's hospitality belied an ulterior motive. Was this his way to rebel or show disregard, to rub his family's nose in something? Given the state of our wetsuits, that could be done at some distance.

Traffic through the cabin continued, this time an old woman with fragile skin and snowy hair. Josh introduced her as his grandmother. She shook hands gamely, but her expression said, *God, Josh, what did you bring home this time?*

We walked outside along the boardwalk overlooking the Pine River. Josh said he had fished it for rock bass and pike. He had also fished in New Zealand for trout, as had his grandmother.

The large trout of New Zealand's small, clear streams are exceedingly tough to catch, Grandma said: "You had to have the fastest reflexes." She said she was soon leaving for the Kamchatka Peninsula on Russia's Pacific coast to fish for steelhead.

"That must be your rod hanging on the cabin," I said. I had noticed a new G. Loomis graphite rod, nine-weight, with a Bauer single-action reel and a sink-tip line. It was expensive and way too much rod for the trout streams of the Huron Mountains.

Yes, that was it, she said. "It might be more rod than I can handle."

As the afternoon wore on, bright sun dispersed the rain clouds. With many miles left to travel, we excused ourselves, climbed into our boats, and paddled off toward the next point.

"Under the best of conditions it's difficult to walk into that rarefied atmosphere of the very wealthy," Susan said. "It's even worse when you come into it like an animal." We were, she said, the great unwashed in more ways than one.

By any apocryphal account, F. Scott Fitzgerald remarked to Ernest Hemingway, "The very rich are different from you and me."

"Yes," Hemingway was supposed to have quipped, "The rich have more money."

Hemingway was familiar with the Upper Peninsula. He might have said, "Of course, the rich have a place in the Huron Mountains."

We had plenty of daylight when we reached Big Bay, a deep bight with a smokestack rising from the woods. Under different circumstances we might have skipped to the next point, but Susan needed to make a call, so we paddled into the bay, where we found a phone at a tiny marina.

As Susan called, I talked to an old man who sat staring toward the lake. "Where's town?"

"Down the road three-quarters of a mile. The big city."

"What was here? What was the stack for?"

A sawmill boiler, he said. "Ford put that in. It was started by Brunswick, you know, the people who make the bowling pins and lanes. They're the ones who started it up. Then some guy out of Grayling ran it, and then Ford finished it up."

Big Bay was so deep, it would have taken us most of an hour to clear the next point, so we decided to stay the night. We roamed town, a simple collection of houses, many with asphalt siding, surrounded by pickups and old cars. A guy by the curb with a large bottle of beer asked, "You been here before?"

"No, never have."

"Welcome to Big Bay. We've got stores down there. Hotel around the corner."

A bed-and-breakfast operated out of the old lighthouse. We eventually found ice cream at a country store. Then we walked back to the marina to fix dinner. After dark, I unscrewed the bulb from the light on the marina building and we pitched the tent in the shadows. No use. Within minutes we were busted by a woman in a nylon jacket that said Perkins Park Security.

"You're not supposed to be camped here. Do you guys have a boat here?"

"Well, no, not exactly. We've got two kayaks."

"You're not supposed to camp here."

"We'll have the tent down by six."

"Oh, no problem. We're just concerned about you because we have bears and things down here. I'll tell my boss so someone will check in on you."

Then she left. Swish, swish went the nylon jacket.

That night wind thrashed the tent and lightning flashed, but we saw no bears. By six, more or less, we were packing. Soon after we cleared Big Bay Point in a brisk west wind.

Rounding Granite Point, a sharp tit of land that blocked the trailing wind, we looked far to the southeast toward Marquette. The city, marked by a couple of stacks, lay behind lines of blue, green, and gray hills, with a long line of red cliffs mixed in, as though a series of veils formed the shore. The shoreline was mostly protected, except as we breasted a point and the following seas surfed and twisted the boats.

Approaching Marquette, we saw more cabins and homes along shore. Many were only shacks in the woods. Some were pleasant cottages. But as we rounded a series of dark points at the foot of Garlic Mountain, we saw a building unlike anything we had seen anywhere on the lake.

It appeared to be a magnificent lodge, three stories high, constructed of fieldstone and logs. It perched defiantly on the craggy shore, supported by a sea wall of stone, and looked across the narrow channel to Garlic Island. The break wall wrapped into a bay to form a private marina. Large windows faced every direction. Nearly a dozen stone chimneys rose from the building. At the top of each chimney sat small elegant birds of stone. We marveled at the building for some time and were about to leave when I spotted a man on shore. I paddled closer and asked him if the building was a lodge.

"No, a house," he said.

A house! I was astounded.

"Literally, lifestyles of the rich and famous," he said. "He's a commodities trader in Chicago. He jets up on the weekends. I'm the caretaker."

The trader, I discovered, was Tom Baldwin. His place, Granot Loma, had been featured in *Architectural Digest*. Even so, it was, as the caretaker said, "one of the best-kept secrets on the lake."

It was built by Louis Graveraet Kaufman, son of a German immigrant, who worked his way up through his brother's bank in Marquette and then married Marie Young, whose father owned much of the real estate in the Chicago loop. By World War I, Kaufman was worth $150 million. He had helped reorganize General Motors and lived in a luxurious suite in the Ritz-Carlton Hotel in New York.

By one persistent story, Kaufman was denied membership in the Huron

Granot Loma, a retreat built by one of the financiers of General Motors, is perhaps the most ostentatious home along the shore. Was it built in retaliation for being snubbed by the Huron Mountain Club?

Mountain Club because he was Jewish, and built Granot Loma to retaliate. But I spoke with a librarian at the Marquette County Historical Society who said, despite having heard the story for years, she had never found any evidence it was true.

Whatever his motivation, Kaufman spared little expense. Beginning construction in 1919, he imported pine logs from Oregon, each wrapped in burlap for protection. Three hundred craftsmen, many Finnish immigrants, built the house, which included a sixty-foot-long great room, twenty-six bedrooms, and two totem poles from the Pacific Northwest. He derived the name from the names of his children. Guests arrived to the opening bash in 1927 by way of Kaufman's private railroad spur. Over the years, guests included tennis star Bill Tilden, who laid out the tennis courts and taught the sport to the Kaufman children, and George Gershwin, who played the grand piano. Fred Astaire, Cole Porter, and Mary Pickford also visited the estate. Plans for the Empire State Building, which Kaufman helped to finance, were rolled out and studied in Granot Loma.

Kaufman died in 1942; Marie Kaufman died five years later. A daughter and her husband, the one-time caretaker, owned Granot Loma for a few years, but from 1950, the house was all but abandoned. Tom Baldwin was attracted to the five thousand acres on which the house was built, but when he toured Granot Loma on a rainy day in 1987, he recognized its potential and historical importance. During the next three years he renovated the house, replacing a third of the original logs, which had rotted. In 1990 Granot Loma was designated a National Historic Landmark.

As the caretaker and I talked, a bald eagle flew overhead.

"We have a young male and a breeding pair down there toward the point," he said.

Susan and I paddled away toward Marquette. We would spend the rest of the afternoon and early evening rounding the innumerable points in anticipation of large following waves that never found us. We ended the trip as we began it—in Marquette, in the dark, in a state of exhaustion. But just as we were leaving Granot Loma, Susan said this, referring to the caretaker and the eagles:

"He made it sound as though he owned them."

It would take a lot of restraint, I thought, not to.

CHAPTER 11

Pictured Rocks: Grand Island
to Brimley State Park

A NORTH WIND HOWLED off Superior. Whitecaps filled the lake all the way to Canada. Rank upon rank of six-foot waves rose, broke, and crashed upon the sand.

Wind bound again.

Still, the Little Beaver Lake campground was not a bad place to be stuck. There were plenty of vacant sites, and I had two weeks of food. I could hike to the beach on a trail that wound beneath old hemlock and mammoth beeches, and even follow the crest of the Pictured Rocks, the brightly colored sandstone cliffs, some nearly two hundred feet high, that flanked the lake. I'd had a chance to meet some of my fellow campers. Walt and Dee Dunlop, a retired couple from Grant, just north of Grand Rapids, had invited me over for chili and Rolling Rock beer. I had talked to an enthusiastic couple from Wisconsin, who, four days into a six-month journey around the continent in a VW van, had backed into a rock as they pulled out of the campground, disabling their air conditioning. A man named Bill, with a sea kayak on his four-wheel-drive, dropped by to smoke Camels and tell me how good the fishing had been in the streams of the Huron Mountain Club—until he was arrested, convicted of trespassing, and fined by a judge who told him he had caught some very expensive trout. I had also met three kayakers who were waiting, as I was, to get out on Superior. Tomorrow, if the wind died, I would paddle to their camp on nearby Beaver Lake.

I was on the last leg of my travels around Superior. This trip had begun several days ago. Susan and I had spotted my car at Brimley State Park, just west of Sault Sainte Marie. We drove her car to Munising, which would have been a fine town, nestled in a deep bay, except that the streets were plugged with tourists—by all appearances a traffic jam that would last the Labor Day weekend. We found a place to park at Sand Point, stuffed gear in our boats, and crossed the narrow channel to Grand Island.

Two hundred years ago a small band of Ojibwa found shelter on the island from the fierce battles between the mainland Ojibwa and the Dakota. They were known as a peaceable group, content to pursue their own interests, until, in a single battle with the Dakota, they lost nearly all of their young men. The band struggled, eventually melding with mainland bands and scattering to the towns that would later become Munising, Bay Mills, and Sault Sainte Marie. According to legend, Powers of Air, the lone survivor of the battle, sang an epic song of the event to explorer and Indian agent Henry Rowe Schoolcraft. The details, considerably altered, became part of the *Song of Hiawatha*. The poem, though wildly popular from the day of publication, was not universally admired. "Longfellow might conceivably have made a great epic out of the Nanabazhoo cycle of Chippewa mythology, in the manner of Wagner's treatment of the Nibelungenlied, but he was hardly the man for that," wrote historian Grace Lee Nute. "Instead, he took the folk tales current about Lake Superior among the natives, was generally quite faithful to them, but softened and tenderized them till they became palatable to the immature taste of Victorians."

Susan and I paddled by the ruins of the Grand Island East Channel Lighthouse, threatened by age and beach erosion. We continued past the cliffs that make up the shore of the Thumb, a one-time island now joined to the larger island by a sand tombolo. The rock exhibited bands painted with leaching minerals. The waves had carved arches and worn the sandstone to the pattern of wood grain. Light-colored gravel in the shallows registered in the clear water as a brilliant blue. Glades of cedar topped the cliffs. Off to the northeast we saw the similar but much grander geology of Pictured Rocks National Lakeshore.

"This is Shangri-la," Susan said. "This is a lost world."

We rounded the Thumb to the sandy tombolo. The island was part of Hiawatha National Forest. The beach was off-limits to camping, but in the crush of the weekend, all other sites were taken. We tucked our tent at the edge of the sand in the fringe of the trees, within a few feet of legality.

Susan could stay only one more day before she had to head home. We hoped to paddle along the Pictured Rocks, which stretched twelve miles

The author maneuvers near a sea cave on Grand Island. (Photograph by Susan Binkley.)

along the shore. Unfortunately, the forecast warned of a strong northwest wind. If that materialized, the waves would strike the cliffs dead on and the reflection waves would be brutal. After breakfast, the wind still had not risen, so we decided to chance the Rocks.

The cliffs were massive and unique, stained turquoise, rust, brown, and white by minerals leaching from higher layers. As we admired the cliffs, the tour boat *Grand Island* roared up behind us. It must have been making ten knots when it passed within a hundred feet with a load of tourists. I didn't mind the tourists, but I didn't care for the three-foot wake or the suspense of wondering whether he would stop or veer before running us over. I shouted an obscenity, but it was a timid gesture, since neither the captain nor the passengers could hear over the roar of the engines and the rush of water. Smiling, they pointed and waved. Minutes later, the *Miss Superior* bore down on us, turning less than two hundred feet away. This time I saved my breath. I used my finger.

We continued up the shore to the place where the Grand Portal once stood. The portal, a cavern large enough to accommodate sailboats, collapsed in 1906 with a crash heard a dozen miles away in Munising. Fortunately, a small arch remained nearby. Riding the waves that sloshed in the confines of the arch, our boats bobbed drunkenly beneath tons of rock.

We returned to Sand Point in advance of the belatedly rising wind. We were accompanied by low-flying airplanes, pleasure boats, and Jet Skis, which had the effect of a dentist's drill on a bad tooth. Everyone was out to see the

Susan paddles through an arch near Grand Portal Point at Pictured Rocks National Lakeshore.

Pictured Rocks today. In many respects, I thought, Pictured Rocks was one of those landscapes that was more spectacular than it was interesting.

The next morning the wind was strong from the northwest, and Susan dropped me at the Little Beaver Lake campground. I waited two days, hiking periodically to the beach to check the waves. On the morning of the third day, the wind subsided. I struck camp, launched my kayak in Little Beaver and paddled through a narrow channel to Beaver Lake, where the three kayakers I had met were camped. They were still fixing breakfast when I arrived. We ate pancakes. Then I poked around the site, the location of an old resort, as they packed their gear.

Their leader was John Henegher, an outfitter from St. Charles, Illinois. The other two paddlers were clients: Bob was an environmental consultant and Steve was a landlord and renovator. Neither had kayaked much, but they were beautifully outfitted, with North Face jackets, headlamps and other gizmos, and more gear than you could reasonably expect to cram into three kayaks. It took them forever to break camp. The long wait reminded me how far Susan and I had come.

We crossed Beaver Lake to the creek that flowed to Lake Superior. It was clear and sandy, and filled with downed timber. We pulled across the obstructions, waded through the shallow spots and paddled when we could. A hundred yards from the lake we encountered a monstrous logjam. We portaged around and launched in the final stretch of the creek, which glided swiftly over a gravel bar and into the lake. I led the way through the low surf rolling into the creek mouth. Steve and Bob followed, plowing eagerly through the waves. John brought up the rear.

As I bobbed in the swells just beyond the surf zone, I noticed, floating in the water near my kayak, a pair of black wings. They appeared to be songbird wings, perhaps from some kind of blackbird, joined by the thoracic bones and some flesh. Nearby were two more black wings, floating separately.

I decided to file this odd discovery under Birds of Prey to compensate for all the times I had watched merlins and eagles fail in their efforts to catch and kill their quarry. I imagined that a raptor of some kind would catch birds near the shore and eat them on a branch overhanging the creek, dropping the wings and other offal into the water.

We paddled together for awhile. Bob and Steve bounced happily on the

At the mouth of this small stream, which runs from Beaver Lake to Lake Superior, we found mysterious black wings.

rolling swells. But John's brood was planning to travel only as far as Seven-mile Creek. I wanted to go much farther—twenty miles to Grand Marais if the wind would cooperate. And so I left them behind as I sprinted down the shore.

This would be the last of my trips around the lake, a mere 120 miles, of which I knew very little. I looked forward to the Grand Sable Dunes, mentioned in the journals of explorers from Radisson to the present, and to the Great Lakes Shipwreck Museum at the tip of Whitefish Point. Otherwise, the shore was something of a mystery.

Twelvemile Beach was aptly named, a golden strand that was nearly deserted. Were I to visit Pictured Rocks again, I'd take a quick look at the cliffs

246

The Au Sable Light stands near the approach to the Grand Sable Banks.

but then spend my time at the beach, partly for its beauty, largely for its solitude.

I passed Au Sable Light, a cream-colored cylinder with a brick house at its base. As I rounded the point, the Grand Sable Banks burst into view. A much reworked deposit of sand and gravel that had collected in a glacial crevasse, the banks rose three hundred feet from the lake at a steep angle. Gullies, wave patterns, and funnels (like the work of great ant lions) had carved the face of the sand. Birches inhabited the ravines. Otherwise, only a few patches of grass tried to gain purchase on the unstable sand. I landed on a beach, too narrow to provide protection in a big wind. You'd be worried about trouble from two directions: the waves from one side and the possibility of landslides from the other. I was surprised to see, among the many

The explorer Radisson wrote of the Grand Sable Dunes: "That place is most dangerous when there is any storm, being no landing place so long as the sandy banks are
under water."

bird tracks, human footprints as well. I assumed these visitors had come and
gone by boat, since there was no evidence that anyone had clambered
down the face of the dunes. I wasn't sure if that would be possible.

Toward evening, as I reached Grand Marais, beachcombers were at work
after the recent wind. I landed at the greatest concentration of people and
hiked up the bluff to Woodland Park, where I found the attendant and
arranged to camp near my boat on the beach. As I set up my tent, an old
man stopped to check up on me.

"Did you know that we have a park there for camping?"

I knew what he was driving at and told him I had permission. At first his
nosiness annoyed me, but then we fell into conversation. He enjoyed pad-

dling himself, he said. In fact, he paddled a small solo canoe. I judged he was about eighty. I told him I was traveling around the lake.

"Your traveling alone just fascinates me."

It was nearly dark. I decided to hike downtown for dinner. Townies with a boombox were having a party across the street from the park. Otherwise, Grand Marais was quiet. Several sailboats, masts bare, sat unattended in the marina. I ate dinner and then crossed the street to the Dune for a beer. Next to me at the bar, two women, in their early twenties, were talking and making out with a couple of guys my age. One of the men ordered another highball, but the gal behind the bar cut him off.

"I'm not drunk," he protested. "I've driven that road plenty of times a lot drunker than I am now."

Finally she gave in and poured another drink. Then one guy said to the other, "Don't fuck with me." And the other replied, "Don't fucking tell me what to do." As this discussion replayed ten or twenty times, I ducked out of the bar and hiked back to my tent, thankful I wasn't driving.

Some days the paddling is difficult. Every stroke irritates like a boil. But other days, you float as if in a dream. Today the boat moved as effortlessly as an idle thought. The beach rolled by mile after mile without end. I saw whitecaps far out on the lake, but the wind, wrapping around from the southwest, pushed me eastward. I might worry later in the day, as the shore curved northward, but now everything was perfect. The act of paddling was simple, harmonious, and nearly effortless.

Beaches and dunes. Dunes and beaches. I reached the mouth of the Blind Sucker River before one in the afternoon—seventeen miles in less than four hours of paddling. Beachcombers searched for pretty rocks with long-handled scoops. I asked one fellow if he was finding much.

"A few," he said.

I thought of people who are devoted to activities that pay nothing. Their children inherit the legacy of rock pickers, fly fishermen, kayakers, freelance writers.

The Two Hearted River (as opposed to the nearby Little Two Hearted River) slid dark amber over a sandbar into the lake. More than a dozen fishermen congregated on the mouth. I asked one spin-caster wading in the lake what he caught. Salmon, he said.

"Big Two-Hearted River" was Hemingway's story, but it was not his river.

That, most likely, was the West Branch of the Fox, across the Superior divide toward Seney. But that didn't matter, for many things were not only what they seemed. Returning from the war, Nick Adams stepped from the train in Seney, expecting to see a hotel, saloons, and houses. But "there was no town, nothing but the rails and the burned-over country." Standing on the railroad bridge, he looked down into the river. Small trout were readily visible. But the biggest trout—they were visible only when he peered hard into the shadows. He left the bridge and followed the river through the woods, where he was alone.

It was a romantic notion—to simply step off the train and then lose oneself in the woods for several days of trout fishing. Yet more than that, "Big Two-Hearted River" was the story of a fragile man, finding what solace he could in the deliberate act. The ritual of a simple thing well done kept his demons at bay. Still, he was unwilling to wade into the darkest waters of himself. "He felt a reaction against deep wading with the water deepening up under his armpits, to hook big trout in places impossible to land them. . . . In the swamp fishing was a tragic adventure. . . . There were plenty of days coming when he could fish the swamp."

I thought of the story as I paddled. I thought of all the days when I wanted never to stop, but only to keep paddling. Stroke after stroke, a thousand strokes to the mile, thirty-eight thousand strokes by seven in the evening, when I reached the Crisp Point Lighthouse. I landed and found a place to camp on the fringe of the woods. I set the tent and carried my gear from the boat. Then I dragged the kayak over the sand to the woods. I drew water from the lake. I brought the teapot to a boil on the gas stove and saved some water in the thermos for later. Then I used the rest of the water for dinner. I laid my gear on a tarp and stepped carefully around the stove to keep sand out of my food. I ate dinner nearly in the shadow of the Crisp Point light.

The light was a simple tower. Paint peeled from the brick, but that was not the worst of its problems. Two winters ago the attached building washed into the lake. The tower itself was not far behind, as sand eroded from under the foundation. Crisp Point was accessible only by a long dirt road followed by a winding path over sand dunes. I saw ATV tracks, but no evidence of other visitors. The lonely tower suggested a link to the supernatural, a pathway to the Kitchi-Manitou, a beacon in stormy seas.

After dinner, I poured the hot water from my thermos to make tea. I smoked a cigar as the sun set. I found comfort in the tea and cigar, as though they held the day together. I heard noises in the dark woods behind me, but when I looked, nothing was there. I thought of all the days when I wanted never to stop, but only to keep paddling.

The coast between Grand Marais and Whitefish Point is known as the Shipwreck Shore, the Graveyard of Lake Superior. Since Europeans began navigating the lake in large boats, more than three hundred vessels have foundered along this shore. The vast fetch of the eastern lake makes for violent waves. While a kayaker or canoeist simply pulls up on the sand to wait out a storm, the captain of a large boat finds no shelter along the endless beach. Many boats have been driven ashore and battered to pieces.

A lifesaving station with surf boats for rescue operated at Vermilion Point, a windswept lobe a few miles east of Crisp Point. Established in 1876, it was considered the most isolated station on the lake. "Vermilion Point was the Alcatraz of the Life-Saving Service, as it was a forty-mile hike one way from Grand Marais," said John F. Soldenski, a surfman with the station from 1912 to 1920. "Yet, homesickness overcomes hardship," he wrote. "Several times I made the eighty-mile, round trip on foot during a three-day pass, just to be at home a few hours." The station closed in 1935, after responding to more than one thousand calls. Today a palatial home of cedar and glass stands on the windblown site.

I reached Whitefish Point before noon. I pulled my kayak far up on the sand, trusting that tourists strolling the beach wouldn't mess with it, and hiked up to the lighthouse and the Great Lakes Shipwreck Museum.

Constructed in 1849, the station at Whitefish Point was the oldest operating light on the lake, though the original tower had begun to crumble soon after it was built because the Ohio contractor had used poor quality mortar to cheat the government. The restored lighthouse keeper's residence was open for tours. Robert Carlson and his wife, Anna, staffed the light from 1903 to 1931. Carlson once saved eleven people from the steamer *Ora Endress*, which had capsized in front of the lighthouse. With two fishermen to help him, Carlson launched a fourteen-foot flat-bottomed skiff in rolling surf and heavy seas. He easily could have lost his own life. A survivor, Byron C. Campbell, reflected that "there is not one man in a thousand who would have attempted to launch a small boat in such a sea."

In the waning days of World War I, Carlson discovered that his new

251

second assistant keeper was a German spy who had been collecting shipping data and who had attempted to sabotage the light. He discreetly summoned help. A government boat and agents arrived to take the assistant keeper and his wife away in handcuffs. The man went quietly, but his wife screamed and cursed in English and German.

The Shipwreck Museum was smaller than I expected. It was also moodier and more somber. It was dark except for the puddles of light on the exhibits. A whole corner of the museum consisted of a diorama of the shallow resting place of the antebellum *Independence*, the first steamer to travel the lake and the first to sink on it. Rippling light suggested the refraction of waves. Stuffed burbot finned over timbers embedded in the sand, and three mannequins in scuba gear descended from the ceiling. Gordon Lightfoot's "Wreck of the Edmund Fitzgerald" played softly.

The exhibits recounted the more notable of Lake Superior's five hundred wrecks, ever since a northwest gale drove the *Invincible*, a two-masted schooner built by the British in Sault Sainte Marie, aground near Whitefish Point in 1816. Most of these accidents occurred along the Shipwreck Shore or in Whitefish Bay itself, where a great volume of traffic passed between the Sault and the narrows at the entrance of Whitefish Bay. In the 1880s, more than thirty-one hundred vessels plied the lake, compared with fewer than two hundred today.

Among the displays were models of various ships that had sunk. Among them was the *Alberta*, a steel-hulled passenger ship and mail carrier, whose captain was notable for his arrogance and immunity from manslaughter charges. Running full tilt in the crowded eastern lake, the *Alberta* had skewered four other ships in a single month. Its last victim was the wooden steamer *Osborne*, which sank with the engine hand aboard. In his defense, Captain Anderson of the *Alberta* had declared, "The *Alberta* carries her majesty's mail. Other boats must get out of her way."

Collisions send many ships to the bottom. In 1909 the *John B. Cowle*, 420 feet, was rammed by the even larger *Isaac M. Scott*. The *Scott* remained afloat, but the *Cowle* plunged into more than two hundred feet of water with fourteen crewmen aboard. One who was determined not to drown was Stewart B. M. Rogers: "When I found myself in that V-shaped hole," he said, "I knew I had a stiff fight on my hands to save my life. I gritted my teeth, strained every muscle and said, 'You're not going to get me this time, Old Man, if I can help it. Not yet, no sir, not yet.'"

Yet the most dramatic wrecks were those that were also the most mysterious, because they disappeared with no survivors, no witnesses, and no tell-
tale signs except for the flotsam that appeared on shores in the days and
weeks that followed. None of these captured the public imagination more
than the wreck of the *Edmund Fitzgerald*, to which an entire corner of the
museum—not to mention the incessant Lightfoot song and the video in
the theater—was dedicated.

On 9 November 1975, a clear fall day, the ore carrier *Edmund Fitzgerald*
had departed from Superior, Wisconsin, with a crew of twenty-nine and a
full load of taconite pellets. During the next day, the wind rose as a cold
front moved across the lake. By four the next afternoon, snow filled the sky.

At the height of the storm, the ore carrier *Arthur M. Anderson* was following about seven miles behind the *Fitzgerald*. The crewmen of the *Anderson*
worried among themselves that the *Fitzgerald*, in an apparent effort to find
some scant shelter from the wind, had strayed northward toward Caribou
Shoals. Captain Ernest McSorely of the *Fitzgerald* had radioed the *Anderson*
that the *Fitzgerald* had been badly battered by the waves and had taken a list.

"Please stay by me until I get down."

"This is the *Anderson*. Charlie on that. Do you have your pumps going?"

"Yes, both of them."

"We're taking heavy seas over our decks," McSorely reported. "It's the
worst sea I've ever been in. We have a bad list and no radar."

As the afternoon wore on, winds gusted to one hundred miles an hour
and seas built to thirty feet. At about six-forty in the afternoon, two huge
waves, estimated at thirty-five feet, crashed over the *Anderson*. The same
waves were bearing down on the *Fitzgerald*. It was perhaps this moment that
painter David Conklin tried to portray in *Every Man Knew*, which hangs in
the museum. The *Fitzgerald's* lights burn feebly in the black night. The stern
is lifted from the water as a mountainous wave crashes over the bow and
washes down the deck.

The two ships continued to communicate.

"We haven't got far to go. We will soon have it made."

"Yes, we will. It's a hell of a night for the Whitefish beacon not to be
operating."

"It sure is. By the way, how are you making out with your problems?"

"We are holding our own."

These were the last words from the *Fitzgerald*. Ten minutes later, the ship disappeared from the radar screen of the *Anderson*. By seven-thirty the snow began to clear, but the crew of the *Anderson* could see no trace of the *Fitzgerald*. A subsequent search by air and water turned up debris, but no sign of the crew. Five days after the ship disappeared, sonar located the broken remains of the *Fitzgerald* seventeen miles northwest of Whitefish Point. The next spring, the U.S. Navy lowered a remote-controlled submarine to photograph the front half of the boat, which rested on the bottom, upright, and the stern, upside-down and some distance away.

No other Superior shipwrecks have lived in legend like the *Fitzgerald*. Only the *Fitzgerald*, to my knowledge, has inspired a popular song. People continue to commemorate the event. Family members of the victims gather at the Shipwreck Museum for an annual memorial, while across the lake, the light at Split Rock Lighthouse shines November 10 to mark the anniversary. The centerpiece of the *Fitzgerald* exhibit is the ship's bell, cut from the pilot house by a diver in a hard-shell suit and replaced by a replica inscribed with the names of the twenty-nine dead.

I wondered why the legend of the *Fitzgerald* endured. Because no one survived to tell the story? Quite a narrative it was, rich with mystery and drama. Did a faulty hatch or damage sustained in striking Caribou Shoal cripple the ship? What do men think in the final moments, when the end is all but certain and choices no longer exist? But more than anything I was drawn to the symbolism—that a ship so large and so modern should crumble before the timeless force of a storm. A storm on a mere lake. In an age of steel ships and radar and meteorology, we are still ruled by Nature.

Yesterday, as I had approached Crisp Point, I had become aware of a mass of land in the far distance. It hadn't appeared suddenly but had gradually emerged from the haze on the horizon, looming darker and more solid until finally it had caught my attention and I realized it was not a bank of clouds, but land. But what land? Was it Whitefish Point? No, I had thought, looking at the map on my deck. Whitefish Point should be hidden behind Crisp Point. Could it be Crisp? No, Crisp Point was a mere bump in the shoreline; this was massive and tall.

I rummaged through my waterproof case for a map of the entire lake. I spread it out and located my approximate position in the far southeastern corner of Superior. Checking the compass, I realized that the emerging hills were Coppermine and Mamainse points and the highlands around

Batchawana Bay, the very shores that Susan and I had clung to when we began our travels.

Today, from Whitefish Point, the Canadian shore was clear and immediate. It seemed I could sprint there in no time at all. That much was an illusion, but I could clearly see the entrance to Goulais Bay, where Susan and I had first emerged on the great lake. The adventure was at an end. In the shelter of Whitefish Bay, where none but the strongest northwest wind could trouble me, I barely felt that I was on Lake Superior at all.

Through the afternoon I paddled southward, down the concave shore, by the communities, such as they were, of Whitefish Point, Shelldrake, and Paradise. Toward sunset I began to look for a place to camp. A broad shoal, which ran for several miles along the beach, forced me several hundred yards out into the lake. Cabins and homes dotted the shoreline. I would have stayed at a resort, if there had been one, but I couldn't distinguish any a quarter mile away from land.

Finally, approaching the mouth of the Tahquamenon River, I spotted a clearing in the woods. It turned out to be a highway wayside. There were no campsites, just a picnic table and an outhouse. As I cooked, I was surrounded by begging gulls, including a small lame bird I fed a bagel. The ground was covered with feathers and scraps of trash. I looked for a tent site among the places where people had walked their dogs. It didn't appear that camping was allowed, so I waited until dark and then set my tent in the shadow of a tree, where it was less likely to be spotted. Cars and trucks drove by on the highway. My car was parked only twenty-five miles away, an easy day's paddle. The thought that this might be my last camp depressed me.

I packed the boat, perhaps a final time, and paddled far out into Tahquamenon Bay to avoid the shoal water. The shoreline was boggy and forlorn. Not until I crossed the bay, a distance of about six miles, did the land rise, and then a road ran along the shore. As I paddled toward Menekaunee Point, I headed into a stiff north wind. The beach was sand, wonderfully sprinkled with boulders. I saw a dark shape on shore. A bear, I thought at first, but it did not move and I soon recognized it as a large rock.

Rounding the point, I began passing cabins. People swam and sunbathed and built sand castles. What a strangely warm season it had been. Hugging shore, mesmerized by the steady rhythm of the paddle, I daydreamed. They were beach fantasies of beautiful women on the sand, of the *Sports Illustrated* swimsuit issue, photographed here on Lake Superior. But these, after all, were the people you would see in K-Mart, but with fewer clothes.

The shoreline of Pendills Bay swung gently northeast. Ahead lay Iroquois Point and, plainly visible across the channel on the Canadian side, the granite face of Gros Cap. One early diarist compared these bookends to the Pillars of Hercules framing the entrance to the Mediterranean. Call them the Pillars of Naniboujou, if you will.

Iroquois Point was the scene of a famous battle between the Ojibwa and the Iroquois, until then the undisputed tyrants of the eastern lakes, to be avoided by whites and other tribes alike. In 1662 a war party of Iroquois invaded the Ojibwa's *Bawating* and camped brazenly on the point, across the channel from the Ojibwa. The Ojibwa crossed the water before dawn and surprised the Iroquois, killing nearly all and securing eastern Lake Superior for their own. The Ojibwa name for the Iroquois tribe, *Nodoway,* now applies to a nearby lobe of shoreline.

I reached Nodoway Point in midafternoon. I could easily make Brimley State Park before dark, but when I saw the gravelly beach and several natural openings in the forest, I thought better of it. Why hurry? I could think of no better way to make up for last night than to camp where the longtime people of the lake secured their homeland, with a clear view of where Susan and I had begun our travels.

I found a tent site and had just pulled the boat to the fringe of the woods when I spotted a bulky fellow with a cane tottering along the beach. Coming to chase me off his land, no doubt. But, no, he said he lived nearby and was taking his walk.

"I quit the rat race," he said. "This is how I get my exercise. If I didn't walk the beach, I wouldn't do anything."

I asked if I could camp.

"This is national forest," he said. "Not to worry."

He looked like Santa Claus, if Santa work a dark blue sweat suit and a red cap that said "Retired, U.S. Marine Corps" in gold lettering. As we chatted, a one-thousand-foot ore carrier plied the channel toward the open lake.

"I just love watching those big ships come through," he said. He advised me that the lake was dangerous. "It scares me. It's too big to go out on."

We talked, too, about the Ojibwa who still lived in the area, including on the reservation just down the shore at Bay Mills, where the tribe ran a casino.

"I don't mind," he said. "After all, we screwed them throughout most of history. I mean, we took everything they had. It seems only right that they get some of it back. And they're getting it back with the casinos."

As he walked off, I felt thankful for my good fortune. I set the tent and made dinner. I boiled water to save for tea. I made spaghetti with extra red peppers. For dessert I splurged—two cups of chocolate and raspberry pudding. As I ate, I looked out over the lake, contemplating a story that had begun more than a year and a thousand miles ago.

Often, the shortest path to knowledge is not a line, but a curve. My own journey had begun long ago with the arc of a stone into water, an arc that existed now only in my mind. Travel by kayak is full of arcs—the swing of the paddle, the path of the boat between each stroke, the foreshortened arc of the shoreline, the curvature of the lake's surface toward the horizon, and ultimately, the greatest arc of all, curving on itself and bringing me back to where I began. By the time the circle was complete, I had learned that my judgment was stronger than my courage, that I could travel alone when I needed to, and that I was strongest in the company of others.

Tomorrow, weather willing, I would travel the last few miles to Brimley State Park. I would stroke the paddle once again and then no more and wait to hear the crunch of the bow against the sand. But there would be plenty of time on the long drive home to brood on that sad finality. Tonight I would drink my tea and savor a cigar and settle one last time into my snug tent, to await the great day that dawns.

Bibliography

Adams, Arthur T., ed. *The Explorations of Pierre Esprit Radisson*. Minneapolis: Ross and Haines, Inc., 1961.

Agassiz, Louis. *Lake Superior*. 1850. Reprint, New York: Arno and New York Times, 1970.

Ahlgren, Clifford, and Isabel Ahlgren. *Lob Trees in the Wilderness*. Minneapolis: University of Minnesota Press, 1984.

Berman, Ann E. "Granot Loma in Michigan." *Architectural Digest*, May 1995.

Betts, M. W., and M. A. Latta. "Rock Surface Hardness as an Indicator of Exposure Age: An Archaeological Application of the Schmidt Hammer." *Archaeometry* 42, no. 1 (2000): 209–23.

Blocksma, Mary. *The Fourth Coast: Exploring the Great Lakes Coastline from the St. Lawrence Seaway to the Boundary Waters of Minnesota*. New York: Penguin Books, 1995.

Bogue, Margaret Beattie, and Virginia A. Palmer. *Around the Shores of Lake Superior: A Guide to Historic Sites*. Madison: University of Wisconsin Sea Grant College Program, 1979.

Bree, Marlin. *In the Teeth of the Northeaster: A Solo Voyage on Lake Superior*. New York: Clarkson N. Potter, Inc., 1988.

Breining, Greg. "Grand Portage." *Minnesota Conservation Volunteer*, March–April 1999.

———. "Savoring Saunas." *Islands*, April 1995.

Canada. Ministry of Natural Resources. *Lake Superior Provincial Park*, 1992.

Carpenter, Edmund. *Eskimo Realities*. Holt, Rinehart and Winston, 1973.

Chisholm, Barbara, and Andrea Gutsche. *Superior: Under the Shadow of the Gods*. Toronto: Lynx Images, 1998.

Coffin, Barbara, and Lee Pfannmuller, eds. *Minnesota's Endangered Flora and Fauna*. Minneapolis: University of Minnesota Press, 1988.

Conway, Thor. *Archaeology in Northeastern Ontario: Searching for Our Past*. Toronto: Ontario Ministry of Culture and Recreation, n.d.

————. *Painted Dreams: Native American Rock Art.* Minocqua, Wis.: NorthWord Press, Inc., 1973.

Dahl, Bonnie. *The Superior Way.* 2d ed. Duluth, Minn.: Lake Superior Port Cities Inc., 1992.

Daniel, Glenda, and Jerry Sullivan. *A Sierra Club's Naturalist's Guide to the North Woods of Michigan, Wisconsin, and Minnesota.* San Francisco: Sierra Club Books, 1981.

Dawson, Kenneth C. A. "Prehistoric Stone Features on the Relict North Shore Cobble Beaches of Lake Superior." In *Megaliths to Medicine Wheels: Boulder Structures in Archaeology,* edited by Michael Wilson, Kathie L. Road, and Kenneth J. Hardy. Proceedings of the Eleventh Annual Chacmool Conference, University of Calgary Archaeological Association, Calgary, Alberta, 1981.

————. *Prehistory of Northern Ontario.* Thunder Bay, Ont.: Thunder Bay Historical Museum Society, 1983.

————. *Pukaskwa National Park and the Prehistory of the North Shore of Lake Superior.* Parks Canada, 1979.

————. "The Pukaskwa Religious Stone Features of Lake Superior." Victoria, B.C.: British Columbia Museum, 1979.

Dean, Pauline. *Sagas of Superior the Island Sea and its Canadian Shore.* Manitouwadge, Ontario: Great Spirit Writers, 1992.

Dewdney, Selwyn, and Kenneth E. Kidd. *Indian Rock Paintings of the Great Lakes.* 1962. Reprint, Toronto: University of Toronto Press, 1973.

Emerson, J. Norman. "The Puckasaw Pit Culture: A Pilot Study." *Ontario History* 51, no. 1 (winter 1959): 69–72.

————. "The Puckasaw Pits and the Religious Alternative." *Ontario History* 52, no. 1 (winter 1960): 71–72.

Farnquist, Thomas L. "Requiem for the Edmund Fitzgerald." *National Geographic,* January 1996.

Friends of the Forest. *Lakehead Regional Green Spaces.* Thunder Bay: Friends of the Forest, 1996.

Friends of Lake Superior. "Lake Superior Provincial Park" (map). Friends of Lake Superior in cooperation with Parks Ontario, 1995.

Friends of Sleeping Giant. "Sleeping Giant Provincial Park" (map). 1994.

Gerstenberger, Thomas. "Island Hideaway: The West Bay Club." *Lake Superior Magazine,* December–January 1992.

Grove, Noel. "The Superior Way of Life." *National Geographic,* December 1993.

Graham, Loren R. *A Face in the Rock: The Tale of a Grand Island Chippewa.* Berkeley and Los Angeles: University of California Press, 1995.

Heinselman, Miron. *The Boundary Waters Wilderness Ecosystem.* Minneapolis: University of Minnesota Press, 1996.

Hemingway, Ernest. *In Our Time.* 1925, 1930. Reprint, New York: Charles Scribner's Sons, 1970.

Holman, J. Alan. *Ancient Life of the Great Lakes Basin: Precambrian to Pleistocene.* Ann Arbor: University of Michigan Press, 1995.

Johnson, Derek, Linda Kershaw, Andy MacKinnon, and Jim Pojar. *Plants of the Western Boreal Forest and Aspen Parkland.* Edmonton, Ab.: Lone Pine Publishing, 1995.

Johnson, Elden. *The Prehistoric Peoples of Minnesota.* St. Paul, Minn.: Minnesota Historical Society Press, 1988.

Johnson, Mary L. "Orphan Light." *Lake Superior Magazine,* April–May 1998.

Johnston, Basil. *The Manitous: The Supernatural World of the Ojibway.* New York: Harper-Collins Publishers, 1995.

Keller, James M. *The "Unholy" Apostles: Shipwreck Tales of the Apostle Islands.* Chelsea, Mich.: Bookcrafters, 1984.

Kostich, Dragos. *George Morrison.* Minneapolis: Dillon Press, 1976.

Lanman, Charles. *A Summer in the Wilderness Embracing a Canoe Voyage up the Mississippi and around Lake Superior in 1846.* 1847. Reprint, Grand Rapids, Mich.: Black Letter Press, 1978.

Legasy, Karen, Shayna LaBelle-Beadman, and Brenda Chambers. *Forest Plants of Northeastern Ontario.* Edmonton, Ab.: Lone Pine Publishing, 1995.

LeMay, Konnie. "Are the Lights Going Out?" *Lake Superior Magazine,* August–September 1999.

Leopold, Aldo. *A Sand County Almanac with Essays on Conservation from Round River.* New York: Ballantine Books, 1966.

Linnea, Ann. *Deep Water Passage: A Spiritual Journey at Midlife.* New York: Pocket Books, 1993.

Littlejohn, Bruce, and Wayland Drew. *Superior: The Haunted Shore.* Willowdale, Ontario: Firefly Books, Ltd., 1995.

Mabry, Marcus. "Alone at Last." *Newsweek,* 27 July 1998.

MacMillan, Colin. "The Discovery of the Pukaskwa Pits." *Wanikan,* newsletter of the Ontario Archeological Society, February 1986.

Mahan, John, and Ann Mahan. *Lake Superior: Story and Spirit.* Gaylord, Mich.: Sweetwater Visions, 1998.

McGuffin, Gary, and Joanie McGuffin. *Superior: Journeys on an Inland Sea.* Minocqua, Wis.: NorthWord Press, 1995.

McIlwraith, T. F. "The Puckasaw Pit Culture." *Ontario History* 50, no. 1 (winter 1958): 41–43.

Merton, Thomas. *Thoughts in Solitude.* 1956. Reprint, New York: The Noonday Press, 1995.

Monette, Clarence J. *Freda, Michigan: End of the Road.* Thirty-fifth of a local history series. Published by the author, 1989.

———. *Redridge and Its Steel Dam.* Forty-second of a local history series. Published by the author, 1992.

Morrison, George, and Margot Fortunato Galt. *Turning the Feather Around: My Life in Art.* St. Paul: Minnesota Historical Society Press, 1998.

Myers, John. "Caribou Still No Closer to BWCAW." *Duluth News-Tribune,* 27 April 1998.

Nash, Roderick. *Wilderness and the American Mind.* New Haven, Conn.: Yale University Press, 1967. Third ed. 1982.

Newman, Lee E., and John Johnson. *Development of a Reintroduced, Anadromous Brook Trout Population at Grand Portage, Minnesota, 1991–1996.* A cooperative effort of the Grand Portage Natural Resources Department and the U.S. Fish and Wildlife Service, 1996.

Nute, Grace Lee. *Caesars of the Wilderness.* New York: D. Appleton-Century Co., 1943.

———. *Lake Superior.* Indianapolis: The Bobbs-Merrill Co., 1944. Reprint, University of Minnesota Press, 2000.

———. "More about the Pictographs." *The Conservation Volunteer,* June 1943.

Ontario Ministry of Natural Resources. *Agawa Rock Indian Pictographs: Lake Superior Provincial Park.* 1991.

———. *Slate Islands Provincial Park: Background Information and Option Plans.* N.d.

———. *Spar Island: Area of Natural and Scientific Interest.* N.d.

Peters, Bernard C. *Lake Superior Place Names: From Bawating to the Montreal.* Marquette, Mich.: Northern Michigan University Press, 1996.

Peters, Bernard C., ed. *Lake Superior Journal: Bela Hubbard's Account of the 1840 Houghton Expedition.* Marquette, Mich.: Northern Michigan University Press, 1983.

Peterson, Bill. "Moose Walking in Circles." *Minnesota Volunteer,* September–October 1997.

Peterson, Roger Tory, and Margaret McKenny. *A Field Guide to Wildflowers: Northeastern and North-central North America.* New York: Houghton Mifflin Co., 1968.

Peterson, Rolf O. "Wolf-Moose Interaction on Isle Royale: The End of Natural Regulation?" *Ecological Applications* 9, no. 1 (1999): 10–16.

———. *The Wolves of Isle Royale: A Broken Balance.* Minocqua, Wis.: Willow Creek Press, 1995.

Pukaskwa National Park. *Management Plan Summary.*

———. *Research Bulletin,* 1995.

Quammen, David. *The Song of the Dodo.* New York: Scribner, 1996.

Racey, G. D., T. S. Whitfield, and R. A. Sims. *Northwest Ontario Forest Ecosystem Interpretations.* Ontario Ministry of Natural Resources, 1989.

Rennicke, Jeff. *Isle Royale: Moods, Magic, and Mystique.* Houghton, Mich.: Isle Royale Natural History Association, 1989.

Roosevelt, Robert Barnwell. *Superior Fishing: or, the Striped Bass, Trout, and Black Bass of the Northern States.* 1865. Reprint, St. Paul: Minnesota Historical Society Press, 1985.

Ross, Brian D. *Of Pits and Petroforms: The Monitoring and Protection of Mysterious Stone Structures in Pukaskwa National Park, Ontario, Canada.* Cornwall: Department of Canadian Heritage, n.d.

Rovit, Earl, and Gerry Brenner. *Ernest Hemingway.* Boston: Twayne Publishers, 1986.

Schlesier, Karl H. *Plains Indians, A.D. 500–1500: The Archaeological Past of Historic Groups.* Norman, Okla.: University of Oklahoma Press, 1994.

Schwartz, George M., and George A. Thiel. *Minnesota's Rocks and Waters.* Rev. ed. Minneapolis: University of Minnesota Press, 1973.

Sivertson, Howard. *Once Upon an Isle: The Story of Fishing Families on Isle Royale.* Mount Horeb, Wis.: Wisconsin Folk Museum, 1992.

———. *Tales of the Old North Shore.* Duluth: Lake Superior Port Cities Inc., 1996.

Soetebier, Virginia M. *Sweetwater Sea Saga.* Blacksburg, Va.: McDonald and Woodward Publishing Co., 1991.

Strong, Paul I. V. "By Way of Paradise." *Lake Superior Magazine,* June–July 1998.

———. *Call of the Loon.* Minocqua, Wis.: NorthWord Press, 1995.

Strzok, Dave. *A Visitor's Guide to the Apostle Islands National Lakeshore.* 1981. Reprint, Ashland, Wis.: Heart Graphics, 1992.

Tanner, Helen Hornbeck, ed. *Atlas of Great Lakes Indian History.* Norman: University of Oklahoma Press, 1987.

Tester, John R. *Minnesota's Natural Heritage: An Ecological Perspective.* Minneapolis: University of Minnesota Press, 1995.

Tilman, David, and John A. Downing. "Biodiversity and Stability in Grasslands." *Nature,* 27 January 1994.

Turk, Linda. "Land of Nirivia: Ontario's Enchanted Islands." *Star Tribune,* 6 July 1997.

———. "Silver Islet, Ontario: There's No Need to Rush." *Star Tribune,* 3 August 1997.

U.S. Department of the Interior. Division of Publications, National Park Service. *Apostle Islands: A Guide to Apostle Island National Lakeshore, Wisconsin.* Washington, D.C., 1988.

Warren, William W. *History of the Ojibway People.* 1885. Reprint, St. Paul: Minnesota Historical Society Press, 1984.

Waters, Thomas F. *The Superior North Shore.* Minneapolis: University of Minnesota Press, 1987.

Week, Robert P., ed. *Hemingway: A Collection of Critical Essays.* Englewood Cliffs, N.J.: Prentice-Hall, Inc., 1962.

Zimmerman, Craig. "Pukaskwa National Park: A Wild Shore." *Explore: Canada's Outdoor Adventure Magazine,* December 1994–January 1995.

GREG BREINING writes about travel, sports, and the environment. His books about travel and the outdoors include the *Minnesota* (Compass American Guide) and *Return of the Eagle.* His articles have appeared in *Sports Illustrated, Audubon, Islands, International Wildlife,* and *Minnesota Monthly,* and he is the managing editor of the *Minnesota Conservation Volunteer,* the magazine of the Minnesota Department of Natural Resources.

If you have any comments about *Wild Shore,* you may send them to Greg Breining at breining@aol.com or visit his web site at http://gregbreining.com.